The Old Man and the Sand Eel

Will Millard is a British writer, explorer and BBC presenter. He spent his twenties criss-crossing remotest West Papua in search of ancient tribal trade routes, before his solo descent of a West African river, which became an acclaimed series for BBC Radio 4. He lived alongside Aboriginal whale harpooners and subsistence-hunting sea-nomads as part of his maiden television series, *Hunters of the South Seas*, for BBC2. He writes regularly for *Geographical*, *Outdoor Fitness*, the *Daily Telegraph* and *Vice* magazine.

The Old Man and
the Sand Eel

WILL MILLARD

PENGUIN BOOKS

PENGUIN BOOKS

UK | USA | Canada | Ireland | Australia
India | New Zealand | South Africa

Penguin Books is part of the Penguin Random House group of companies
whose addresses can be found at global.penguinrandomhouse.com.

First published by Viking 2018
Published in Penguin Books 2019

001

Copyright © Will Millard, 2018
Illustrations copyright © Anna-Sophia Watts, 2018

The moral right of the copyright holders has been asserted

The publisher is grateful for permission to quote from: *Fishing for a Year* by Jack Hargreaves (Medlar Press 2011), reproduced by kind permission of Jack Hargreaves's stepson Simon Baddeley, owner of rights in all Jack Hargreaves's 'Out of Town' films for Southern Television; *John Wilson's Fishing Encyclopaedia* (Boxtree 1995), reproduced by permission of Pan Macmillan; *The Secret Carp* by Chris Yates (Merlin Unwin Books 2000), reproduced by permission of Merlin Unwin Books; *Blood Knots* by Luke Jennings (Atlantic Books 2010), reproduced by permission of Sky Horse Publishing, Inc and Atlantic Books Ltd; *The Book of Eels* by Tom Fort (HarperCollins 2002), reproduced by permission of HarperCollins Ltd; *Somewhere Down the Crazy River* by Paul Boote and Jeremy Wade (Hodder and Stoughton 1994), reproduced by kind permission of Jeremy Wade; *A Game of Thrones* by George R. R. Martin (HarperCollins 1991), reproduced by permission of HarperCollins Ltd; 'Pike' from *Lupercal* by Ted Hughes (Faber and Faber 1960), reproduced by permission of Faber and Faber Ltd; *A River Runs Through It* by Norman Maclean (University of Chicago Press 1989), reproduced by permission of University of Chicago Press; *Fish, Fishing and the Meaning of Life* by Jeremy Paxman (Penguin 1995), reproduced by permission of David Higham Associates.

Every effort has been made to trace copyright holders and to obtain their permission for the use of copyright material. The publisher apologizes for any errors or omissions and would be grateful to be notified of any corrections that should be incorporated in future editions of this book.

Typeset by Jouve (UK), Milton Keynes
Printed and bound in Great Britain by Clays Ltd, Elcograf S.p.A.

A CIP catalogue record for this book is available from the British Library

ISBN: 978-0-241-97770-5

www.greenpenguin.co.uk

For the great man
who once taught me to fish

Contents

The Greater Sand Eel   1

The Striped Assassin   13

The Water Wolf   81

A Never-Ending Golden Sun   133

The Fish Everyone Hates   191

The Great Game   243

Coming Home   295

Acknowledgements   321

The Greater Sand Eel

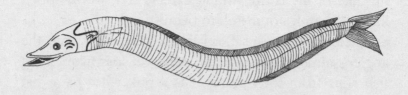

What do they know of fishing who know only
one fish and one way to fish for him?
Jack Hargreaves, *Fishing for a Year* (1951)

I depress the playback button on my phone for the fifth time in five minutes. It's killing me to keep watching, but I'm desperate to find something, anything, positive amid this total horror show of a film.

'That is one of the biggest sand eels I've ever seen in my life!' it begins.

I'm shouting, partly out of excitement, and partly because the wind is whipping up so hard around the Dorset coast that it's distorting the sound on the video.

In one hand I'm trying shakily to film with my mobile phone, while, in the other, I'm struggling to hold a British record fish. I don't know what else to say. 'It's a whopper!' I eventually stammer, sniffing back a runny nose and punching the 'stop' button.

I gently place my phone on my table and smash a cushion directly into my face. I've just made the biggest mistake of my entire fishing career, and, worse still, I know I've only got myself to blame.

There are few sensations in life that can match the angler's almost immeasurable sense of loss when a big fish slips from their grasp. It is a poker-hot pain that continues to burn as bright in the memory as it did in the moment itself. Losing the sand eel record set me on a redemptive pathway that spanned the length and breadth of Britain. For over a year of my life I allowed the eel to completely take over, and, in the end, my angling would never be quite the same again. But that was all still to come. For now I was stuck in an angling purgatory, with bent hooks, broken dreams and that video for company. I pressed the playback button once more.

When I was a boy I used to revel in going around my grandparents' home, a small bungalow that for me meant warm milky tea, chocolate sauce on ice cream, well-worn furniture and *John Wilson's Fishing Encyclopedia*. My grandad would take the heavy hardback book in his thick fingers and, when I asked him, rest it on his enormous belly and thumb through the various sections. As far as I was concerned John Wilson was a god. He had a long-running series called *Go Fishing* that used to crop up for a few weeks a year on Anglia Television. It was on pretty late at night so I'd either try and stay up to watch it or get Mum to record it on VHS by laboriously punching the long code printed in the *Radio Times* into our tape player. *Go Fishing* spanned the period of time as a child when I was only ever allowed to catch tiny red-finned roach from the creek directly outside our house, roughly the ages of four to twelve, or 'Argos Introduction to Fishing Kit' through to 'Kingfisher Coarse Supreme Kit', if you prefer. The titles always began with John Wilson's silhouette walking on an animated, but minuscule, planet Earth. He lumbered over the surface of our world as a giant, striding with remarkable ease from continent to continent, passing signs that simply read 'fish' and 'more fish'. Pretty remarkable in itself for an adoring young super-fan from an insular village in the Cambridgeshire Fens, but the best bit about *Go Fishing* is that, despite what you might infer from the titles, Wilson rarely left Britain. His world was the chalk-fed River Wensum in Norfolk, the Royalty stretch of the River Avon, expansive gravel pits, beautiful Irish lochs and picture-postcard-perfect fish. *Go Fishing*'s gift was that it made catching fish, often of a specimen size, seem attainable. By catching well from his own backyard, Wilson made me, a novice angler, believe I too could catch well from mine.

Wilson placed equal value on all species of fish, a sort of 'Martin Luther King' of the fishing world, so it was to be expected that in *John Wilson's Fishing Encyclopedia* no one species, method, bait or habitat was over-represented. From A to Z as much page space was dedicated to boilie baits as bread, carp as catapults, wire traces as wobbling dead baits. This was important because, to juvenile eyes, it presented the world of fishing not as a game to be completed, but as a near infinite set of variables where it was possible to utterly lose yourself in the discovery and mystery of the sport. Anything was plausible, because nothing was predictable.

In the *Go Fishing* era, any catch I deemed to be 'highly unusual' was hastily reported to Grandad with perhaps the same level of enthusiasm as an ecologist might have on discovering a new species after decades of fruitless toil. It mattered not that the fish species were, in reality, just slightly less than common, the days I caught my first zander, ruffe and bleak were moments to be celebrated from the highest platforms possible (from the narrow selection available to me from within my grandparents' bungalow), climaxing with the highly ritualized inspection of the John Wilson *Encyclopedia*. The reason for this was three-fold: first of all, the book allowed me to glean the definitive facts on the 'new' species from the highest authority in the land (John Wilson), secondly it made me feel one step closer to my idol (also John Wilson), and, finally, it was a cast-iron guarantee that I could get the full and unadulterated attention of my grandad, a living breathing angling (demi-)god, of sorts.

I inherited the Wilson *Encyclopedia* when my grandad passed away two years ago. For a few weeks I couldn't even bring myself to open it. It smelt of him and his bungalow; a precious bridge back into those memories before the body and mind of this once strong man gave way to life and death in a nursing home. It just didn't feel right to read it without his permission and his bookstand stomach to open it from. It sat on my shelf untouched, the magic spilling from its pages.

Then the sand eel slithered into my life and changed everything.

I had never caught a sand eel before; let alone one within the 'greater' species definition. I strongly suspected it would be featured in the *Encyclopedia* – pretty much all the common species in the British Isles had made some sort of billing – so, with curiosity eventually getting the better of me, I decided this would be the appropriate time to finally peel open the pages of the formerly forbidden tome.

I found my fish wedged between the obscure Corbin's sand eel and the squid-eating scad. With a supporting image resembling the scabbard of a dagger, the greater sand eel entry read: 'the largest of the sand eel . . . The body is long, thin and smooth with a greeny-blueish back, blending down the sides into lower flanks and a belly of silvery white.' Wilson goes on to say that you can only catch them on exceptionally small feathers armed with tiny hooks. That's funny, I thought to myself. I had mine on the vulgarly named 'Flying Condom', a long hefty lure only really designed for the gaping mouth of the large sea bass or a sea-sprung salmon. The hooks on that lure are massive, thumbnail-sized and thick. Strange I managed to land that sand eel then. I supposed.

For a moment I just let that thought rest on top of my brain. A few more precious seconds of blissful ignorance after what had, up until that point, been a very enjoyable weekend. Inevitably, though, the thought drifted its way into the centre of my skull, fired up the synapses responsible for reasoned thought, and caused the horrifying implications of the Wilson suggested hook size, versus the ones I had used, versus the size of the fish I had managed to land, to dawn on me with force.

I recoiled from the book. What if the reason I landed that fish was that it was, in the modest world of the sand eel, an absolute monster?

The greater sand eel description had taken me onto a second page. I knew the layout of this book as well as if I'd written it myself. At the start of each species section Wilson always details the British record weight, which meant, just one page previously, the auspicious number was lying in wait for me. I felt a tremble somewhere deep within my bowels.

Just close the book, Will.

Close the book, put it back on the shelf and never open it again.

I turned the page back.

Eight and a half ounces. It was staring me right in the face, in black and white, directly below the drawing of the distinctly smug-looking greater sand eel.

Eight and a half ounces. That's a pot of Marmite, a tin of beans, a four-pack of Mars bars, surely not a new British fish record?

I didn't need to review the footage I shot that morning to know with certainty that the fish I had caught was in excess of 8.5oz, but I did it anyway, multiple times, and there it was: as bold as brass, wriggling along the length of almost my entire forearm. A fish clearly over 10oz, possibly even knocking on the door of one pound, a cast-iron miniature record breaker, and I had quite literally thrown it away.

To say I was fuming for the rest of the week would be to put it mildly.

Not only did I not speak for a good few days, but I could hardly even bring myself to look at the offending fishing tackle. I'd had my scales in my bag the whole time, the coastline had been packed with people, including my girlfriend, who had patiently waited for me at the top of the rocks, and I'd even had my camera with me. Getting that sand eel officially registered with the golden trifecta of witness, weight and photo, required by the British Record Fish Committee, would have taken less time than it took me to come up with my stupid little speech on that stupid bloody video. A video, I might add, which now only exists as little more than an everlasting record of my own unbelievable ignorance.

Let's be honest, no one is going to be particularly rushing to break the doors down at the British Record Fish Committee to register a new shore-caught sand eel

7

record; nor are the editors of the national angling press waiting, poised over their typewriters, for the sensational scoop of my 'against the odds' battle with sand eel destiny, but that is precisely the point: no one actually wants the greater sand eel rod-caught record, which means it was the perfect record for me to break.

In truth I am still something of an amateur fisherman. Sure, I know my way around several different styles and techniques, and have had more than my fair share of luck, but realistically that sand eel was absolutely my best chance of making it onto the list of official record breakers, and I had completely blown it.

During the golden years of the John Wilson *Fishing Encyclopedia*, back when I was twelve years old, I would fish only two waters: the Well Creek, outside my childhood home, and Popham's Eau, a vast drain which I would venture to once a week with my grandad. I may have gone to the local school but this was where I truly received my education. More than just the places I caught my first fish, these twin rivers were where I learnt my watercraft and discovered the workings of the natural world, where I made my first real friends, and endured the rain and cold without running home to Mum. Very occasionally they were also the settings of the purest personal triumphs I will ever experience in my life. I would go on to catch much bigger fish from hundreds of different venues with far greater names than Popham's or the Creek, and yet the memories of my time on those banks remains undiminished. I ask myself now, looking back, am I truly more knowledgeable as an angler now than I was then? In my childhood, thanks to the *Encyclopedia*, I knew every single British fish species, and its record weight, by heart.

How could I not have realized I had caught a new record then? The answer was obvious and it was staring me right in the face. On the wall of my study I had pinned two sheets of A4 paper. One is the optimistically titled 'fishing targets', and the other is a list of potential venues and tactics. The list includes king carp, crucian carp, eel, perch, pike, salmon and roach, with ample space for notes.

Many years ago the plan was to work my way through the entire list, breaking my lowly personal bests, and introducing myself to as many new species and varied environments as I possibly could. Just as John Wilson did, and, it pains me to say it, just as my grandad would have liked.

I look up at that list now and know I've badly let him down. The pages next to all the native species are barren, whereas the sections dealing with the introduced and very foreign king carp are absolutely crammed with information: Monument, Linear, Redmire, popped-up plastic corn; 4G squid; the Source, crab-mist, chod, braid and spod. The list goes on and on, years of accumulated information on a single species, from a single type of venue, that has completely suffocated my childhood knowledge of the wider piscatorial world; pushing king carp facts in one ear and everything else I've ever learnt about fish and fishing right out of the other.

That lost greater sand eel was a sign from above. I'd stopped caring about where I fished, as long as there were fish. For two decades straight, the places I fished were near identical commercial ponds and lakes filled to bursting point with artificially reared carp and brought to my net using much the same methods and baits. As a result, I failed to identify the record breaker in my hands and rightfully lost my chance. Now, with the rediscovery of the *Encyclopedia*, I have all the ancient wisdom I could possibly require on virtually every single species and fishing technique within the British Isles, and that sand eel which slipped between my fingers is the kick up the arse I fully deserved and desperately needed.

I prise the list off the wall – it's been up there for a while, the Blu-tack has gone hard and takes a small flake of paint with it – and select the biggest, thickest black marker on my desk. Striking a meaningful cross through the entire king carp section instantly makes me feel better. 'It's catching, not fishing,' Grandad always used to say every time I talked up my latest carp conquest at the local commercial fishery; I'd give him the withering teenage eye roll reserved for uncompromising adults, but it's only now I realize he was bloody right all along. I scribble all over the freshly drawn cross for good measure and focus in on all the other names left on the list, taking delight in rolling my tongue over the names like I'm reading a fairy tale to a child. These are legendary fish, steeped in history, yet bullied to the periphery of most anglers' imaginations by this nationwide king carp obsession. To find the native, truly wild populations of these fish I'm going to have to travel to the sorts of places that exist well beyond the public gaze. Spots where most wouldn't think to cast a line: tangled underworlds, crumbling docks and urban rivers, the dwellings of the truly abandoned, where a unique kind of freedom survives distinct from the regentrified, reimagined and sanitized versions of wilderness that I've just wasted the last twenty years fishing in.

I spread a map of Britain out on the table and am immediately struck by just how well watered this nation really is. The rivers and lakes stretch right across this island like a giant central nervous system, easily dwarfing our roads and motorways through their sheer scale and abundance. Obviously not all these waterways will hold record breakers, and I wouldn't get very far attempting to wet a line in every body of water in Britain, but I know there are definitely ways of shortening the odds in my favour before I set off.

A quick search on the internet finds me the British Record Fish Committee's record-coarse-fish register, which helpfully includes all the places the fish were caught and by whom. That feels as good a place as any to start out, but I know I must avoid becoming completely hamstrung by someone else's list. A lot of these venues will have seen serious angling pressure since they produced their record, and doubtless some of them will also be part of expensive and exclusive clubs that I just won't be able to access. But records are there to be broken and fish die or move on elsewhere. If I'm going to give this a proper crack I need to look to offshoots of pre-established record-breaking waters, speak to local people and be prepared to take seriously the near-mythic stories of park lake monsters and river beasts. After all, just sticking to the beaten track was pretty much what got me into this mess in the first place.

I take a deep breath. It feels like I'm learning how to fish all over again. I know this is going to take patience and extraordinary amounts of luck, but the night before I attempt the first fish is utterly sleepless. I feel like I can actually sense the monsters of my imagination queuing up to be caught, pressing against the inside of my eyelids, willing me on to success.

The Striped Assassin

I am haunted by waters.
Norman Maclean, *A River Runs Through It* (1976)

Proper fishermen would never set up their rods before seeing the water they intend to fish, but I'm not a proper fisherman and have learnt the hard way that I make a much more proficient job of putting together my tackle in the dry confines of my kitchen than on the bankside. By the time I've made it out of the door and down to the river, lake or pond, I'm usually far too excited about the prospect of the first cast to concentrate on tying my knots properly, and thus set myself inexorably on the path to experiencing the devastating parting of fish from angler, right at the point of least resistance: my crap knots.

The line peels from the reel's silver barrel with a series of soft clicks and glides over the wooden top of my chair. I plan to keep this set-up extremely straightforward as big perch hate complication.

I squeeze an extra-large shot of weight, the shape and dimension of a rabbit dropping but heavy and hard, on one end of a short, six-inch length of line. That'll keep my bait pinned hard to the lake bottom. To the other end I attach a swivel, a tiny barrel of metal with two small rings at either end, which I then thread onto my main line. The swivel allows the weight to slide sweetly along the length of line without registering any resistance should a big perch pick up my bait. It slides down sweetly; free and smooth, right along the length of the line till it hits the rod's tip with a satisfying 'plink'.

Perfect. Zero resistance. The perch won't even know it's hooked.

My whole life has been one spent surrounded by water and my happiness can be accurately measured by my proximity to it.

I was born in the Cambridgeshire Fens; one of two, five minutes before my twin sister, Anna, with a little brother, Tom, coming along some seven years later. Ours was a house filled with nature, thanks, in no small part, to the unbridled enthusiasm of our dad.

He was a magical figure to me as a scabby-kneed under-five. I didn't really understand why he was so often not around, the demands of his job as the local village doctor frequently taking him away from us for longer than we all would have liked, but when he was there he poured his love of wildlife deep into the souls of his children.

Through him I learnt to seek pleasure in bird-watching walks in fenland waterscapes, or to train my eye onto the very tiniest of life forms, dissecting the underside of a carefully lifted log with forensic precision, in the hope of snaring one of the worms or pungent ground beetles that lived there.

He seemingly hadn't inherited his father's passion for angling, but in those early days he armed me with the essential patience and respect I would require to winkle out fish later in life.

My earliest memories are really just a haphazard collection of senses and emotions, but they all revolve around the natural world brought to my palms by Dad. First there was Norman, the Airedale terrier. Unwisely purchased just before Mum gave birth to us twins, he was a mix of hyperactive, ginger, hard wire wool and smelly wet tongue. Next was the mustiness of Dad's vast butterfly collection, which had a sort of pungent, slightly oppressive, perfume-like smell that you might also find around the embalmed corpses in the British Museum. I have always associated that scent with the dark wood and glass that contained his treasures and, if allowed, I would open the drawers with real care and reverence. The residents of these cases were frozen in time. Ossified and rigid, captured and sacrificed, all in the name of science. Even if I removed the glass they were trapped behind they could never grow or float through the sky again. I knew that this was not a time to smile or make jokes as the creatures that lived in there were actually just dead.

Living animals in the house, apart from Norman and the occasional woodlouse that made it (very) briefly into the room I shared with Anna, were accommodated in the circular conservatory at the back of our home. This pleasure dome for captive wildlife all but guaranteed victory for the Millard twins on the Upwell County Primary School 'show and tell' table, something that was of extreme importance to me at that time; plus, it was perfectly placed at the foot of the garden, providing a thrilling portal between the familial and the feral.

Dad would often hatch foreign moths and butterflies in the warmth of the glass house, the death's-head hawk-moths were easily my favourites. With their human skull patterns emblazoned on their thoraxes like bikers' tattoos, I thought they had to be just about the coolest insect that ever lived, but it was in the careful handling of the giant Atlas moths that I learnt the value of being gentle with any living creatures. Even the smallest brush of a wingtip could leave a guilty trace of their dust on my fingers. It was the Atlas depositing tiny scales from their bodies and would dull their colour instantly. Even today, despite having pulled a fish through the water with a hook in its mouth, I chastise myself at the loss of a single scale as a result of any rough handling on the bank.

Dad taught me that it was sometimes okay to catch animals to study and admire, but, as he aged, his focus became less on capture and more on the observation. Photos replaced traps, his butterfly collection waned, and the insect population of the conservatory began to dwindle.

I guess that was where Dad and I differed in our approach to nature. For him it was enough to simply observe and understand from afar; for me, it was necessary to get as close as possible, and, ideally, hold the creature in my hands. It wasn't a case of wanting mastery over the natural world – I wasn't one of those cruel kids who would pick the legs off a daddy-long-legs for a laugh. I just seemed to get infinitely more from something I could actually hold, touch and, years later, catch then release.

One day, a new resident was installed in the conservatory fish tank. It was to be my first close encounter with a fish, and, my goodness, what a fish it was.

In researching for this book I have since learnt from Dad that the brook lamprey was actually with us for only a single night, caught in a willow wicker-work trap by an eel-catcher from our local creek and given to Dad because he was 'into that sort of thing'. Yet I remember it like it was there for the entirety of my early childhood. For the under-fives, time lengthens and memories compress in unusual ways; that one-night stand with the lamprey made a massive impression.

According to the Wilson *Encyclopedia* the brook lamprey 'rarely exceeds an adult length of 10 inches', which is quite extraordinary as I was fairly convinced our specimen was the size and girth of a Burmese python.

Wilson goes on to note that its 'sucker-like mouth is used only for adhering to the undersides of stones'. Now, not that I wish to accuse a fisherman, of all people, of understating the facts somewhat, but at no point does Wilson highlight that this fish has to be one of the most bizarre-looking creatures in Britain, if not the planet Earth. Not only does it have no fewer than seven separate gills, running in a hole-punch-like line right down its body, but he also neglects to mention that its 'sucker-like mouth' is, in fact, a horrific circular suction pad filled with a truly nightmarish series of studded teeth.

For hours my sister and I stared at the curious fish in the tank; utterly transfixed. It didn't seem to move much, preferring instead to spend its time stuck hard to the glass side of the fish tank. Perfect for me, though, as it afforded a close-up view of those extraordinary mouthparts for the brief period it was in our custody.

It was a highly unusual capture anyway. The brook lamprey is most often found in fast-running streams where it can happily breed on gravel deposits; in the turgid murky waters of the river outside my home it seemed an absolute imposter. That thought delighted me. Out there, beneath a brown theatre curtain of surface water, was a subaquan wonderland just waiting to be discovered: a place where real monsters lived and died, well away from the gaze of us land-dwelling, air-breathing mortals, yet it *could* be accessed briefly; if, and only if, you learnt how.

Dad took its picture, and the next day the lamprey was gone, returned to live out its unlikely, and doubtless quite lonely, life in the water running around our tiny village, and I was left to advance an obsession with what else might be caught from water.

In the ironed-out landscape of the Fens, water is absolutely everywhere and, as a result, I grew up an extremely happy little boy.

I needed guidance to access water for the first time of course, but Mum and Dad were never afraid to let me go near the water's edge, with supervision initially, and later on my own.

I was lucky; lucky to have so much space to play in safely, but also lucky to have parents that understood the importance of allowing me to discover the outdoors and water for myself, by myself.

I'm at that stage of life now where all my friends are starting to have children of their own. It only takes moments in the company of a young person to realize that a fear of water is inherited and not innate. Last week, my two-year-old niece Edie was utterly mesmerized by my fish tank, desperate to dip a net in and learn the names of the fish; her wild eyes reflected in the glass sides as her mind hungrily consumed every new scale pattern and plastic leaf. Eventually she reached out her tiny hand and ran it along the tank corner and on into the wet within, learning, in that moment, the curious interplay between glass and water.

It's fascinating to see, and I believe a vitally important part of development, yet most children these days are absolutely forbidden from taking any interest in water outside of the bathtub. How many times have you seen anxious parents grasping the hands of their children in horror as they approach the six inches of 'deep' water at the edge of the municipal park pond? Or adolescents getting terribly scolded for daring to place their fingers in a perfectly clean town centre stream? Eventually these irrationalities rub off and those children grow up with their own unnatural fear of wild water, and, somewhat inevitably, so do their offspring in turn.

Not all of those fears are completely without foundation. Tragically, the last decade has seen an average of 390 people per year drown in accidents in British inland waters; but look a little closer into the figures and you will see that doesn't automatically mean that the water outside our home is inherently dangerous for young children.

Of those 390 the single largest category is males aged between their mid-teens and mid-twenties. Many instances are alcohol-related, most are avoidable: young people looking to prove themselves by swimming distances beyond their ability or fatal injuries caused by diving head first into surprisingly shallow water, or water that is dangerously fast, or too deep, or just shockingly cold. Instead of teaching young people to be aware of the risks and guiding them towards safer areas to play and wild-swim from an early age, the prevailing attitude seems to favour putting up warning signs, locking gates, building barriers and telling our children that natural water should not be entered under any circumstances, and especially not for your entertainment. Let's face it: since when have any of those sorts of measures stopped your average young person hell-bent on besting his or her peers?

Year on year more obstacles to accessing our waters appear, and year on year the number of deaths stays more or less the same. Surely it is better to invest in teaching our children how to manage risk in water, and thereby avoid tragedy, than to let them stay indoors, where they live their lives vicariously through the internet and television?

There are reams and reams of studies proving the physical and mental health benefits of just being near water. More than that though – perhaps most importantly in fact – our fresh water desperately needs our attention.

Thanks to myopic human development, rampant pollution and climate change, freshwater habitats are now easily the most endangered environments on earth. In the last half-century the doubling of freshwater withdrawals for our own ends has caused 50 per cent of wetlands to vanish altogether, and fewer than seventy of the planet's 177 longest rivers remain free of manmade commercial obstructions.

For freshwater fish, the news is even worse: one third of all species are threatened with extinction today, compared to 21 per cent of mammals and 12 per cent of birds. Yet if you cast a speculative eye on the adverts for all the major wildlife charities, you'd be forgiven for thinking our fishy friends are doing just fine; but if you are beginning to think it's bad for them, you should check how awfully the amphibians and freshwater invertebrates are faring.

You may well like to believe it is in the developing world, in the sorts of places where populations are dependent on harvesting freshwater fish just to survive, that the results would be at their worst, but looking at Europe in isolation we see that the number of fish species facing extinction is nudging up to a shameful 40 per cent, and, according to the European Environment Agency, half of our rivers and lakes are polluted. Things aren't much better in the United States either. Over the pond, the rate of fish extinction is now over 800 times faster than in the fossil record.

We are marching to the brink of a worldwide environmental disaster, and yet there is little more than a whimper of protest.

Of course we should all be up in arms, but how can you reasonably expect people to care about saving an environment that they are preconditioned to believe is irrelevant and dirty at best, or a dangerous menace at worst?

Every garden should have a pond. Ours was oval-shaped and about ten feet wide. At one end there was a neat little shallow area that allowed amphibians to come and go as they pleased and provided a safe nursery area for frogs and toads to spawn. It dropped to a depth of no more than a couple of feet from that shallow point and was stepped in at the edges so Mum and Dad could submerge baskets filled with aquatic plants and water lilies. In the summer the centre was near solid with Canadian pond-weed, an invasive species that shrouded the pond's surface with its green pipe-cleaner-like tendrils while providing oxygen as well as shelter to the host of invertebrates that lived within its bulk.

It was here I learnt how to hunt frogs, the first living thing I ever knowingly caught from water (the first living thing I caught unknowingly from water was a 'miller's thumb', a three-inch-long micro-fish with a fat head and rounded tail that slipped inside my wellies when I fell into a stream in Yorkshire).

I was appalling at first. My ham-pink hands slapped the water's surface like a drummer's cymbal each time a frog dared to lift its head above the weed. The first rule I learnt then was to be patient and observe.

Soon enough I realized the frogs in the centre of the pond were never to be caught: they always had a couple of feet of water below them to sink down into, whereas I was aiming at only about half an inch of a frog's head. To go for them in the middle was to disturb the whole pond for hours; the best bet was to wait for them to approach the edge, as the shallower water would significantly narrow the frog's options for escape.

At first I would leap up and try to grab them the moment they came within reach, thus breaking the second rule: keep your profile off the horizon.

Down the frogs would plop en masse. It took me some time to realize that if I stood up, particularly with the sun behind me, the frogs would see my silhouette ten times out of ten and scarper before I could get anything like close enough to catch one. So I took to lying on the grass, obscuring myself with the pond's bordering plants and watching like a tiny blond otter.

It was to be the beginning of a lifelong fixation with peering into water. As a child I couldn't really make out the difference between a natural or a man-made habitat, but that hardly mattered as nor could the wildlife. I remember being amazed to discover that if you left rainwater to puddle in a bucket it would quickly become inhabited all by itself. Usually this just meant a colony of tiny waterbeetles or millions of species of swirling zooplankton, but sometimes I would find mosquito larvae jerking in the water like a tiny hairy finger trapped in a door, and, in bigger, older, water traps, like the defunct water butts or abandoned cattle troughs that got left around farms, it was possible to find small fish, thick black leeches, and, very occasionally, even an eel.

Not all ponds are the same but the best times to observe, and afterwards to fish, were early mornings and later in the afternoon. In most ponds at such times, a background hum of life builds in a crescendo like an orchestra tuning up before the performance begins. This was when our pond was at its most magical. Bright damsels and acrobatic dragonflies, the assassins of the sky, hunted on the wing above my head as fearsome diving beetles plundered the unfortunate larvae living below. I had a soft spot for the alien-faced waterboatmen: they seemed like gentle souls who didn't need to attack anything in the pond, but the pond skaters were always the most impressive. With their fine displays of nimble skills on implausibly long legs, these thumbnail-sized insects comfortably outmanoeuvred the birds and beasts that wanted to eat them by propelling themselves along the pond's meniscus at incredible speed. Dad taught me that everything which lived in the pond relied on the health of its tiniest living organisms, and if I scooped the pond water into my hands and viewed it with my pale palms as a backdrop I could just make out what he was talking about. Hundreds of tiny haphazard dots made up a dense concentration of zooplankton: water fleas, daphnia and the water worms that held this whole environment together. Their presence was why he didn't want to stock our pond with ornamental goldfish or koi carp. Pet fish would soon eat all these miniature friends, as well as the beetle larvae and the frog's tadpoles, until, eventually, the entire system in the pond would stop being able to support itself. Then we would have to buy food to feed the pet fish, food which, I later learnt, was largely made from wild-caught baby sea fish, fish oils and even the krill that provided the foundation of the ocean ecosystem. It all seemed a bit crazy really: damaging one ecosystem to artificially prop up another, so we stuck with the wildlife pond.

If I was really quiet I might be able to see the garden

birds – the song thrushes, blackbirds and sparrows – bathing in the shallow end of the pond. They would do this all year round, even in the middle of winter when the pond had a skin of ice and I could scarcely stand to put my hands in the water, but it seemed to happen most often towards the end of a long hot day. They would shake themselves vigorously afterwards, puffing out their feathers and finery as if they had been placed in front of my mum's hair drier and towelled down. As darkness fell, the pipistrelle bats with their coats coloured like old bricks, their dark ears, faces and wings, would funnel down flying insects by the thousand. I knew I would soon have to go back into the house for tea when that performance began, but not before I checked my surroundings for a repeat appearance from my most exciting discovery of all time: a small shrew that once crawled along the pond's bank and right along my side as I lay there. It sniffed the air with its comically conical nose and screwed up its tiny eyes in disgust. It knew something was up, but I don't believe it ever realized I was there or what I was, before it shuffled its way back into the undergrowth.

The frogs had a curious habit. They would actively hunt and, to my juvenile mind, play in the deeper water, but they tended to come to a standstill when they were submerged in the shallows right in the gaps between the planting baskets. They felt safe there, I guessed, and with that I had cracked my third rule: find the sanctuaries and exploit the routine.

Soon I had my first definite touch of slimy flesh; next I briefly clasped a leg and then, finally, after a summer of study, I proudly held my first frog. I only had it in my hands long enough to splurt out the 'M' of 'Mum', before it released its stripy legs from my clutches and powered its way back into the pond, but it was, in my mind, a massive accomplishment.

I would tell everyone in the family several times of my heroism, establishing a lifelong fourth and final rule: always amplify any special capture, especially if there was no witness.

Finally, with no one else in the house left to tell, and my sister getting visibly irritated by my boorish antics, I made my concluding performance to my grandparents.

'Impressive, son,' Grandad remarked at the curtain call. Lifting an enquiring white eyebrow from behind his large, wire-framed glasses, he casually dropped an absolute thunderbolt into my life:

'So what would you say to trying to catch a fish?'

A spark flickered into life; somewhere well behind my out-and-proud bellybutton and the small of my back: a truly great journey was about to begin.

I was almost five years old when I caught my first fish but I can't tell you what it looked like. I was so excited by the prospect of catching and holding a real live fish that when my float eventually slid under the water, I struck so hard that I projected my catch directly out of the river, over my head, and deep into a field filled with sugar beet.

'A little too hard perhaps, Will,' said Grandad after a short spell of mutual silence.

He took the rod, freshly baited the hook with a couple of maggots, and re-cast into the middle of the Creek.

Technique wasn't all that important in those seminal days. With Grandad it was all about experiencing the first fish on the bank, by whatever means possible, and enjoying time spent in each other's company. That meant size was an irrelevance also. Our best bet, clearly, was with the vast shoals of roach that teemed within the Well Creek right opposite the house. They never seemed to grow beyond a few inches in length, but that didn't mean they were foolish – far from it in fact.

With the float now bobbing happily in the centre of the Creek once more, I was passed back the rod. It was my first, a bright-red two-piece number with a smooth plastic handle and reel loaded with light monofilament line and I loved it more than anything else I have ever owned.

'I'm just going to feed a few maggots to get them interested,' said Grandad, selecting a pinch of the wriggliest bait tin residents and flicking them around the float with extraordinary accuracy. The float bobbed. 'It's another bite!' I screamed, standing up, blowing our cover, and forgetting to strike. Grandad pulled me back into the seated position via the elasticated waistband of my bright-red shorts.

'You've got to stay calm, Will,' he implored in hushed tones, his eyes sparkling with suppressed laughter tears.

I refocused, pleading with the float and river to give me just one more chance. A couple more maggots flew out and then, finally, mercifully, it happened.

In the photo of that first fish, I am sat next to Grandad with a look of utter disbelief plastered across my face; my eyes are as wide as they could possibly be, gripping a length of line with what can only be described as 'a miracle' on the end of my hook.

Incredibly, given how many roach were in the Creek, my trap had worked its way into the mouth of a small skimmer bream. Like the roach, the skimmer appears to be a silverfish but it is, in fact, the juvenile form of the darker and much larger common bream. It differs from the roach in its elongated, slate-grey anal fin on the underside and its generally much flatter, wider appearance; hence its 'skimmer' name, in homage to a skimming stone.

To be honest, it could have been any fish of any species ever; my reaction would have been just the same. In that moment I was the king; the master and commander of the river; the man who had unlocked the secrets of the deep and tamed the great beasts that lay within. It mattered not that this was, in reality, an extremely small specimen either; in that brief moment I had been handed the keys to a lifetime of pleasure and study, and in Grandad I had a more than willing teacher.

*

The five years I then took to reach the age of adolescence revolved around fishing and an endless supply of fishy stories and patient tuition from Grandad. The pond, the conservatory of animals, my family and, later, school all dissolved into the background. I had a new magic man now, capable of conjuring the most almighty tricks with a dainty flick of his thick wrist.

We float-fished for the Creek's roach at any opportunity. He couldn't say no: I was irrepressible. He would rock up to ours usually on a good sunny day as Grandad really hated being cold, even though he did always like to claim: 'There's no such thing as bad weather, just bad clothes choices.' He would be wearing a floppy sunhat, and a T-shirt usually several times too small for his enormous stomach, and would often have a large pork pie secreted somewhere on his person, wrapped within a capacious handkerchief and brought out well away from the interfering eyes of my grandma.

I had the rod and reel of course, a couple of cheap floats, and a handful of hooks and weights he had given to me himself, but he would always ask: 'Got all your stuff then, Will?' as if my collection of tackle were vastly larger, and not, in fact, comfortably able to fit in his top pocket.

Grandad was both a thrifty man and extremely industrious. His fishing gear was as ancient as it was immaculate and his favourite floats were all handmade from drinking straws. 'McDonald's ones are the best,' he often claimed, usually before adding: 'it's the only time you'll see me in that bloody place.' Repetition and consistency are a key component of any good angler, as well as any good grandparent.

The session would begin with my taking ten times longer than him to prepare my rudimentary tackle. I would first thread a small orange-tipped float onto the line by a tiny hole at one of its ends, and then secure its tip with a small rubber float sleeve, a finely cut piece of tubing that fixed the float to the line. Next I would carefully tie on a hook from Grandad and pinch a small line of lead shots intended to cock the float till just its top half-inch would show above the water. Finally, I was ready for bait. I would take an age to decide which two of the tens of thousands of maggots would be skewered onto my hook, usually drop a couple of hundred on the floor by accident, and then spear the grubs through the wrong end and have to start all over again.

When I was eventually ready to make a cast I would either overdo it and chuck the whole lot straight into a tree, or I would forget to release the line on the reel and tangle my float approximately one million times around the rod tip. Both eventualities took time to fix, and would nearly always result in me having to start the whole process again from scratch.

Grandad would never fish on through my dramas, but he wouldn't just sort it out for me either. I had to learn to do things properly, and, as tackle cost money, it paid to learn quickly.

Time passed and gradually I improved. In the early

days any fish was a real bonus, but several seasons in I was beginning to catch nearly every time we went out. Expectancy is a terrible thing in fishing: it murders the heady rawness of feeling you get from the first few fish you ever caught by suffocating it under a fixation with catching as many fish, or as big a fish, as you possibly can. Sadly, a bit like the first time you ever fell properly in love, or saw a magic trick, or rode on a rollercoaster, that exhilarating feeling of holding one of your earliest fish can never be matched by simply catching more of the same.

With the sheen fading from the silver scales of the roach I began to wonder what other challenges might be living within the depths of the Creek. One day, while quickly retrieving a red-fin roach along the Creek's surface, a massive impact tore my fish clean off the end of the hook. My line fell limp at the rod tip and I turned to Grandad, near rigid with shock.

'Pike, son,' he said, with a solemn and knowing glance at the pathetic remains of my roach, which was now little more than a smattering of tiny silver scales descending to a murky oblivion.

I had just been humbled. That was a man's fish and I knew I wasn't ready to take it on, but luckily there was another, more pocket-sized, predator lingering close to my diminutive grasp.

The temperature gauge on my van tells me it's a dispiriting 4°C outside. I flick the indicator to take a long right-hand turn at the roundabout by the football club, and steam happily away from the commuter traffic trailing into Cardiff for work.

It feels like the wrong day to begin this challenge – the Vale of Glamorgan strikes me as particularly numb and lifeless this morning: lumpen, cold and grey, like the contents of a mortician's drawer. I turn up the fan heater and squeeze the accelerator.

It's overcast too but that doesn't bother me nearly as much. Big perch hate bright conditions. To be fair, even 4°C isn't truly the end of the world – there's plenty of fish willing to feed in those conditions; but this is the first major temperature drop after a sustained period of double digits, which is very bad news indeed as fish really dislike sudden changes in temperature, and, worse still, the opening frost of winter is forecast to arrive tonight. That's an event guaranteed to put every fish in Britain off its food.

After a frost some fish species will remain on the bottom; hidden, in a trance-like torpor, just subsisting off their reserves until the warmer months stir them back to life. Others, like the perch, will adjust to the colder climes after just a few days and will gradually come back on the feed.

The worst possible time you can try and angle for them is just after a frost; the second-worst time is right now: just as it's starting. By rights, I should have stayed under the duvet this morning, but I felt I had one very good reason for wanting it today more than most.

Fishermen are among the worst offenders when it

comes to believing in 'signs'. I've seen the most hardened atheist turn clairvoyant when it comes to the desperate search for a fish-filled future; scientific anglers who, no matter what the conditions, will only fish their lures and flies in a certain order; and those who sincerely believe that a specific choice of socks or the sudden appearance of an auspicious bird or favourite mammal can conjure a fish for the fishless. Even my grandad, a no-nonsense engineer throughout his working days, would never fish the river if there was even a hint of a westerly wind.

What was sticking in my craw that morning was that it was precisely a year ago to the day that I lost the biggest perch of my life: I simply had to go fishing.

A little perch is almost always every little fisher's first ever fish. It wasn't quite mine of course, but they were an ever-present pleasure in the Creek, ready to step in and save my blushes when a blank day seemed otherwise inevitable.

'Like a Japanese Warrior in his medieval armour,' intoned Jack Hargreaves in his 1951 classic book, *Fishing for a Year*; and what a perfect simile that is for this classy little predator. With its hard, sharpened gill plates, black eyes, and spine-tipped and sail-like dorsal fin, the perch is absolutely built for a fight; but it's a strikingly handsome fish too: its flanks are marked by a series of immaculate black stripes blended perfectly over a dark olive backdrop. With striking blood-red fins and a whitened-cream belly that is wonderfully plump in the bigger specimens, it really is one of the best-looking of all the freshwater fish.

Unsurprisingly, it was one of the most in-demand fish to pass under the taxidermist's scalpel in the Victorian era; but it's the perch's mouth that truly must strike the fear of God into any fish or bait unlucky enough to fit inside, for the perch must be the greediest fish ever to have lived.

Its jutting jaw is specially hinged, allowing its over-sized mouth to engulf surprisingly large prey. As a boy I would often catch them fishing on lures intended for pike ten times larger, such is the perch's capacity to sense weakness and an opportunity. When they are in the mood, they will bully their patch of water and intimidate others with a yobbish enthusiasm.

On the Creek we would catch them near boat moorings, reed-lined banksides or, more often than not, directly beneath wooden jetties: right in among the pilings, where they can leap back and forth from their ambush point. Clearly, they are comfortable in large shoals. I remember one astonishing day with my little brother when we simply could not stop catching them. Like shelling peas, we flicked them out one after the other from an area under a landing stage no bigger than a ping-pong table. Eventually, it got so embarrassing we had to stop and upended a keepnet filled with at least a hundred little stripy fish.

On a clear day I would observe the Creek's vast perch

shoals, tucked tight into the holes and structures they preferred, allowing their zebra stripes and dorsals to fuse with the reeds, wood or each other, till the individuals were near indistinguishable from the shoal. From here they would conduct their remorseless assaults: plundering the roach-fry like a marlin destroys a bait ball, sending their panicked prey scattering on the surface in great shimmering plumes of silver.

On occasion I would spot one or two that were clearly a lot larger than the rest: hump-backed and aloof, these were the adults. These wise old fish were given respectable space by the smaller fish in the shoal, most likely not out of deference, but because big perch have a cannibal's reputation.

They would observe me with an infuriating indifference as I made cast after cast in their direction, never once looking even remotely likely to come to my hook. Eventually they would tire of my intrusion, and would simply disappear with a flick of the tail; leaving a boy with a face redder than his rod, kicking up clods of turf in wretched frustration.

The Wilson *Encyclopedia* describes a 'mega-specimen' as any perch over 3lb, and lists the British record at 5lb 9oz, but, as I write, the current record is now headed by two separate fish caught just a year apart, and which tipped the scales at a whopping 6lb 3oz.

What I wouldn't give to catch such a perch. I can't think of any other species where the gulf in skill between catching the smallest member and the largest is so vast. It has to be one of the biggest challenges available to the British angler. Once hooked the perch is unmistakable. The pugnacious jag-jag-jagging fight, as they repeatedly dive back for their cover, is like having your line attached to the sword of an Olympic fencer. It singles out the striped assassin every single time. In the bigger ones this pulsing motion is only magnified, till the shudders on your rod register with the force of a piledriver.

As a child, having blown my opportunity to snare a big one for just about the millionth time, I consulted Grandad on the appropriate method for snaring the larger of these princely predators. 'The tail of a lobworm, nicked through the bloody stump,' he opined simply, in much the same manner as a witch might recommend a wicked potion for curing warts.

'Is that really all there is to it, Grandad?' I enquired, my heart full of hope.

Grandad was a keen devotee at the church of lobworm; they were the only alternative bait he would consider when his maggots failed to work. He dug his mud snakes, the largest of the British earthworm species, out of the sweet-smelling compost heap he managed out the back of the bungalow. From there, he would roll them tight within long leaves of newspaper and stick them in his large white chest freezer.

I recall the first time he showed me his supply. 'Don't be shy about using a big hook; it'll work, but, look,

Will . . .' He stopped and fixed me with his big brown eyes. '. . . big perch need patience. You can't be jumping about and re-casting all the time. You have to learn to time it right: early mornings or the last hour of light.'

He placed his giant forearms on the chest freezer's top and leant forward. 'You must be prepared to wait for him to make the first mistake. Otherwise,' he added, 'there's not much point in you even trying.'

In much the same way that I discovered collecting conkers was actually more fun than playing with them, I took to collecting worms with more enthusiasm and early success than catching big perch. Of course, Grandad had me pegged. Totally.

I had heard the best time to look for the biggest worms was in the dead of night, just after a summer storm, preferably on the outfield of a cricket pitch. That seemed like a ludicrous number of variables to me, and with night-time cricket matches in the rain particularly thin on the ground in my patch of Cambridgeshire, I took to re-creating a rain storm with a washing-up bowl filled with Fairy Liquid suds, and the tactical deployment of a gently wiggled garden fork. Once I got it right it was like raising Medusa's hair from the turf. Up the worms would pop en masse, no doubt poisoned from their homes by the sudden influx of soap, and I would scoop them up and into my bait tin with unbridled glee.

One week later the largest and juiciest of all my incarcerated lobworms landed within an inch of a big creek perch's mouth with a resounding thump.

It was the stealth equivalent of hiding behind a door for an hour to quietly surprise your mate, and then slapping him round the face with a draught excluder the second he walked into the room. Naturally the big perch flushed immediately from its hole in fright, leaving me sat impotently watching my giant worm squirm its way along the bottom without a single fish anywhere else in sight.

What was it about these cursed bloody worms? Perch holes and playgrounds: lobworms seemed to clear them both with ruthless efficiency.

For thirty seconds I waited, roasting from the inside out with a furious impatience. How did Grandad do it? When I did give up, I made sure I gave the turf the most solid kick I had in me before heading straight home to catch more worms, swearing blind that day I would never bother trying to catch big perch ever again.

After the sand eel was lost and the Wilson *Encyclopedia* found, it made sense to me to start my quest with big perch. Not just because they had such a presence in my childhood, but also because it was the perch that had slowly begun to ease me off my carp addiction in the months before the sand eel hammer blow.

It started with a few speculative casts with a worm a couple of years ago; purely to fill in time when the carp weren't biting. I wasn't expecting anything to happen, but, to my sheer delight, my float zipped away with a familiar jagging riposte and I found the swarms of little perch had been dutifully waiting for me, almost as if they had been following me around since I was a little boy.

With a bit more managed neglect of my carp rod, a slightly bigger hook and the careful chumming of the water with broken lobworm, I soon found I could even winkle out the odd larger perch in the shoal. Okay, they weren't that big, perhaps only a pound or so, but I was at least aware that these were indeed the striped 'monsters' of my childhood memories and so venerated them sufficiently.

The following year I made my first concerted effort to target even bigger perch. I did some research, modified my tackle, and shipped in 200 live lobworms that I established in a garden shed bucket and fattened up on vegetable scraps. Within the year I had my first 2lb fish: a stunning, bristling specimen that scrapped all the way to my net in a heart-stopping account of itself. As I held it in my hands I felt a sort of electrical pulse of excitement that I hadn't experienced since I was a boy. Just why had I wasted the last twenty years fishing almost exclusively for one species of fish? I slipped her back, the dorsal slicing the water like a serrated knife through an apple, and would meet the sand eel on my very next trip out.

In the past twenty years of fishing almost exclusively in stocked carp lakes I had inadvertently stumbled across a very modern phenomenon. With commercial carp waters sprouting up all over Britain, big perch have found a habitat where they can absolutely thrive. In these lakes there are generally no pike present to cull their numbers or compete for the baitfish, and barely any angling pressure from the hordes of Cyclopean fishermen targeting only carp. As a result the perch in these ponds have been allowed to grow to prodigious proportions. Out of the biggest fifty perch caught in Britain nearly half have come from commercially stocked lakes in the last decade; a staggering result that is hardly matched in any other fish species mentioned in this book.

Year on year the established perch records are being pressed and even the 3lb Wilson mega-specimen has seemingly become a happy resident in almost every carp pond you care to mention. You shouldn't be foolish enough to think that means they are easy to catch; big perch will always continue to play their cards very close to their chest, and only the best of anglers will regularly snare the largest specimens. It took me two winters' worth of outings before I had my first decent one, and another year before I had a brush with my very own perch-of-a-lifetime, right here, at the very venue whose gates I was swinging into.

White Springs is pretty much your blueprint for any commercial pond complex you care to pick in the country. It's got a variety of manmade lakes offering everything from pleasure fishing for carp over double figures, right up to a specimen lake with carp over 45lb stirring up the waters. So far, so similar; however, what really set my pulse racing were the reports of the resident perch in one of the ponds: they sounded mega, even by the high standards of this golden age of perch fishing.

I read an article where the author details snaring not one, but three, perch over 3lb in a single session here, which he then topped off with a truly ridiculous fish of over 4lb. Surely, I thought, this had to be one of the greatest big-perch hauls in history, but a few clicks of the mouse proved these ponds had even more to give. A fish of over 5lb is resident here. I've seen its picture. It's a brooding, menacing predator with huge flanks and an appetite to match.

Three-pounders, four-pounders, and even a five: if you were to place that against carp, it would be the equivalent of having a lake holding a fish over 55lb with a head of fish over 40lb as a back-up. It would be among the most celebrated fishing lakes in the country, yet as I roll down the tarmac road and into the complex it becomes apparent that I am going to be fishing the perch ponds almost completely on my own.

I settle right back into the swim where I lost the big one the previous season. It's on a lake known as the Big Pit, an area of water where the White Springs management have fused two lakes together, removing the earthen bank between one lake, which resembled a small canal and held some of the big perch, and another, larger, rounder pond that housed some of the bigger carp.

I have to avoid those carp at all costs now. My perch

tackle is light, so a hook-up with one of the lake's golden mud pigs will necessitate a long and laborious fight which I'm most likely to lose, plus it will certainly scare off any of the big perch that I'm hoping to persuade to my hook.

This cold front will do me a real favour in that respect – carp really don't like the colder months; but there's still a chance I might snare one that's ignoring the forecast, so to boost my chances further I'm avoiding all the baits I would commonly use to target carp (pellets, corn and boilies), and I'm also steering well clear of any parts of the pond where the carp might still be active: the warmer, shallower areas which get more of the limited sunlight, and those fishing platforms which have seen a lot of regular angling activity and feeding. This still might not be enough, though, so I'll also be ready to cut right back on my loose feed of red maggots and broken worms if it looks like I'm attracting the unwanted attention of the *Cyprinus carpio*. Make no mistake, this is a seriously challenging prospect given the intensity of my addiction to that species – a bit like offering a free cigarette to a recently reformed chain smoker – but if I'm going to take this challenge seriously I have to focus my mind solely on the perch.

This corner of the pond absolutely screams 'perch'. It's the area with the thickest banks of marginal reeds, the largest overhanging bushes and, if my depth plummet isn't lying to me, the deepest, darkest holes around.

I can almost feel that big perch's presence; pressed up,

somewhere in the darkness, tight against the sunken tree roots and reeds, perfectly camouflaged, waiting to strike me down with those wild black eyes.

I begin by scooping a dozen red maggots into my catapult. I'm aiming to keep these going in every minute or so. Hopefully the 'little but often' feeding routine will bring into the swim the shoals of little baitfish that the bigger perch like to feed on. If that fails, I've got the crutch of these broken lobworms to rest back on. Chopping them up into pieces will release a slick of worm's blood into the swim: catnip for the big perch. The scent will draw them in, then they'll find all the baitfish, then 'bang': they'll inhale my irresistible bait.

I hook a juicy lobworm through the tail and give it an underhand flick right into the dark shadows at the foot of the reeds. I'll have to be vigilant: any signs of scattering baitfish or big swirls could well be the perch's dinner bell sounding. I may only get one chance to snare a really large one.

Gently, I tighten the line between my hook, the weight and my rod tip, till I can register a bite simply by watching for any minute movement at the end of my rod. Satisfied, I settle back into my chair; and immediately hook into a massive carp.

'For fuck's sake!'

The rod arches down to breaking point and the reel screams in deference as the fish ploughs directly between two small islands. I tighten everything down as much as

I dare, and apply side pressure. My rod forms an almost perfect parabola.

Hold it, Will; just hold it. If it gets behind the islands it's game over.

The line whines in the wind, I'm dancing on the very edge of catastrophe here, but finally I feel the great fish start to turn. Weakness: it's hammer time. I reel down hard and gradually gain ground, steering the carp successfully back through the island maze towards me.

This is a nightmare. The worst possible start. I daren't even begin to think about the damage this carp has already done to my chances with the perch. I prepare my net but the fish is still nowhere near ready; with one giant thump of the tail it cuts its passage straight up the pond, ploughing away from the islands, and my corner, and out into the open water.

That I don't mind at all; it's well away from my traps and there are no obstacles out there. Keep sustaining the pressure and let the rod do all the work. It'll soon start to tire. I'm back in control now. It's just a matter of time.

Actually, this might not be that bad after all. If the grand culture of fishing superstition is to be believed then all that is happening here is that history is repeating itself. This happened last year too. First cast: giant carp. Second cast: giant perch.

The fish reveals itself: it is a stunning ghost carp with golden-white scales and a dark-grey skull pattern framing its head. It's a bit smaller than last year's carp, but for some reason the ghost carp always seem to punch above their weight. I slip it into my landing net first time and walk the fish safely down the pond; as far as possible from my perch spot, and to a place where hopefully it can warn all its carpy mates not to come bothering me up in my corner.

Resettling after such chaos takes time. Lines and bait boxes are strewn everywhere. It's important after any big fish that you don't just cast straight back in. Heart rates and water need time to settle back into a rhythm and hurried casts can result in lost fish and tackle.

After that carp I feel like I'm chasing my shadow, ghosting right back into my mis-steps and mistakes from last year. I remember clearly my next act a year ago: I flung the worm straight back out before I was properly ready and not thirty seconds later the rod tip thumped down hard. I lifted, but I didn't initially feel that familiar perchy fight: I felt a sustained pressure without quite the reel-stripping runs of a truly large carp.

'A small carp,' I supposed then, and bullied it back towards me.

It wasn't till it was almost under the rod that I had the first obvious clue that this was in fact a truly massive perch. The rod suddenly buckled down as the fish dived hard for the wooden posts by my feet. I remember leaving my seat at that point, falling dramatically to one knee and leaning right across the water with my rod outstretched in my hand. The line grated up hard and horrible against the posts and I was convinced I was about to lose it, but, much to my surprise, the perch erupted on the surface right before me.

Time stood still; and, unfortunately, so did I.

I came to my senses at precisely the same time as the giant perch and made a hurried grab for my net just as the perch turned its giant head. It was so large you could have fitted a tangerine in its mouth, and with a single pump of its tail it brought my rod tip back down with tremendous force.

The next scenes unfolded in a bit of a blur. I realized, with sheer horror, that the line had somehow tangled intractably around the arm of the reel. I tried desperately to free it but big fish rarely give second chances and, in that split-second window of weakness, the giant perch freed itself from the hook and was gone. For ever.

It sounds ridiculous, but I bet if I had never seen that perch reveal itself on the surface I would have landed it. The realization that I had my dream fish within touching distance caused me to lose all reason and form. I changed from the confident bully into the horrified victim in an instant. It still makes me shudder at the thought.

'Anyway. You can't let that happen again now, Will,' I tell myself for what feels the millionth time.

I catapult out another pouch of maggots and flick the worm back into the danger zone. Ice cool. I refocus.

Very sadly, history shows no interest in repeating itself. Several hours later, by the time I finally decide to give up and go home, the mercury has plummeted to such an extreme extent that my landing net has frozen solid to the grass. On the drive back, as my fingers come screaming back to life in front of the van's heaters, I swear blind that this will be my last trip to White Springs this winter.

After last year's disaster I have spent a week of my life traipsing up and down the M4 on a hundred-mile round trip, desperately hoping to snare that giant perch again. It has been as torturous as it was futile. I haven't caught a single decent fish.

That all has to stop now. If I am to catch a record, I want it at least to have been fun. Not just me sat static at the most boring end of fishing, freezing cold and achieving absolutely nothing.

It would be all too easy now to simply blame my venue choice for my own shortcomings as an angler. There is nothing actually wrong with White Springs, and those spectacular perch certainly haven't gone anywhere, but it is every inch the commercial fishery. From its sculpted islands to its trimmed shrubs and manicured fishing platforms, it is precisely the sort of place I was supposed to be weaning myself off during this challenge. If I'm going to keep coming to places like this, then I may as well just chuck the Wilson *Encyclopedia* in the lake and carry on catching carp.

I can hear what you are thinking: I bet if you had landed that big perch you wouldn't feel that way. Of course I wouldn't. But I didn't, did I?

*

As the frost settled into something of a rhythm and temperatures stabilized once more, the memory of the various White Springs debacles began to fade. I took up a permit with my local angling club and filled my boots on big perch from a remote farmland pond, finally cracking the 2lb barrier, and snaring more than a dozen fish over 1lb 8oz in one quite remarkable evening. My confidence was restored. I hardly lost a fish that month, and felt far more comfortable with the haphazard rhythm of the big perch's fight. In fact, I can quite honestly say I only broke sweat on a couple of occasions: once, when I accidentally locked the van behind the lake gates, and then lost the key, and then experienced my first serious breakdown; and next, while leaving the lake on another occasion, when I blundered directly into the path of a massive boar badger and almost shit my socks.

I wasn't closing in on that Wilson mega-specimen, though, and knew in my heart of hearts it was probably time to take a long hard look at Grandad's traditional techniques.

Really, as undoubtedly effective as worms clearly still were, I hadn't done anything to update my approach in over twenty-five years; I'd just picked up from where Grandad had left me, rolling his worms into the giant chest freezer.

I began a trawl for new methods and was very surprised to discover that perch fishing was practically everywhere: multiple blogs, on the covers of magazines, all over the internet forums, and in many, many, viral videos. Catching perch seemed suddenly very 'in', and, dare I say, actually, a little bit 'cool'.

Without a doubt, the single greatest piece of public relations to come out of the sport has been the impact of light-rock fishing (LRF) from Japan. In the past, lure-fishing meant shapely chunks of metal, spinners or spoons, and wooden 'plugs', moulded to resemble the features of a wounded baitfish and pulled through the water in a manner designed to fool predatory fish into a take. The trick of LRF is to take these basics and radically lighten the approach. In this way new, infinitesimally small spinners appeared on the market alongside thousands of micro-lures, -jigs and -jerkbaits made of ultra-lightweight rubber and malleable plastics in a bewildering array of colours, shapes and designs.

The masterstroke of LRF is that it has even made fishing for smaller predatory fish really exciting. For fishermen armed with short rods, matched with lightweight reels and hypersensitive braided lines, even the little wasp-like perch are a tantalizing target once again, their attacks registering on the subtle line with an extraordinary jarring force, every run, lunge and headshake transmitted down the rod with surgical precision.

LRF isn't just for small fish though; most of our recent record-breaking perch have been caught using these tactics and, believe me, when you actually do hook into something substantial the feeling of that first heart-stopping run never leaves you.

*

Thanks to LRF, urban fishing is back with a bang, and it was on those previously overlooked waterways that I decided to focus my gaze now.

Armed with a packet of inch-long, rubber, snow-white lures known as 'grass minnows', I scanned through a long list of options for a big-city stripy. The obvious choice would be somewhere on the Thames. The perch-fishing pedigree of this river placed it somewhere among the very best perch rivers in the country, and, according to the perch record list, a 6lb 4oz unclaimed record was landed there just a couple of years ago by a man listed only as 'Bill'. How cool is that? According to reports he had to be forced into declaring any element of his catch at all. I desperately wanted to meet this 'Bill'; a perch-fishing Jedi master to my young Skywalker; but most of all I wanted to meet his perch.

Of course, only a fool would target a river as long as the Thames for just one fish, but Bill's perch was far from the only big one. There's barely a week that passes without a Wilson mega-specimen popping up some-where on that river, either in the press or online, and the overwhelming majority of them are falling to the new LRF techniques.

I had only fished the Thames once before, from a town park in the leafy Berkshire town of Pangbourne, but even then I conspired to lose a very big perch that had engulfed a small roach just as I was about to get it into the net.

That was a 'free-to-fish' spot, and with a little research

I soon found there were actually many more miles of free fishing along other parts of this iconic river. Perfect. It felt too good to be true. I bought a new, ridiculously small rod, coupled with an even smaller reel, and spooled up with braided line. Then I got very over-excited, very prematurely.

Within twenty-four hours Storm Barney had ripped through the nation, bringing gale-force winds and heavy rains in its wake. That rain didn't let up for a week and soon nearly every river in Britain had swelled to bursting point.

I didn't even need to leave the house to know for sure that the Thames would have gone into a serious state of spate; a sort of turbulent chocolate milkshake condition that would need at least another week to settle back down.

The free fishing was irrelevant and my lightweight gear was useless. I chewed my fingers down to stubs.

That's not to say you can't fish flooded rivers – some of the best catches I have ever made have been in the calm areas and eddies where fish are forced to take refuge from the chaos of the main flow during a spate; but LRF fishing in heavy water isn't much fun at all. Even if you do manage to find clean runs away from all the storm detritus, getting the fish to see the lure in heavily coloured water is extremely hard, and getting your light gear to behave in a natural way is nigh on impossible.

*

I had an interview in London coming up that was within a stone's throw of the Grand Union Canal. It wasn't a patch of water I knew very well at all; in fact, I could comfortably count on one hand the amount of times I'd even seen it, but I did know that canals are always a sound bet when the weather is rough.

Canals had to be constructed to allow for the year-round passage of cargo during Britain's industrial heyday. The canal engineers certainly couldn't afford to let a few drops of rain stop traffic, so, with a deliberately even depth and flow provided by numerous manmade gates, locks and drains, you can get far more fishable water in rough conditions; plus, these days, with all the canal boats, low-slung bridges and concrete pilings, there are plenty of features for big perch to hide around and under as well. But the Grand Union Canal? In central London? Really?

The catch reports I read were very mixed, and in some cases downright dangerous. News articles detailed fishermen who were robbed of all of their gear at knife-point, and others who had actually been pushed in by thugs looking for a laugh. The perch stories ranged from the ludicrous – one man claiming to have landed a seven-pounder from the Paddington area – to the plausible: a head of three-pounders dwelling somewhere within the deeper locks of Camden. But to get anything more specific than that required a more effective knowledge of code-breaking than the employees of Bletchley Park had.

I guess I could understand the need for some secrecy. Having put in so much work to locate a fish you wouldn't then want every jolly perch fisher or poacher from W7 to E6 to descend on your mark and clean up; but some of the anglers had gone to truly ludicrous lengths to hide their knowledge: pictures of giant perch clutched by men who had blurred or blackened the entire background of their image, and others who had even gone so far as to obscure their own faces, as if they were part of a perch-based witness protection programme.

I didn't really get it. If you didn't want people to know where you were fishing then why bother putting up pictures of you with fish on the internet in the first place? Unless, of course, you are just showing off and hyper-inflating your own sense of self-importance by blurring your face and background, in which case, why not go the whole hog and come up with an entirely new social-media profile to complete your disguise, instead of posting with your actual name, actual address and actual school leaver's details just one mouse click away?

What really irritated me on all of these blogs, pages and sites was the sheer amount of vitriol reserved for people who did not conform to the rules of the perch-fishing clique. Anglers who posted pictures with specific details of where their fish were caught were slammed for not caring about the welfare of the fish, and those who held their perch with arms outstretched in pride were ridiculed for making their catch appear bigger than it actually was, as if that matters at all at the end of the day.

The worst of the wrath, however, was aimed at those who dared post a picture of their catch with a weight that was not deemed plausible by this, extraordinarily sad, minority of armchair anglers.

I remember one young lad in particular who caught the absolute perch of a lifetime from a town centre pond. It was a fish that looked every inch a record breaker: a glorious, solid-looking perch, which I would happily give away every rod in my household to catch. Doubtless, he was extremely proud of his catch, and, quite reasonably, thought it might be a good idea to post it on the 'Perch Fishing' Facebook group. However, for daring to post the location, weight and method of his catch, he was thrown to the virtual lions and torn to absolute shreds.

Within the hour the picture was gone, as was this boy's Facebook profile, and no doubt any intentions he may have had to learn more about perch fishing from the adults.

If it had happened at that boy's school they would have all been suspended for bullying, but on this platform I'm in no doubt it was pats on the back all round for another job well done. That's what the internet is all about these days though, isn't it?

And so it was as I watched legions of newcomers to the sport turned off for good, derided simply for wanting to publicly celebrate their perch, and feel part of this bizarre little club.

*

It had been a while since I had been in London but I felt I knew the city fairly well, having lived here for a year in my mid-twenties, a piece of my own history I shared with Grandad.

He had actually been part of the engineering team that had helped design the Thames Barrier in the 1970s, a pioneering construction built near Greenwich to stop the city from being flooded in the event of a storm surge or exceptionally high tide; but it's fair to say Grandad revelled in telling anyone and everyone he met about what a truly miserable place he thought our capital city to be.

I remember the first time I visited as a teenager, and, on returning to the village, made the huge mistake of relating to him the following comment by a bus driver: 'In London you are either looking at a shithole or living in one.' Grandad, I recall, nodded along sagely, as if Buddha himself had crafted this singular piece of crude wisdom. 'Well,' he eventually said, 'he's right. Lonely too.'

I swore there and then that I would never go to London through choice, but somewhat inevitably, given the lack of entry-level employment opportunities for a budding Factual Documentarian in the Fens, I ended up in London anyway, and, to my great surprise, absolutely fell in love with the place.

London, despite its faults, is one of the greatest cities on Earth, and don't let anyone tell you otherwise. For me, by day, it may have been: 'I simply can't understand

why you're still stood in shot and not bringing our sandwiches', but by night I was free to enjoy deliberately long
strolls home in the darkness, through the buzzing Car-
ibbean markets of Shepherds Bush, along the Royal
Parklands, and down past the glitzy West London casi-
nos where I watched Manny Pacquiao knock out Ricky
Hatton live from the MGM Grand, and once lost a
month's wages in just twenty minutes.

For a young man from a small village simply living in
London was like getting my own star on the Hollywood
Boulevard. I could not believe I was living in the capital
and seeing instantly familiar sights like Tower Bridge,
Big Ben and Piccadilly Circus with my own eyes and not
just on TV. It was the sheer scope and cultural diversity
of the place that truly blew my socks off though.

'London isn't a place at all. It's a million little places,'
commented Bill Bryson, and I have to say I wholeheart-
edly agree. I feasted on all the pleasures to be had by
throwing myself fully into this city's life and began to
wonder if Grandad had simply been overwhelmed by
it all.

Of course, it isn't fair to write anywhere off with a
sweeping statement, but having now lived in several big
cities I have to say they can dish up a very special brand
of isolation if you let them.

When faced with such diversity, opportunity and
choice, to be incapable of seizing any of it for yourself,
through no fault of your own, is to feel like the loneliest
leper in the colony. The city then becomes the problem,

and will provide evidence for your chosen prejudice wherever you wish to seek it out.

As much as I loved and appreciated all the parklands in London it never once occurred to me that I might be able to fish the canals. In my mind they were irredeemably dirty, the haunts of pimps and muggers and certainly not places to be spending any of my free time in. Whenever I peered into them I saw not near limitless opportunity to fish, but waste and weed, beer bottles and piss; an environment devoid of any life worth looking for.

It's extraordinary looking back to think how easily I turned my back on fishing that year, and so it was that the delights of the Grand Union Canal remained hidden from me, until today.

My alarm sounded at a little past 6 a.m. I was staying with friends right out in East London. Ordinarily this would pose a real barrier to a day's fishing in the city centre, as just the thought of piling on the Underground during rush hour with all my fishing tackle is enough to give me heart palpitations, but that is the beauty of LRF: no one would even have to know.

Just what do you wear for an interview when you know you're going to spend the rest of the day fishing? I suppose the obvious answer would be to favour whichever of the two activities is more important to you and dress accordingly; but that's a dangerous path for me to be walking down and one I suspected wouldn't ever lead to an economically sustainable future, so I had opted for a halfway house: fishing trousers paired with a smart shirt and my fishing jacket to go on top, but within moments of boarding the Tube it becomes apparent that I have got it very wrong indeed.

In the bright light I realize I had been happily spraying Lynx Africa deodorant over what is quite obviously a large circular patch of fish slime on the breast of my jacket: I smell like a teenage boy who has just rolled along the floor in a fishmonger's and then stuck a shirt on.

We pause at Stratford and my aroma wafts in and out of the doors as commuters stream on. A few people scrunch up their noses in disgust, so I do the same, with a shifty sideways glance in an attempt to palm the smell off onto some other unfortunate on the Tube.

Thankfully I'm ignored. Smells on the Tube are simply another inconvenience to add to the thousands of others these Londoners will have to face down today.

I wonder who else here might want to go fishing for a half-hour and what a difference it could make to their day. We pull into Liverpool Street station and dozens of smartphones flicker into life. Emails are coming in. Even down in this hole you can't escape work. These people don't actually have half an hour: they are 24/7 slaves to their emails and work.

I've been in those offices. You procrastinate through half the day but wouldn't dare admit you could get your work done in half the time; you eat your lunch at your desk and then wait to be the last person to leave at the end of the day; you send emails in the middle of the night to give the impression of diligence, when in fact all you're doing is confirming your total servitude to a group of overlords who'll never even notice the extra hours you put in.

We're losing out on our leisure time right across British cities and largely it's a problem of our own making. I moved from this city, worked fewer hours, got out more, and surprisingly got a lot more work done as a result.

Capping the mind-bending and inefficient seventy- to eighty-hour weeks made me much more focused when I was in work, and much happier when I wasn't. I was largely getting to do what I wanted to do outside of work (which was fish) and I slept much better due to the increase in physical activity and fresh air.

I'm determined to prove that it is still possible to go into work, even in our capital city, and find some time to fish somewhere nearby; but it doesn't even need to be fishing – you can do whatever *you* want to do with *your* time as long as it's not illegal and you're back in work on time. The only thing I ask is that if you are a boss employer that you don't read this to mean that I'm promoting the idea of fishing in the lunch break purely to increase productivity for your company: this is about my readers escaping your clutches during the break they richly deserve; it's for them, about them, and your work doesn't come into it – in fact I recommend you try it out for yourself as long as it doesn't become an official 'work outing', 'a team-bonding exercise' or something else as excruciatingly lame.

A man spots my rod so I give him a little smile. He looks at me with large, doleful, baggy eyes: 'Get me out of here,' they plead.

My interview finishes at a very agreeable time. I think it went well: they didn't once mention the smell from my jacket and I reckon they thought the fishing gear was actually pretty charming.

Stepping out of the shiny glass building and onto the Euston Road it's clear I'm not going to get everything my way today. The heavens open and it starts pitching it down hard. Clearly, Storm Barney hasn't let us go yet. I pull my cap over my eyes and head towards King's Cross station.

In keeping with most areas around major train stations the world over, the immediate vicinity of King's Cross is truly one of London's grimmest areas. It really shouldn't be – the station itself is full of Victorian splendour with its neat bricks, grand arches and glass façade, and just down the road is the equally stunning St Pancras Renaissance Hotel and British Library, but the fast-food restaurants, ugly coffee shops, horns, sirens and shouting give it a feel of a place where people would only ever wish to arrive or leave.

Moments later I felt like I was in an entirely new city. The black atmosphere diminished with every squelching step I took down York Way; there was water around here for sure, and it had already cast its comforting net wide down this street.

I pop my head over a low wall, hoping to spot it, but only find rows of parked trains. A little further on I spy the unmistakable shape of a bridge, but it's got traffic piling over it and doesn't look like a particularly inviting spot for my first look at the canal. You can't mess up your first approach to water. It has to feel right; you've got to give your patch space to display itself in its best finery – otherwise you might find yourself writing the water off prematurely and miss out on something truly special.

I take the next right down a narrow alley. I'll catch her out further downstream. Soon I'm passing behind a posh business building, and there, at the alley's end, the world opens out splendidly into wonderful calm water. This is Battlebridge Basin. Victory.

It is hemmed in on all sides by up-market housing developments and the noise from King's Cross is totally suppressed here, leaving this blissful oasis jutting fully 150 metres inwards from the main flow of the canal.

It's wide too, fifty metres across I later learn, and, better yet, it has relatively little weed and no obvious 'no fishing' signs: the perfect place to have my first speculative cast.

I extend my telescopic travel rod and check the sharpness of the hook point by gently pressing it against the cuticle of my thumbnail. There are not many places to actually cast a clean line. The rows of brightly coloured canal boats on the far side look well worth a chuck, but on this bank I've got about fifteen metres of the alley end and a covered walkway leading across a marbled floor at the back of an architectural firm. Still, fifteen metres is better than nothing, and there is at least enough room to put a couple of long casts into the centre of Battlebridge Basin, and probably a couple more along the weeping brickwork running along the water's edge.

I'd better get on with it, at any rate; I'm being eyeballed suspiciously by a security guard with biceps like coiled ropes.

The grass minnow plops into the drink and the time it takes to settle on the bottom tells me that this place is a hell of a lot deeper than it looks. From this point on, I'm fishing on faith and feel.

The braided line and soft rod are incredible; I twitch the minnow through the water and can feel every single bump, nook and cranny, as I make my first retrieve. The rain pours on the surface, flattening it and obscuring any potential signs of schooling baitfish, but I don't mind that at all as the water is painfully clear so a bit of natural cover plays into my hand and obscures my outline.

I'm going to have to box clever today. There's no point taking all my time to cover every single inch of water: the fish are either there or they're not. I need to target specific features: something that casts a shadow and makes its residents feel safe. A couple of tries in each spot and then move on; accuracy, a methodical retrieve and determination are the keys to success here.

I can't be a river snob either; the perch in this canal are just as likely to be living inside a car tyre as in a bank of reeds; it's only us humans who get really fussy about the look of our real estate.

I fish between the canal boats, right along a thick ribbon of duck weed, under my first bridge, round a submerged traffic cone and along the length of a flat-bed trolley. No luck, but I've got to stay confident. Crossing a road out of the Basin I pass a sign giving fishing the thumbs-up and immediately feel buoyed. This place just feels right for a fish.

The next likely feature is another bridge right opposite the King's Cross Theatre. I'm going to be leaping from bridge to bridge like a troll today. The rain clearly isn't going to stop so they'll be my only possible shelter, but the artificial darkness will also appeal greatly to the perch.

A couple of speculative casts into the murk bring my first proper take, but it's short-lived: a single spirited headshake sees the hook easily disgorged. A pity, but a positive sign for sure. I must be doing something right.

I try again, taking care to slow my retrieve right down, and this time the hook finds something far more solid: but this is no fish.

I heave hard and get nothing back bar unyielding resistance. Obviously I've hooked into a heavy piece of solid waste: a trolley, a washing machine or perhaps something more sinister? I try and change my angle but there is still no give. This will have to be my first donation to the canal then. I snap the braided line under the strain.

The very best of fish live in the hardest places to catch them. Of course they do; they've grown in age and weight by being canny feeders, avoiding bigger predators, and picking the best spots to ambush food, but here that doesn't mean supple tree roots or the soft tendrils from an overhanging bush – this is solid city centre litter dumped off the bridges by the lazy and feckless, in short: a tackle graveyard.

Another cast yields another aborted take, but this extra scrap of evidence allows me to narrow down the size and location of the fish.

It's a small perch for sure, hidden somewhere tight against the heavily graffitied far wall. There's no walkway over there so it is clear of human debris, but right in the middle of the canal is a ceiling fan and a billowing white sack. It's a tough cast. I steady myself. I reckon I've got one more crack at this before the little fish spooks for good.

'Any luck, mate?' comes a thick West African accent from over my shoulder. I turn to meet a large man in full train guard uniform, his head topped with an immaculate black cap.

'Not yet, mate, just had a take down here but I missed it, I think.' We both look into the water. 'Ja. There's fish here all right.' He leans over the railing, hoping to spot one on demand, and then gobs into the canal: 'It all depends on the weather.'

I ask about his job and it turns out he isn't a train guard at all.

'It's just a good thick coat and a snappy hat, don't you think?' I nod in approval and smile. I haven't heard the word 'snappy' for over twenty years.

'Plus you get plenty respect on the train.' He laughs heartily.

My new friend and I both agree that there is a little perch under the bridge but, after a couple more casts, we surmise he's probably not going to get caught today.

He shuffles off and so do I, downstream, passing Camley Street Natural Park, which had a couple of volunteers gamely tending to the shrubbery in the torrential rain, and on into my first lock.

St Pancras Lock is really very striking. A cute little whitewashed cottage guards the thick oaken lock gates and a string of canal boats line up along my side of the bank.

Each boat is a tiny commercial venture in itself; there are a bookshop, a garden store selling shrubs, even a floating coffee and cake shop and micro-theatre. I feel like I've been transported to the Cotswolds or the Norfolk Broads. The canal boat life looks undeniably quaint and, dare I say, quite attractive. I wish I'd thought of this when I was living here.

Sadly, I have only been on a canal boat once. It was on a stag do along a stretch of this very canal, much further upstream, somewhere between Leighton Buzzard and

Milton Keynes, but, let me tell you, you get a very different experience with thirty drunken blokes dressed as pirates from the one you would onboard the artisan boats of King's Cross.

Still, it was enough to let me know that the canal boat life probably isn't for me after all. It's cramped in there, with or without Long John Silver hogging the toilet, and it gets very cold in the mornings when you wake up at water level.

I forsake the immensely tempting cake and coffee and keep heading downstream in search of the elusive first fish.

Under a large railway bridge I finally get a rattling take that hangs on. After a short fight I've got a spiky London prince in my fingertips: a picture-perfect perch with beautiful markings. It has probably never seen a hook. I gently ease him back and re-cast. Another bite! This could be the mother lode! The next perch is near identical to the first, as is the next, and then I lose my hook on some lumpen piece of sub-aquan detritus.

That's the game: every other cast is a bite and every one in between is a snag. I've got to keep it slow and steady to induce a take, but there's always that risk of snaring up. It's well worth it though: there's a pod of perch hunting in here for sure.

Next cast I hook a much better fish that strips line from the reel, races through the legs of an office chair and manages to transplant my hook into the metalwork.

Bad news. I curse my luck. I've heard it said that big perch are the brainiest of all freshwater fish, and I know a good few anglers who always release them well away from their fishing mark, firm in the belief that a big one can get an entire shoal to back off the feed for the rest of the day, if they so wish.

I rest the swim for five minutes. A couple of long trains shake the thick, grey girders above my head, displacing a shower of pigeon poo into the water. I re-cast and 'bang', the fish are right back on it again.

For a while I'm getting savage bites but I just can't seem to hook up. I try a firmer strike on the next take and the rod buckles down under an immense weight. This time it's animate, and begins to move steadily downstream. There's no jagging fight to be had here; I feel almost certain I've just hooked into a really big pike.

My tackle is light so I've got to be very careful now, but equally I can't just let this fish dictate terms.

I walk downstream and everything goes solid once more. For a moment I think I've been snagged up by the fish again, but then, slowly, carefully, it starts moving upwards, towards me.

Hands shaking with adrenaline, I reach into my pocket and fish out my pike glove. I might only get one crack at this.

'You take it?' An extremely drunk man, who tells me he is from Poland, clutches his can of Tyskie lager and laughs so hard it echoes like thunder around the bridge walls.

I try again to get my hook out of the sleeve of the suit jacket. Some bloody pike that turned out to be.

'Maybe you sell at fishmonger's, get good price!' There are actual tears streaming down the Polish man's face now and he even starts to choke.

For a second I wonder if he's having a heart attack, but he fortifies himself with a generous swig from his can of lager.

'Yeah, very funny, mate.' I try to conceal the rage gnawing my insides and with a hard yank finally free my hook.

I didn't even see this man coming as I was hauling up the coat; it's as if he just materialized from the water like a large, drunken canal spirit.

The jacket slopes back into the murk where I can't retrieve it.

It hangs there with one arm in the air, like a creepy scene from an Asian horror movie: an indistinct demon crawling out of the water ready to feed on livers; mine, obviously, not the Polish man's.

The very next cast brings me another perch. 'I take it.' I turn to see my new friend. He's not laughing any more, in fact he's deadly serious, eyeing me glassily, with one fat red hand outstretched towards me.

'No, mate,' I say casually, 'it really should go back.' I reach under the railing, ready to place it in the water, and feel his hand pressing heavily onto my shoulder.

'No.' He leans in. 'I eat it.'

His hot, drunk breath slaps my face like a bar-room

drip-tray and I realize I'm in a bit of a bind: on the one hand I've got the totally unnecessary and near-certain death of a tiny fish from a recovering canal, and on the other I've got this man bearing down on me with the real possibility of violence should I not concede to his demand.

With little time at my disposal I attempt to make it look like I just dropped the perch back in by accident.

'You fucking English idiot!' The man explodes, screaming with such force I almost jump into the canal in terror.

He throws both hands to the heavens and hurls his can high into the air until it comes crashing down in the middle of the canal with an immense splash.

Fishing's over then, I think to myself, before rationalizing that I'm probably about to get beaten up very badly.

'Look, I'm sorry, mate.' The ability to reason with drunks has long been a skill I admire; my landlord friend tells me the trick is to speak to them like they are three years old: 'I just think the fish should go back, it was only a little one anyway.'

This time round, I place my hand on his shoulder. It was *only* little, I've had bigger fish fingers, yet he looks at me like I've just insulted his wife.

'Pizda!' he screams, inches from my face, before storming off.

Later I check Google Translate and discover he was not actually asking me to buy him an alternative dinner.

I decided it was probably best to head down to the next bridge after that.

Perch after perch come to my line until I've had at least a dozen in ten minutes. Leaning, with my back to an impressive-looking piece of skull graffiti, I attempt a massive cast and watch my lure arch through the air to near certain fish; however, just as the hook strikes the water, I notice two approaching policemen. Instinctively, I just know it's me they're after.

'Any luck so far?' they say in unison.

They look almost identical; with neatly trimmed ginger beards and a slightly unnaturally chummy disposition that makes me feel deeply uncomfortable.

'Er, yeah, quite a few perch,' I stammer, trying to look as 'not guilty' as possible.

I've always been nervous around the police. Not because I've ever done anything really wrong, but because my mum's dad used to find it funny to grab me in a headlock and shout: 'I've got him, officer!' at the top of his voice whenever he saw a police car. That feeling of latent criminality just kind of stuck with me.

'Got your permit then, have you?' they enquire with a well-practised airiness.

I actually do, of course, and happily present my rod licence. If that is all this is about, then I should be back fishing in seconds, I think.

'Nah.' They both look at me sternly.

Oh shit.

'We want your Canal and River Trust permit.'

I don't have one. I don't even know what one is. I had simply assumed it was free fishing on this stretch of canal. The first time I've heard of this permit is right here, right now, in front of the Thompson Twins ginger edition.

I shuffle nervously and think about what prison might be like. 'I'm really sorry, lads, I honestly didn't know. I thought it was free fishing,' I proffer desperately, appealing to their sense of compassion by being completely honest.

They consider my words, obviously sizing up the extent of my law-breaking behaviour, then, without warning, they suddenly change tack: 'Look, we really don't care, mate, between you and me this is a total ballache . . .' answers one, looking at his feet sheepishly. '. . . but you've picked the wrong day to try this sort of stunt. The Canal and River Trust are actually here today,' continued the other.

They both then give a worried glance over their shoulders.

Jesus, I think, who are these guys? If they've got the police anxious they must be the canal equivalent of the SAS.

'Okay, guys, I'm not looking for any trouble. I'll sling my hook.'

I hope that little joke at the end there might crack a sympathetic smile, but I'm sadly misguided.

'Good,' they say in harmony, before clicking their heels together and heading back in the opposite direction.

I don't feel much like risking another cast after that and head back to King's Cross with the deeply satisfying smell of perch on my hands: I've already had a brilliant day.

When I eventually made it back home I looked up the Canal & River Trust and discovered, to my eternal shame, that it was only £20 for a permit that covered this section of the Grand Union Canal and a great many other canals right across the UK as well, for an entire year.

They had an email address for contact, so, with a little Dutch courage, I fired off a few words requesting a chat.

I noticed I had another email in my inbox. It was from the interview earlier that morning and it informed me that I hadn't got the gig.

Maybe taking your rods to work isn't always the greatest move after all.

John Ellis had such a nice lilting accent and calm manner that I struggled to associate him with the threat of spectacular violence over the wrong fishing permit, but I thought it was still best to play my cards very carefully.

Whenever I've encountered the people who work the closest with nature they almost always exude a Zen-like sense of eternal perspective. It is as if they have already realized their life's work will last long beyond their graves and 'that's just fine, thanks'.

It is more than just a job to these people, and their knowledge of their area is usually encyclopedic, and so it was with John, the National Fisheries and Angling Manager for the Canal & River Trust: 'We look after every water the CRT owns, that's some two thousand-plus miles of canals and seventy-odd still waters right across the UK,' he effuses. 'Last year there were 61,000 members of our canal clubs, making us the biggest owner of canal-fishing rights in the UK.'

I was far too ashamed to attempt a question about the number of people that fish without permits, plus I didn't want to stop John in full flow. 'The second thing we do is asset management: looking after the fish stocks, the engineering works, repairing riverbeds or draining the locks; right up to fish rescue, when we've had to drain a canal or temporarily relocate fish.'

My ears pricked right up next to the phone receiver: 'Really, John, so it's probably fair to say that if there was, say, a record fish to be had from a canal then you would be the man to ask?' I gently probed.

'Absolutely!' he replied enthusiastically, as I fist-punched the air. 'On the Grand Union Canal for example, just up by the Watford Gap service stations, we found the most massive eel: it was eight pounds, two ounces!'

I was gobsmacked. That is basically an anaconda. I made a note to hit that very spot later in the year for eels.

'It wasn't alone actually,' continued John, perhaps

mistaking the silence on the line for indifference from my end, 'there was another with it, which weighed six pounds, fourteen ounces.'

'Jesus Christ, John!' I exclaimed. 'That's two fish, probably several feet in length, in one stretch of canal!' I was on the verge of losing it, but there was more to come: 'They weren't just in the same stretch of canal, Will! They were both in the same lock together: trapped!' I was basically beside myself; this was a truly astonishing piece of information.

'If you are interested in eels –'

I interrupted him: 'I am, John, VERY interested . . .'

'Well,' he continued, 'then you've just got to try the Monmouth and Brecon Canal, there's plenty of two-pound fish in there; it's practically paved with the things, who knows how big they'll go? But I'll tell you what else, Swansea Canal near to you is absolutely full of brook lamprey as well.'

I could scarcely believe what I was hearing. The brook lamprey from my childhood had returned, thriving in another body of turbid water. Perhaps it wasn't such a rare occurrence as I first thought?

'In September we did some dredging works to remove the silt and caught over a thousand in just one four-hundred-metre stretch. They are thriving, they just love the silt!' John continued with a schoolboy's enthusiasm.

Our chat went on at a feverish pace and by the time we were through his list of potentially record-breaking canals I thought my writing hand was going to fall off:

15lb slab-sided bream from the Regent's Canal, pike over 30lb in the Ashby and Coventry canals, giant perch from the Leeds and Liverpool; it was quite conceivable that I could have attempted this entire challenge from Britain's canal systems alone.

However, there was one irrefutable and unavoidable detail: although the heavy weights in themselves were undeniable, the sheer number of big individual fish coming out of the commercially stocked lakes far outstripped those that came from the canals.

'Well, the management of those commercials is always going to have a big impact on the weight of any fish. What with all those piles of protein-rich baits fed in just to attract the carp.'

There was a pause on the line. I knew what John wanted to say next, it was obvious: 'But ask yourself this, Will, would you feel a greater sense of achievement catching a known giant artificially reared in a pond, or a wild unknown that's built the foundation of its size and strength purely on its own cunning and guile?

'For years the record tench came from a canal,' John lamented. 'It was from the Grand Union Canal's Leicester line. That record stood right through till the 1960s, seven pound something it was, but today the tench record stands at over fifteen pounds; over double the size of the record that once stood for decades.'

Commercials had changed everything. Even I had caught a tench over 7lb from a commercial fishery in the past; a great fish without doubt, but I had no idea it would once have been a new national record. I don't even think I thought to photograph it.

'It's possible that the canals could still turn up a record one day; I don't believe those big eels will find their way out of the canals and back to the sea too easily; and canal catches have never been better, you know; but without doubt the biggest threat to our canals is the lack of anglers,' continued John flatly. 'There are many, many more people choosing to seek their thrills from commercial fisheries, and some of our best canals are falling into a state of serious neglect.'

John believed the mentality of the angler had fundamentally altered. 'We are missing a whole generation of people that learnt to fish on the canals. I grew up on the Llangollen Canal, it cost me my place in medical school,' he quipped, 'but all the kids want is the guarantee of big fish these days.'

I offer my theory that most people, including myself once, didn't actually see the city canal as a place where fish live; that we have this prevailing myth that a lot of them are completely devoid of life.

'Yes,' John agrees, 'then we make these school visits and netting trips and the kids are absolutely amazed!'

It had been fascinating chatting to John, but also really quite sad to think that this iconic natural resource was falling into a state of such serious disrepair through little more than neglect and ignorance. What was for sure, though, was that the Canal & River Trust desperately needed the funds from fishing permits to keep all their important work going; so, feeling like a first-class 'pizda', I sheepishly promised to make a donation to the Trust and swore I would never fish again without double-, triple-, checking I had the right permits.

Sometimes in life it isn't the threat of trouble, or getting caught out, that makes you follow the rules, but actually the idea that you might not be taking your very own opportunity to help preserve something you love.

Storm Barney gave way to Storm Desmond and the rain did not stop until the middle of January.

I had arranged to fish with the wonderful-sounding Perchfishers club on the River Ivel in December, but the weather soon put paid to that, and with John Ellis's ringing endorsement in my ears I decided the time was probably right to try another canal for my next predator.

I had made a start in my quest, but really, in terms of catching a record, my time with the perch had been an absolute failure.

This was obviously going to be a lot harder than I thought, and there are no advancements in fishing tackle or increases in the number of specimen fish that were going to gift me a first-class catch without a great deal of hard graft and sacrifice beforehand. Still, I had made a start and thoroughly enjoyed targeting something new, and that definitely counted for something.

*

My grandma passed away that Christmas. It was heart-breaking, but dementia had taken a hold on her to such an extent that this utterly charming and dignified lady had been reduced to just two sentences: 'I'm managing' and 'Yes, boss.'

Grandma and Grandad had been happily married for over sixty years, the pair of them champions of the life and love that could be extracted from our waterways; him from the end of his rod, her from the tip of her paintbrush.

Twenty years ago Grandad caught a truly big perch. 'You should have seen it, Will! It was massive!'

I remember him splaying out his palms as if he were holding aloft a priceless china plate; re-enacting the precious moment he had held it for the very first time.

I dearly wished I had only been there to witness it. His finest captures always seemed to happen away from me. I wasn't even sure it had actually happened.

I should clarify that Grandad was no liar; he had definitely caught a big perch, but we were both fishermen after all. Memories blur and sometimes the distance between our palms can widen with time.

Grandma left behind an old plastic ice cream tub filled with pictures when she departed, and right there, somewhere in the middle, I found a picture of Grandad with his most magnificent perch.

I hold that image between my fingers as I type this. That picture is more precious to me now than any big perch of my own.

The fish's stripes are a darker shade of green than the stripes on his jumper. He props up the perch's dorsal with the tip of one of his big thumbs and his mouth is wide open in a self-satisfied and slightly stunned grin.

It is a Wilson mega-specimen, and I am in absolutely no doubt he caught it on a lobworm.

The Water Wolf

> It was as deep as England. It held
> Pike too immense to stir, so immense and old
> That past nightfall I dared not cast.
>
> Ted Hughes, 'Pike', (1960)

When I was around nine years old I owned one VHS tape that I kept specifically for Mum to record John Wilson's *Go Fishing* series on direct from the TV. There was one episode in particular, filmed, I think, somewhere in the Norfolk Broads, that I had watched so many times that the tape itself had started to warp and go fuzzy.

I could recall that episode near verbatim. In fact, I'm pretty sure I still can.

The episode begins with a slightly awkward 'Hello'

from a thick-rimmed-bespectacled gentleman who bore more than a passing resemblance to a giant land tortoise. I didn't realize at the time that this was in fact the legendary Dick Walker, a true fishing icon.

In this film Mr Walker was playing the role of surrogate grandad to the thousands of young fisher folk tuning in across the nation; explaining the rudiments of pike angling and biology in a safe environment, before the hero, John Wilson, took over at the sharper end of the spear.

'Pike are predators, and they're scavengers too,' he begins, with a grim-looking stuffed pike staring on blankly from the wall behind. 'They are very well equipped indeed for both jobs,' he continued, 'they will eat practically anything, dead or alive, that will give them some nutriment.'

A pencil-drawn otter is framed over one of the old man's great oaken shoulders and ancient-looking books surround him. Everything about this office, from the interior to Dick himself, looks like it has been dipped in sepia and warmed up with wood smoke. It was the sort of place where I wanted to be for all time and I poured my consciousness into its cosy security to such an extent that I could well believe Mr Walker was addressing me directly; from right across his well-worn hardwood table to the rug of my parents' lounge, where I would sit cross-legged, inches from the TV screen.

'Now, here you can see what I've been talking about,' continues Mr Walker. He reaches down and produces the giant head of a stuffed pike. The warming atmosphere of

Dick's Den is extinguished in an instant, a brooding malevolence creeps into his office and my sense of longing quietly tiptoes back out.

Mr Walker works the head carefully around his fingers, gradually illuminating the business end in the dull light of his table lamp. He says it is from a 43lb giant caught in Ireland but all I can recall is its enormous jaws. Row upon row of razor-sharp fangs along the jaw-line backed up by hundreds more, pinned hard to the roof of the fish's mouth.

Mr Walker notes how all the teeth angle slightly backwards towards its blackened throat. Whatever goes in there isn't ever coming out, I thought. 'Never put your hand in a pike's mouth,' says Mr Walker, while clearly running his own thumbs and fingers over the teeth. He was my kind of man.

The film cuts to the heroic Wilson rowing his way alongside a tall reed bed. There is a vast expanse of wild-looking fresh water opening out right behind him; it's February, it's bleak, and he even says it's cold, so just what is he doing in that tiny wooden rowing boat with just a tweed hat for company? I grip the remote tightly and pray nothing bad happens to John.

Somewhere along the edge of the deep water he drops anchor and plucks a small live roach out of a bait tin. He says something nonchalant about only using 'small' live baits these days but I can't help noticing that the roach he has selected is actually the same size as my personal best from the creek. A highly unpleasant sense of shame burns at my cheeks, a feeling I later learn to interpret as a sense of inferiority combined with instant emasculation. I remember how it felt to land that best-ever roach, the euphoric 'championship-winning' sensation carried me through the whole summer and the glow stayed with me every night I closed my eyes and thought of that fish. In one swift move by Wilson that feeling had been obliterated: my best was his bait. How, even after a few years of fishing, could it be that the gulf between Wilson and myself, between being a man or just a little boy, was actually widening? He had no idea what he was doing to me of course. Hooking up the roach, he simply swung it out into the water under a large bright-red float and confidently commented: 'When that goes I'm in business.'

The final pike of the programme comes from 'the middle of the hole', which is how Wilson describes the slate-grey no man's land where he has cast his bait. It is, of course, the beast we have all been waiting for, but incredibly, as Wilson battles it to the side of the boat, he describes it as 'only a small one'.

The giant pike writhes on a foam mat after he's got it into the net. It's long – three or maybe even four feet – with a dark, muscular back leading on to a crocodilian head.

'As fat as butter!' exclaims Wilson jubilantly.

He holds his fish up for the camera and I get a good view of its mossy flanks. It is as if an artist had taken the time to delicately flick light-yellow paint along a green pike-shaped canvas, then decided to finish the job by scraping through the lot with a yard brush. The fish's thick, olive sides may be interspersed with pretty blond flecks and subtle vertical stripes, yet the overall look and feel of the fish are of pure brute savagery.

At the rear of the fish a russet-red and black-striped dorsal fin stands erect and rounded. It is set so far back along the body it almost meets the tail fin. This intentional back-loading of the pike's powerhouse affords it all the explosive forward motion it needs to intercept prey from a stationary position. Like the perch, they prefer to ambush their prey, but they can also take fish, frogs and even ducks, well out in open water, such is their confidence in their own turn of speed.

Somewhere towards the end of the programme, Wilson rotates his fish so it is head on to the camera lens. The skull is uniquely flattened in appearance, with large, predatory eyes set unusually high on the sides; perfect for peering up from the depths and selecting its next victim.

The grim jaw of Wilson's fish hisses open like a trapdoor and I can't help but imagine what it must be like to have that as your last view on earth. Horrid, I would expect. 'Absolute magic!' says John victoriously.

When the theme tune kicks in I am left alone with a feeling of raw inadequacy. I was nine, almost ten, and quite desperate for a pike of my own. It represented much more than just another fish. It symbolized growing up, doing something on my own, facing my fears – in short: being a man; but if the fish that Wilson caught in the film really was 'only a small one', and the bait he used as big as my personal best, then how could I ever expect to manage a pike for myself?

The beginning of the winter of '92 saw me fish like I had never fished before. For three months straight I was out almost every single night, drawing a triangular-shaped piece of shiny metal through every inch of the Creek's brown water, but trapped deep in a piker's purgatory.

Spinning for pike was my first major new fishing skill after five years of float-fishing for the Creek's roach and perch. Until that point I had been pretty much sat on my hands waiting for a bite, but spinning required constant movement of both myself and my hook: to animate the spinner – literally, to get it to spin, and make it flash through the water like an injured silverfish.

Winding the spinner in on my line would only last about twenty seconds in the narrow Creek, which meant I was now casting many more times in a day than ever before. Given my earlier problems with this most basic of fishing skills, I felt I was now risking my end tackle almost twice a minute. To make matters significantly worse, I also learnt the most likely pike-holding areas were right under the trees and along the reed beds: the very obstacles I had spent the previous half-decade try-ing to avoid casting towards. The arms of the trees and roots of the reeds might have been tackle thieves, but the shade and shelter they afforded the pike made them the perfect ambush points for any unsuspecting fish. To stand a chance of a pike I had to land my spinner perfectly: firmly in the pike's lair and within an inch of the devastating grasp of the bankside bush.

Grandad wasn't interested in helping at all. 'Pike fishing is too easy,' he would say dismissively. Perhaps he understood this was a fish I needed to meet by myself, but the effect of his words was to heap yet more pressure on my infantile shoulders. If it really was easy, then why couldn't I just catch one?

Looking back, I know precisely what the problem was: my retrieve was always too fast and too uniform. I would never let the spinner drop beneath the top six inches of surface water, meaning any interested pike would have to come right up off the bottom to grab it; nor did I vary the speed of my draw to allow the lure vital space to flit and flutter along like a wounded fish, meaning, in the eyes of a predator, that my spinner was in fact a turbo-charged superfish with a full bill of health.

Zipping my spinner across the Creek's surface merely served to give onlookers the impression I was a man out pike fishing, the man I wanted them to believe I was, while, in reality, I was never really giving myself a chance of hooking my quarry. Effectively, I was a rank boxing amateur dancing round the undefeated prizefighter without ever getting close enough to throw a meaningful punch, or get hit myself. I was simply too terrified of the potential consequences of hooking a pike, and too bloody-minded to just give up.

*

There is a unique existential crisis brought on by anyone seriously into pike fishing.

'Why am I here?' is a question that will inevitably pass the lips of this peculiar breed of angler.

Fish are as much a product of their environment as are the people who angle for them. Carp, with their fat scales, soft mouths and friendly curves, have the look and feel of summer, to be had from lily-strewn ponds and picture-perfect lakes. The typical carp angler prefers fairer weather and appears built for comfort, not speed; paradoxically, though, the fatter the carp, the slimmer and more pathological the bent of the carp fisherman, and no one should doubt that even the laziest-looking carp, and carper, has an extraordinary turn of pace when it is required. The barbel's golden hue is classic autumn; its angular fins are shaped and coloured like an early leaf drop and the torpedo shape marks this fish out as a specimen of fast water. The barbel fisherman, like the fish, is a shrewd and romantic character, a lover of nature and hardy too – easily capable of withstanding stormy weather and early starts – but this angler can't match the pike and pike angler for sheer durability. They are the embodiment of winter and both thrive on a rare form of neglect.

Of course, you can catch pike in the summer, and there are many anglers who fish for all fish species all year round, but the pike are at their largest in mid-winter, and it takes a very special breed of fisherman to convincingly morph their own character to match up to the deep cold their quarry prefers. As a child, I was a pretender, a mere sheep in wolf's clothing, but, unbeknown to me at the time, my dad was about to give me a big helping hand.

On the Creek you know spring is around the corner as soon as the daffodils outnumber the snowdrops. Time was running out for my first pike and me. Soon the water would warm and the river-fishing season would close till 16 June. I lay in my bed near wild with frustration.

I couldn't sleep that particular night for two distinct reasons: firstly, I had discovered Dad had taped over *Flash Gordon* at the precise moment he begins to turn things around in his fight to the death with Barin, and 'Flash! I love you! But we only have fourteen hours to save the Earth!' was now for ever jump-cut with Geoff Hamilton talking about manure on *Gardeners' World*. Naturally I was furious, but the second reason I was counting sheep was considerably more devastating.

Just as Mum and Dad had been going to bed I had overheard them have the following conversation right outside my room:

'Will is spending a lot of his time fishing at the moment, even more than normal,' said Mum, standing on the landing as Dad came up the stairs.

'He's trying to catch a pike,' replied Dad.

'Really?' answered Mum, with audible concern in her voice. 'Isn't that dangerous?'

'Not really,' said Dad, 'but don't worry, he won't get one in. He's not strong enough.'

The words slapped my eardrum and tore straight into my heart. Instantly, I could feel hot tears filling up my face and bee-lining for my tear ducts. It was the first time I had ever heard Dad doubt I could do anything. We had always been brought up on the principle that you can succeed at anything if you just try your best, yet here he was saying that, despite everything I was putting into it, I was never going to be good enough.

I tried to cover my ears with the pillow and will his words to leave my brain. Every fear I had suppressed to that point had been realized in full; the shadow of self-doubt reared up and smothered me in my bedsheets.

Hours later I was still very much awake. I gritted my teeth and thumped my fists on the duvet. Why would he say that? How dare he say that?

I got up and looked at myself in the mirror; my sense of my own shortcomings was quickly being replaced with a wild rage. That was a total betrayal from Dad. I glowered back at myself. I would show him; I would prove I did have the strength.

In its elemental form pike fishing necessitates in an individual a curious brand of madness: crumbling dock-lands, isolated rivers and windswept reservoirs – the last places your average anglers would choose to spend their time; but the purist piker casts into these locations with a sort of masochistic thrill, fearlessly fishing a fearful landscape for a fish seemingly without fear.

In my late twenties I fished a handful of times for pike

in a long, narrow fenland dyke called the Cuckoo Drain. You could probably spend a lifetime searching through the names of waterways and not find one as ill-fitting as the 'cuckoo' moniker given to this place. The cuckoo throws up more than simply the iconic bird sound of spring; it is the vision of renewal: a glade filled with fresh-sprung wild flowers, an oaken woodland rousing itself after a week of rain, the resurgence and resilience of life – a clarion call to heat the soul, reminding us that winter has passed and the good times are here once more. The Cuckoo Drain in winter was miles of pure brutality. Its near unrelenting misery placed it well among the hardest places I have ever fished. Thus it was near perfect for big pike.

It took some time simply to find the place, tucked, as it was, tight between a pumping station and a dip between two brown fields that stretched ad infinitum. As all fenland drains contain pike of some measure, and with Cuckoo both being deep and sporting a good head of shoaling roach and bream, it seemed fair to assume there might well be some decent-sized resident fish. This assumption was backed up by the only person I ever saw down there besides me: a typical piker, tall and grizzled with a rugged ginger beard and slightly gaunt appearance; he strongly resembled a starving Viking.

Few words were wasted between him and me. 'Anythin' doin'?' he would mumble. I would answer in the negative, and repeat his question back to him. 'Nuffin' doin',' he would respond with a sniff. I was really quite intimidated.

I decided to take a small spinning rod and had huge early success with a trio of fine averagely sized fish on my first outing; but from that moment forward I really struggled. It was as if the drain itself had lured me in with the promise of pike, only so it could then enjoy watching me endure an endlessly barren ice-cold search along its desolate banks.

After a dozen or so visits I began to seriously question whether those early pike had been a mirage. Pike-shaped sprites, kelpies, spirits or sirens? Even the Viking was nowhere to be seen by the bitter end of that bitterest of seasons. A barn owl would usually emerge when there was an hour of daylight remaining. It offered cold comfort, haunting the banks and circling my position like a ghostly vulture, just waiting for me to drop so it could pick apart my frozen carcass.

It would take until my final visit for the drain to yield me another pike. A slamming take and dogged fight marked it out as a decent fish, a good double for sure, but, as I reached down to slip my fingers into its gills, a hard headshake left only the tip of one hook in its stiff upper lip.

I had been fishing with two treble hooks on a wire trace specifically designed for the bony mouth of the pike. The extra hook points (six in this case) should give you a greater chance of landing this hard-mouthed fish, but with just one hook-hold left I now stood a very slim chance of success unless I acted quickly.

I tried to get a solid grip on the fish once more, but another violent headshake brought a tearing sound and the warming feel of fresh blood spilling across my hands. The numbing cold had dampened my pain receptors to such an extent that it took several seconds more than it should for me to realize that all the blood was my own; and several more still to discern that it was not my fingers that had been sliced on the pike's teeth, but that one of the higher treble hooks had torn right through my trouser leg and embedded itself deep within my shin.

Pike fishing leaves scars both real and imagined. I have two you can see: one livid white on my shin, the other, right across the cornea of my right eye, where I almost lost my sight to the hooks of a spinner while pike fishing as a teenager; but these are a small price to pay in the mind of the truly serious piker. I needed to be made of sterner stuff if I was ever to land a monster.

I drew a curtain over my last serious attempt at pike fishing that evening: bum shuffling and whimpering my way back up the bankside of Cuckoo Drain, a hook impaled in my leg, and a 10lb pike dangling around my ankles.

I've heard the pike once described as a 'Gothic' fish, and although I get where this reference is coming from, what with the pike's shadowy behaviour and angular appearance, I think 'prehistoric' is a far fairer depiction of this truly primeval creature.

The earliest British fossils of *Esox lucius*, to give the pike its Latin name, are dated at half a million years old. It is believed the fish first made its way to British shores via the North Sea land bridge, way back when the

River Thames was connected to the River Rhine in the Netherlands, but the latest fossil dating of the *Esox* genus far predates even this, placing the pike in northern America some 80 million years earlier.

The pike's evolutionary masterstroke came sometime during the Cretaceous period when the early *Esox* developed jaws capable of swallowing far greater-sized prey than the other species within the herring–salmon order. From that moment forward the pike had set itself on an extraordinarily durable pathway that would see it survive several Ice Ages and spread its presence from America and right across Europe, eventually spanning almost the entire boreal forest region of the northern hemisphere.

With its elongated body, sharpened head and penchant for aggression, the 'pike' name stuck with the fish from the Middle Ages, aptly chosen for its resemblance to the tall thrusting spear favoured by the infantrymen of the time, and used for taking down knights on horseback with ruthless efficiency and maximum bloodshed; much like the fish might, given the chance among a shoal of roach.

The Wilson *Encyclopedia* describes an average size of between 5 and 12lb, with a mega-specimen topping out at over 30lb. When I was still stuck angling for my first, Roy Lewis shocked the pike-angling world with a whopping 46lb 13oz beast from Llandegfedd Reservoir in South Wales. That record still stands today, taken on little more than a small and humble-looking wooden lure called the 'creek chub pikie'.

There is no other fish species on these shores to have sprung quite the same degree of myth and legend as the pike. The Yorkshire terrier that didn't make it home from its paddle in the park pond, the toothy beast that supposedly went for the ankles of a small swimming boy, the bleached bones of the 90lb fish washed up on the banks of some far-flung Irish loch – all unreliably witnessed, yet all somehow difficult to debunk completely. Just look at that image of the pike caught by Roy Lewis. It is an enormous spawn-filled female fish that appears almost as long as Roy himself. Is it such a leap in imagination to make real the violent water monsters of our childhood then?

The answer is probably 'Yes, it is.' The genuinely big fish have nearly always fallen from the drains and lakes that have seen very little pike-angling pressure or human presence; the pike certainly would not attack a human without any prior provocation. In this day and age the real specimens are to be found lurking safely within trout-fishing-only reservoirs, or concealed somewhere within mile upon mile of undisturbed lake or drain. They prefer the forgotten edges of our nation, you see, the sorts of places where you could still quite easily fish for a lifetime without even laying eyes on a Wilson mega-specimen, and the big old pike can while away their lives well away from our disturbing habits.

Big pike need food though, and lots of it – that's why, I'm told, many of those stocked trout lakes tend to do so well in sustaining monsters – but more than that they require a healthy ecosystem and a relative lack of competition. You should never consider culling pike in order to produce a bigger, better stamp of fish, though, or to protect the other fish in the water, for that matter. Many a world-class pike venue has been destroyed by the unwise attempt to remove its resident predators, and, unless you get them all (and, really, why would you want to do that?), there will inevitably be an explosion of smaller pike that would have otherwise been controlled by the larger, cannibalistic fish. In a pike's world, the only fish that truly controls the pike is the pike.

I first began looking for a big pike for this book in January, but it took until the middle of the month before a sudden break in the rain seemed to offer a true chance of a catch. Overcast, grey, a slight rise in temperature from single to double digits – it wasn't consistent with the forecast at all. I rushed from my desk and straight out to the garden pond to find my goldfish milling around the surface and even feeding. Potentially the biggest catch of the season was on.

Pike feed at ill-defined times. You can convince yourself there are no pike at all in a place and then a small change in atmospherics brings them onto the feed and suddenly you're in. I've heard of anglers catching nearly a hundred pike in just a few hours of ferocious action, then, as quickly as they are turned on, they're all off again, often for hours, sometimes even for days. Of course, the pikers are left scratching their heads and wondering where they're all hiding, but there is a widely held belief that these small rises in temperature can bring the pike out of their stupor. With even the goldfish showing some signs of life this morning, it was all looking very good indeed.

The problem I faced was that it was now far too late to grab a ticket at any one of the certified big pike venues; and with all the rivers still flooded I needed to think out of the box. John Ellis. The canals, of course.

I flicked the laptop on and used Google Maps to zoom right in on the small network of drains and canals that ran around Cardiff. The one area I was particularly interested in stumbled off a giant space of disused industrial-era docks called the Atlantic Wharf. If big pike thrived on neglect, then this place surely hid a giant. It is only about half a mile from a glitzy shopping centre but it may as well have been on Mars. The blackened remains of rusting high-tower cranes hang over this place, looming large and lifeless over the water like Jurassic-era herons. An unattractive busy main road runs right along one side of the water too, but there were big fish to be had here if you only knew where to look.

I had already started my quest for a big pike there at the year's turn, but I hadn't yet had much luck. I did have some definite follows, though, predatory swirls at the surface, as my lure came back under my rod tip, and, on one occasion, a savage take tore my rubber lure clean in two, narrowly missing the hook, and leaving me with little more than the grinning head of my replica eel.

The other people who fished there tended to be a special breed, but they were friendly enough as long as you didn't ask too many questions about permits or carry on like a member of the Cardiff City Council.

The first time I ventured down there I met an enormous shaven-headed man in a state of some despair: 'Fuckers nicked all my meat and my rods in the night,' he raged – eyes popping from their sockets and his mobile clutched firmly to his ear – I presumed to the police. 'I was a bit pissed up last night to be fair, but they could at least have not cooked up all my fucking meat on my fucking BBQ not ten fucking metres from my fucking tent . . .' He was near apoplectic with rage, which was understandable given he'd just woken to discover nearly everything he owned had been stolen.

There was no fishing club looking after Atlantic Wharf back then, so the fishing was effectively free; but there is always some price to pay.

Some of the local pike fishermen here had an uneasy relationship with both the law and the rules. A few openly admitted to fishing illegally in nature reserves and one even told me he was banned from the local Glamorgan Anglers Club for using live ducklings as bait. Grim, almost beyond belief. Eventually I was trusted enough to be shown the pictures of the pike they had caught: blurry pictures of half-cut anglers with what were quite clearly significantly large fish in their hands.

Some of the pike looked to be over 25lb, perhaps one was even pushing the magic 30lb mark. 'Just beware fishing too long alone after dark . . .' I was warned, '. . . and keep an eye out for the poachers and prostitutes.'

The Royalty stretch of the Hampshire Avon this was not.

Poaching is a growing problem in Britain, particularly in these little-visited urban hinterlands that kiss up against large populations of people. For years I had disregarded those who talked of 'poachers taking all the fish' as just having fishermen's excuses, but John Ellis had been quick to point the finger too, claiming all it takes is a replica lock key to drain an entire stretch of canal in the middle of the night and make off with fish worth upwards of £2,000. In recent times I'd encountered more less-than-formal approaches: gill nets and long-lines dumped on the banks, tragically emptied of their quarry when no one else was around.

Many of my non-fishing friends don't really see the point of the sport if all you are ever doing is catching fish only to put them back. I know plenty of anglers who also believe there is no harm in taking the occasional sample, but the hard reality is that our inland fish stocks would simply collapse if everyone started to take their catches home. The few places where you can do it – trout and salmon fisheries, for example – have very carefully managed and monitored restocking programmes, strict limits on your catch and fastidious attention to the paperwork every angler must complete if he or she intends to take a fish home. Our island nation is too small and too over-populated to expect our recovering fresh water to handle anything other than catch and release, and when it comes to removing pike, the top fish predator, the resultant effect on an ecosystem can be devastating. It was one of the many reasons why predator anglers are so secretive about their catches.

I felt the canals feeding the wharf were easily my best bet for lure-fishing. The wharf was deep enough to take giant coal tankers and industrial container ships in its heyday, so this little spike in temperature wouldn't have even registered in those depths; however, in the relative shallows of the canals, the water would be responding almost instantaneously. I hoped to find the shoals of over-wintering silverfish holed up somewhere in there, which would, in turn, be drawing the big pike up off the wharf and deep into the canal system to feed; like great white sharks on the trail of a great chum-slick of African sardines.

I parked up with just an hour of light remaining in the day, the 'witching hour' for predators the world over, and headed over to a small bridge overlooking a canal. It's hemmed in on all sides by a housing estate; a small ribbon of gently flowing water no more than ten metres in width and a few feet deep. From this point it's only a short walk to where it spills into the vast basin of water that forms the wharf, but upstream from here the canal disappears under the ground, cutting a subterranean path until it pops up behind a posh hotel and meets its maker: the River Taff.

I'd looked into entering those underground canal workings while researching stories for a BBC series on the river, even going so far as to find a local artist who had worked out a plan to sail them on the inflated inner tube of a tractor tyre, but the council had thwarted our plans. The king rats and giant eels of the perpetual dark would have to wait. Still, I peered hopefully off the bridge and into the water below, willing a daylight giant to materialize somewhere in the void below.

Superficially, it couldn't be less welcoming. Hard slabs of concrete encase this narrow patch, and the water is clogged hard with storm-swept branches that reach to the heavens with their long skeletal fingers.

The litter here is far worse than the stuff on the Grand Union Canal, and there's certainly no caring edge or quirky canal culture to be found in this forgotten space. The slack water teems with beer bottles, cans and plastics, and as the streetlights flickered into life, a grimy orange hue was cast right across the scene, lighting up the canal like some bargain basement red-light district.

A series of gently expanding rings appear suddenly on the water's surface. Even here, there are signs of wildlife. It is a shoal of feeding fish, moving around in the upper layers of water, just as I'd hoped; basking in the relative warmth, and snatching the very occasional fly or grub ensnared in the surface film. Perhaps I can dare to dream?

Removing the four-inch rubber lure from the end of my line, I quickly switch to a tiny spinner. These topping fish are small; I don't want to stand out too much from the crowd. I make my first cast and the water stirs with mass movement. Clearly there are a lot more silverfish here than I'd first thought. Seconds later a pluck on the line is converted into a jarring take. It feels small and awkward, possibly a perch, but more likely just a foul-hooked fish.

Yes. I've accidentally punctured a pristine roach right through its silvery side. I've massively underestimated this place – there are quite literally thousands of fish holed up in here; there's barely room in the water to work my spinner without risking hooking one in error.

Another cast sees me lodged into something solid and inanimate on the canal bottom. I yank hard in an attempt to free the hooks and spook something very large to the left of my tightened line. It sends a V-shaped bow wave down the water and scatters hundreds of frightened roach across the surface in its wake.

It just has to be a pike.

A man with a pram filled with plastic bags wanders past, eyes down, followed by a jogger whose music is cranked up so loud I can almost hear the lyrics of the R&B song blasting from his headphones. I re-cast and immediately hook into a tiny pike. It writhes on the line as I ease it in to the canal's side, splashing the surface and disturbing the water. That was a very bad move on this little pike's part: with little warning the V-shaped wave is back; but this time it's coming straight for us.

Time slows and my heart rolls up towards my gullet. A monstrous pike emerges right beneath its victim. The little pike, the big pike and I, we all know what is coming next. In a flash the larger has ingested the smaller, spinner and all, without any of it needing to touch the sides.

As my line is still attached to the small pike, we both now have quite a problem. Realizing it is tethered the monster projects itself clean out of the water in fright, using the power of its tail alone to skip impressively along the surface before crashing back into the pool with a thunderclap. I receive a full view of its extraordinary length during these acrobatics; it is in excess of 10lb, perhaps not a big fish in terms of big pike, but a true giant for such a tiny canal.

I try to keep tension on the line but a microsecond of slack sees the hook dislodged and, as the fish belly-flops its way back into the water, I realize we are sadly no longer in contact.

A steady rain blisters the water as night falls hard and cold. The supreme power of the pike's re-entry has sent shock waves slapping into the canal's concrete sides. Briefly, a single tennis ball is projected up onto the walkway. It rolls a wet trail for a few feet before landing back into the murk with a 'plop'.

I walk downstream towards the wharf breathing heavily. I need to pull myself together, fast. There is still a chance that the fish hasn't yet felt the steel of my hooks – it might just take another bait, but I know I must rest the swim before attempting anything else. Both the pike and I need time to consider our next moves.

Clearly, I'm on edge. A grey heron explodes from a thicket at my ankles and I momentarily leave my body in fright. Come on, Will, it's only a fish. Except it wasn't, that fish was a miracle out in that squash-court-sized patch of water, and right now, in this very moment, I'm probably the only person in the world that even knows it exists.

In the desolate car park just before the wharf, a fight between two drug dealers breaks out. I try not to catch their eye as they scream each other down about some aborted deal. With their identical enamel-white parka jackets and fur-lined hoods they look like a pair of duelling swans, puffing out their chests and jostling for territory. I duck down and take a couple of speculative casts into the darkness of the wharf, snagging some weed and finding a sense of calm just in the process of removing the soft green matting from the trio of hooks at the end of my spinner. It's soon time to go back and try again.

I underhand-cast the spinner back into the same spot and get an instant slamming response from the monster. He's ready, and this time so am I. I heave hard against its bulk, in my mind setting the hooks securely into its fang-filled mouth, but, again, I feel the gut-wrenching give of a slack, fish-free line.

I don't understand. Under a downstream bridge a pair of boys smoke marijuana from a roll-up they're sharing. Its sweet smell drifts on the night air right down to my latest disaster. Edgily, they flick their lighter on and off. They haven't noticed my fish, my crisis or me. I reel up and to my surprise discover that yet another small roach has found its way onto the hooks.

This roach is in a truly sorry state: heavily lacerated with a severed spinal cord and a frozen expression. It has been thoroughly mangled by the pike. Stone dead on arrival. Gently, I place a hook through its lower lip and flick it back in. This is now my last chance.

Almost imperceptibly the line starts to shudder and slide. Unbelievable luck. I wait, imagining the giant pike first taking the roach sideways in its mouth before turning it slowly towards its final journey on this earth. I take a deep, deep breath, wind down, and lift into the fish as hard as I dare.

Massive resistance gives way to a thunderous charge towards the bridge. The pot-smokers have gone now and my reel screams as line escapes the spool at speed. There's no acrobatics to be had this time around: just dour, dogged confrontation.

The pike steams right through the bridge and out the other side. I didn't think I was going to be able to stop it from rounding a bend in the canal at first, but, at last, it starts to yield to pressure.

As the great pike inches to the surface I drop to my knees. Here she comes, like a thick, green submarine. I steady myself as the head presents itself. There is only one spot on a pike where you can grasp it by hand without lacerating your fingers or hurting the fish: it's inside the mouth, right underneath the lower jaw by way of its hardened gill plates. With no time to put on a glove I slide my hand into the cavity and lift.

She's beautiful. A spawn-filled female, thick and so darkly marked that you could easily be staring right at her without ever realizing she's there; a metaphor for this canal system if ever there was one.

I roll out a soft mat to safely remove the hooks without causing any more disruption to her day, and spend a few moments on my knees simply gazing at this precious sword from the stone.

A man in a suit walks right past me without even acknowledging our presence. Even with the fish out of water the canal's secrets remain invisible to those incapable of belief.

I lie down on my chest and attempt to self-take a photo at arm's length, but I'm interrupted. 'Jesus Christ, mate!' It's one of the boys from beneath the bridge, back with the remains of his spliff hanging at a comedic angle from his trembling lower lip. 'What dafuk is that!?'

He pulls down the hood on his black Adidas tracksuit to reveal a tightly dreadlocked scalp. He attempts to take a photo with his phone, but his hands are shaking uncontrollably.

'Oh my days,' said the lad, wiping his brow at the sheer intensity of the experience, 'I'm not going to lie,

I've seen some crazy shit down here but I ain't never seen anything like that.'

Together, we sat down next to the great fish. Paying gentle homage as I showed him its mouthparts, fins and armour, before sliding her carefully back into the canal.

Momentarily the pike just sat on the shallow bottom glowering right back up at us.

'That's crazy,' he said.

'I know,' I replied.

It really was.

A waft of her tail eventually sent her back to a life of obscurity beneath a floating mat of litter, and my partner decided it was also time to make his own way back into darkness.

I watched him as he went, pulling his hood back over his head and sparking up the biggest spliff this side of Jamaica.

If Grandad had been around today we would've talked about that capture for weeks, but all I had was the Wilson *Encyclopedia* to pour my experience into, and all that came back was the cold hard fact that my fish wasn't a record breaker. In fact, it wasn't even anywhere close to being a Wilson mega-specimen.

A 30lb pike is a very rare beast in itself, but a forty-pounder capable of threatening Roy Lewis's 46lb 13oz record is almost beyond the realms of possibility. Scanning the list of the fifty biggest pike ever caught, and immediately discounting the sketchy records, repeat captures or those that are likely to now be deceased, I felt it was probably realistic to say there were fewer than twenty known 40lb pike alive in Britain today; most of which were highly nomadic individuals living within immense expanses of water.

Llandegfedd, the water that provided Roy with his record back in 1992, would have seemed the obvious place to start, but by the turn of the century the water had headed into such a state of pike-fishing decline that a five-year hiatus on predator angling was called in 2010.

By the time it reopened in 2015 there was already a new contender firmly on the block. Fifty kilometres to the south-east, Somerset's Chew Valley Lake, or 'Chew' as it is affectionately known by pike anglers, was crushing all comers. 2015 saw an astonishing trio of pike over 40lb grace Chew's banks, and with a further seventeen fish of over 30lb falling in just the first week of the pike season, it was no longer a question of whether Chew was the No. 1 pike water in the UK, but whether it could actually be one of the greatest of all time.

From the moment Chew's super-sized pike started hitting the angling press I was quite literally desperate to fish there. If I was going to stand any realistic chance of catching a record-breaking pike, then clearly Chew was the place to go, but simply getting tickets to pike fish the place represented an immense challenge of will and patience.

There are only two periods in a year you can actually

fish for pike on Chew: one two-week spell in February, and a second, longer spell, running through October and November. These are known as the 'pike trials', and the only way of getting tickets is to call the Lodge landline on the first Saturday after the Christmas and New Year holidays. With every serious pike angler in Britain jamming up the line, for the strict limit of twenty-five boats and twenty bank tickets, the odds of getting a result are extremely slim. No one could say it wasn't fair: everyone is equally unlikely to win this lottery.

It endeared Chew to me no end. Predominately it was a trout-fishing water that happened to contain monstrous pike. No one wanted to outright deny pike anglers the opportunity to catch the fish of a lifetime, but equally the owners felt they had a duty of care to their bread-and-butter trout anglers, and, as we already know, big pike hate attention.

As if the odds weren't already stacked against me, the great Chew phone-in landed on 9 January: the morning after the World Darts quarter-finals at the Lakeside. It took the most almighty effort just to find my phone that morning, but I was present and correct at 9 a.m., albeit barefoot and surrounded by pizza boxes and screwed-up tickets from the night before (our hero, 'Scotty-Dog' Mitchell, had been knocked out). I took a deep, fortifying breath, and began punching in the number.

An hour passed as I notched up my first hundred unsuccessful calls. I was then joined by my bleary-eyed mate Stuart, who deployed both his landline and his mobile phone, effectively tripling my chances, but it was all to be in vain.

We ceremoniously called it a day once we had heard the engaged tone for the 1,000th time. 'I guess that's why they call it the pike "trials", mate,' said Stuart while looking for his van keys. He could see how much it meant to me, I appreciated that. We sloped off to the semi-finals and I tried my best to thoroughly drown my sorrows.

I eventually got through three days later. The polite West Country man on the phone told me all the spots for 2016 were long since gone. The horse had not only bolted before the stable door was closed, he was in the next town and midway through a national lecture tour on farm security. The man told me there were now a raffle and an auction to try for. I failed in the former and the latter topped out at an extraordinary £880 for a single day on a boat. There was nothing more I could do. I was just going to have to look elsewhere for my chance.

With Chew gone and Llandegfedd out of the running, I had to find another big trout water fast. Closer to my childhood home there were the Graffham and Rutland reservoirs, but the really big pike had been curiously absent there for the last few seasons; over in the Brecon Beacons there was Llangorse Lake, famously referenced in *The Domesday Book of Mammoth Pike* for producing the world's biggest-ever pike (in 1846 to the rod of a Mr Owen, a giant fish weighing an alleged 68lb), but that was unsubstantiated, and would have been dead for well

over a hundred years. I called up the kindly owner anyway, and he readily admitted that, although the lake
certainly had potential, it realistically couldn't ever compete with Chew for the sheer size of pike. The last big
fish there was a thirty-two-pounder in 2007. It wasn't
looking good. I had one last avenue to try, but I knew
this was an even longer shot than Chew.

Scarborough's Wykeham Lakes had a lot going for
them on paper. Currently the biggest known living pike
in Britain, a giant 46lb 11oz fish, was resident in their
waters, and at only seven acres (to Chew's 1,000-plus)
the odds of a record-breaking hook-up were dramatically reduced. However, access to pike fish the water was
strictly restricted to members of an exclusive syndicate.
I fired off a hopeful email and was extremely surprised
to get a quick response inviting me to speak to Jake
Finnigan, the fisheries manager.

Jake was a politely spoken and articulate northerner
who clearly cared deeply about the fish in his lake. I
wanted to get a feeling of what it must be like to look
after a water with such a legendary fish, a real-life Loch
Ness monster, a proper, tangible lake beast; and then I
wanted to nonchalantly request special permission to
have a crack at it.

I was going to have to play my cards very carefully
indeed, but Jake tripped me up within moments of
answering my call.

'She's been out on six occasions over the last five
years,' he began. 'First she was thirty-nine pounds,

fifteen ounces back in November 2010 . . .' He paused. 'It was me that caught her then actually.'

'Sorry, Jake, can I stop you there?' I presumed I'd misheard. 'You just said you caught the pike first?'

This was an absolute bombshell. I stammered on but my carefully loaded questions on fish care, leading up to a request to fish the lake, had just flown clean out of the window.

'Tell me exactly how it happened.' I leant into the phone and tore a fresh sheet of paper from my notebook.

'It was just a trout lake back then and this fish was a total unknown. People aren't totally sure how she even got in there. Some think she was placed in, but I reckon she most likely travelled up the becks and streams that flow to the River Derwent; right back when this whole place was flooded some years ago. From that point, she's obviously just gotten bigger and bigger.'

It was more than plausible that a small pike had made its way into this trout lake, and with rich pickings and freshly stocked trout, she would have piled on the poundage: up to 4lb a year for the best weight-gaining predators.

'The water here is deep,' Jake continued, 'twenty-eight foot in places, and has been stocked with trout for some thirty-odd years. It wasn't hard for it to hide, I guess, but the occasional trout angler talked of seeing a really big fish chasing their trout on the retrieve.' He took a deep breath. 'Honestly though, Will, we all thought the most it could be was thirty pounds.'

I had seen a few photos of this pike from its most recent captures. It was incomprehensibly enormous: a long, fat, female fish, with a back so wide you could fit it with a saddle.

My personal best pike was a 22lb fish caught from the depths of the Fens when I was twenty-five years old. I couldn't reasonably imagine tackling a pike nearly twice that size, and nor, it turned out, could Jake.

'A couple of trout anglers had returned their boat early one evening, so I just hopped in for nothing more than a twenty-minute mess about.' I liked that: a 'mess about' that led to the biggest single pike discovery since the turn of the century. 'I went out in the boat around the edge of the lake. It was right at the end of the day and I was on my last couple of casts, making my way back to where the boats were all kept, when suddenly the big girl took my spinner.

'At first I thought it was just a trout of a couple of pounds; she didn't really do that much, just headed straight in towards me. Then I saw it for the first time. That's where the fight truly began. I couldn't believe it.'

I couldn't believe it either. What a story. He went on to say that by the time he had the fish under control he realized the net he had with him wasn't anywhere near large enough to fit her in, and that he had then been forced to use the electric motor on board to get within shouting range of the shore. By a supreme stroke of good fortune a colleague eventually managed to net her tail first before the fish could free itself from the tether.

He had just landed the fish that would go on to become both the English record and the largest known living pike in the United Kingdom today. His previous personal best was just 14lb. It was, and still is, a fishing miracle.

'You just don't know how to feel when it happens. You're gobsmacked.'

That was where the good times ended for Jake and the pike. News of the giant fish travelled fast and Wykeham had to immediately limit the number of pike anglers allowed on the water. She next came out just four months after Jake had first caught her, but, astonishingly, the fish was some 6lb heavier. Now, with her just one meal away from being the next British record, interest in the fishery reached fever pitch. Jake was soon bombarded with requests to fish the lake for the pike.

'Look, it's a trout lake at the end of the day,' he said, with more than a touch of exasperation. 'Trout fishing was getting compromised. I had guys ringing up to enquire about trout fishing that couldn't get through because of all the interest from pike anglers. The syndicate seemed the best way to go then: limit it to ten anglers with a maximum of four a day on the water. I know it's very exclusive, but I prefer this run as a trout lake with the pike as something of a bonus. The amount of pressure she'll get is overwhelming if I don't do something. At least on Chew they've got more than one forty-pound fish and over a thousand acres for them to disappear into: here she's on her own with just seven.'

That last comment struck me hard. I started to feel a sense of real guilt. This wasn't what fishing should be about.

'Pike groups are getting more and more abrasive, just like the carp groups in fact,' continued Jake, 'you can't post a photo anywhere without someone tearing into someone over something. Every time our fish gets caught you've got one big group of people saying we're running it like an exclusive club and then another big group of people saying it's going to be a dead fish within a year. We've had one guy who said this time around: "I know I said last time it'll be a dead fish next year, but this time I really mean it: next year it will be dead." What are we supposed to do? We just can't win.'

Clearly Jake had a point: you've got to really look after these big individual fish. I started to wonder if this pike was more of a curse than a blessing.

'If only I could turn back the clock, I would make this lake invitation only for pike fishing and that's it,' he said, with finality.

For the first time in my entire fishing life I didn't want to catch a fish. Jake was right, pike fishing was going the same way as carp fishing and chasing named and known fish into potential oblivion on small waters was not cool at all. It was actually quite disturbing.

By the end of our conversation I no longer wanted to ask him for permission to fish; in fact, I was quite embarrassed at myself. I wondered what Grandad would make of it all. I knew what he would think actually: he'd laugh at me and question why anyone would ever place value on such a shortsighted pursuit.

Without me needing to say, Jake offered to set me up with a couple of the guys on the syndicate, and potentially, with their permission, have a little fish for the big one.

I told him how grateful I was for the offer, and really meant it, but there was no real mystery around this pike any more. It was still a challenge of sorts, but Jake's original discovery and capture were the real purist piece of angling. That's what was really impressive. That's what I wanted for myself.

Barring a miracle, any hopes I now had of angling for a record pike were fundamentally over. There wasn't much more I could do. Jake was spot on for trying to keep his fish safe in a small water and Chew were doing the same by massively limiting their numbers and restricting the pike-fishing windows.

The start of Chew's February pike trials saw bad weather and a few blowouts. The £880 angler didn't get his day out due to high winds and I managed a couple more sessions down the wharf and canals, but returned empty-handed.

One afternoon I went to Garry Evans Tackle, my local Cardiff shop and a tackle enthusiast's haven, and chatted to my friends Rich and Andrew about pike. 'I reckon there's a chance of a big one in the bay,' suggested Andrew, 'we've all been catching big perch down there all year.'

I told them about the fishing I'd been doing on the canal and down the wharf, and Andrew showed me a picture of a young bloke with a huge 16lb sea trout from one of the feeder streams. 'Yeah, the docklands are doing really well,' continued Andrew, stowing his phone back in his pocket, 'I've had loads of small pike down there, but the carp fishermen reckon they keep seeing really big pike battling it out with the rats.'

That sounded pretty much in keeping with that particular set of docks. It's a pike-eat-rat world down there. 'I've had a really big pike, and I mean a really big one, chasing my floating frog lures down there on several occasions,' Andrew continued, 'but there is something about that lure that the big pike really doesn't like. He keeps turning away right at the last minute . . .' He looked to his fingernails with a touch of embarrassment. '. . . So I've bought a lure shaped like a rat.'

I didn't even know there was such a thing, but Andrew knew everything that was worth knowing about lure-fishing, and, besides, it wasn't like I didn't get it; I'd once spent an entire afternoon fishing with a Pot Noodle on a whim.

'I'm going to be trying that soon,' he said, suddenly far surer of himself, before a ringing phone took him back to his work.

I left the tackle shop wondering about making a proper effort on the wider docks, as well as the wharf, or at least buying myself a rat lure and joining Andrew. In my heart, though, I couldn't help but think that this was feeling very much like needle-in-a-haystack time, or at least floating-rat-in-giant-rat-infested-dock time.

I went home feeling a little defeated, but on the journey back my phone pinged to life with an email. It was from a man named John Horsey, a legendary fishing guide who led trips to Chew during the pike trials, if you had already been lucky enough to snare a ticket of course.

I had contacted him a few weeks before the great phone-in but there didn't seem any point following up, given I hadn't managed to get a ticket. The email read:

Hi Will

Just to let you know there are guided boats available on 5, 7 and 16 Feb with me as the guide. This is a new initiative by Bristol Water.

If you want one of these boats then ring Chew ASAP.

Kind regards
John Horsey

Frantically, I hammered the now very familiar number for the Lodge. No answer. I left a voicemail, wrote an email, and tried to get through four more times, before finally, mercifully, I heard that glorious West Country accent once more: 'Hello, Chew Lakes.'

The words of my request spilled from my mouth at such a pace I was surprised the man on the end of the receiver could even figure out what I was trying to say.

'Ooh, I'm not sure.' I could hear some riffling of papers in the background. 'Possibly they are all booked out, possibly there is one left.'

I tried to sound cool, but it was pretty difficult given how badly I wanted this to work out. My heart was firmly in my mouth as the riffling continued, back-dropped with the occasional 'hmm'.

Eventually he answered.

'Yep, one left.'

16 February 2016. My date with pike-fishing destiny.

It was more money than I'd spent on a single day's fishing in my entire life, but I was over the moon. I had my ticket and I was absolutely determined to make the very most of it. All my ethics about chasing pounds and ounces and being part of a pike-fishing circus were firmly buried; I was boarding the clown car with a front-row seat for the big top and the undisputed ringmaster for hire. I just prayed we had a run of good weather.

The days quickly passed and I started to feel increasingly nervous. A feeling of inadequacy I hadn't felt since I was listening to Dad in the stairwell started to creep into the back of my mind. Am I actually up to these fish? I opted to spend yet more of my dwindling savings on tackle: bigger lures and a beefy braided line that felt like woven rope.

Extraordinary reports from Chew began to filter in. By all accounts this was shaping up to be one of the best February pike trials of all time. By the time my big day eventually came around, twenty pike over the 30lb barrier had already been snared, with two truly enormous fish topping out the scales at 41lb. To give that some sort of perspective, Martin Bowler, one of the best all-round anglers in Britain (who also just happens to be John Wilson's nephew), landed a 34lb 12oz fish and commented to the *Angling Times*: 'If I'd caught that fish at any other venue it would be a safe bet that it would be the best of the day, but I think the day I was fishing it was only third-biggest.' One man even commented on Chew's pike-fishing Facebook group that he wasn't sure it was even worth him posting a picture of his fish as 'it was only 28lb'.

Twenty-eight pounds. Six pounds bigger than my biggest all-time pike. Not even worth posting. I spooled up my strongest reel with my all-new braided line and selected the three most powerful rods I owned from the garden shed.

'I remember a fisheries scientist saying to me, "A pike doesn't know how big he is." I thought that was a silly thing to say, but actually it isn't, is it? It's not like they've got a mirror to look in, is it?'

I liked John Horsey immediately. He was a bright, liberal man, with an exceptional knowledge and enthusiasm for his sport. His heart lay with fly-fishing, particularly in competitions where he had captained England at world and European levels, and had even won the World Championships back in 2009; however, unlike many professional fly-fishermen, he wasn't the sort of person who would turn his nose up at coarse fishermen purely on principle. Plus he had a 40lb pike to his boat, caught, remarkably, on a fly. For all of that, I was extremely grateful.

His point, regarding the pike and the mirror, was that big fish don't necessarily change their feeding habits just because they are big fish. They are able to take bigger baits of course, but it is prudent not to assume their diet exclusively matches their size. Almost every animal is still partial to the food it grew up on, and therefore you shouldn't be surprised if, every once in a while, you encounter a fish of far greater size than your diminutive bait would expect; the biggest carp I've ever caught simply swallowed a single kernel of sweetcorn.

'Everyone always says it has to be a heavily stocked trout water to break a record, where there's plenty of big trout for the big pike to eat, but I don't believe that's strictly true,' explained John.

With his shock of white hair hidden beneath a baseball cap and neatly trimmed goatee beard, he had an air of the 'rock star' about him. 'Chew is the best pike fishery in Britain today because the levels of biodiversity here are exceptional. It's not just the pike; everything in this water is big: big trout, big tench, big eels, big roach; it's all thanks to the rich aquatic insect life that lives and breeds here' – he cast out an arm across the water in front of us – 'especially the black chironomids. The pike here are full of them.'

I had to look up 'chironomid' later. Essentially they are a variety of midge and closely resemble small mosquitoes, but don't let that put you off; this species is non-biting and, according to the Natural History Museum, they are a vitally important indicator species of the health of any water. They are extremely sensitive to any kind of pollutant or acidity in water, so their presence in numbers is a good sign of a first-rate environment; fantastic news to fish of all sizes, from giant pike to minute stickleback, which readily gorge on the flies and their larvae. John mentioned an autopsy on a mid-sized dead pike that revealed a stomach literally crammed with these small, jet-black insects, and my friends, who had fly-fished Chew in the past, claimed to have actually seen the pike scooping the insects right out of the lake, breaching the surface like packs of dolphins.

Chew is just that sort of place – where accepted logic is warped to such a degree that you genuinely start to believe in miracles. The lake looked truly serene at first light and sight. A clear, deep-blue morning had left a light ripple, and a blanket of wispy fog was playing on the water's surface. Chew dwarfed the Cardiff docks, of course. It appeared oceanic in comparison, but it wasn't as intimidating as I'd thought it might be.

As I perused the map on the back of my fishing permit I noted it resembled a hen's chick in profile, albeit with a slightly oversized head. There were a few attractive-looking bays, a pair of trench-like 'legs', and a large island, placed somewhere around the eye of the bird: lots of potential fish-holding areas that broke up the immensity of the venue then.

With John I was far from fishing blind at any rate. He purposefully hung back to see where all the other boats would go. 'Pike fishermen can be a bit like sheep,' he declared, placing his tackle in the bottom of the boat, 'they all tend to go where big fish have been caught that week and will follow each other around throughout the day. It's always best to give them all a wide berth and find your own place to start. There's no rush anyway; the best time on this lake is often the late afternoon to the sunset.'

John elected to start just left of Wick Green Point, a slight protrusion on the far bank from the Lodge, somewhere around the centre of the chick's back. It was lined with a thick growth of reeds that had been bleached a starchy white in the winter air. Instinctively, I would have taken our boat right in among those reeds, looking for a take from a pike hidden up against the beds. This, I learnt, would not have found me a record.

'These are big open-water fish,' explained John, 'they don't even know the meaning of the word ambush. The average depth here is only about thirteen feet, so quite shallow, but you've got to get the bait down there to catch the really big ones. They won't come up to get it, especially not when it is cold like this. They are immensely fat, and immensely lazy.'

I picked up the pair of lures that I'd bought brand new for this trip and handed them over to John for inspection.

They felt sticky, like they were fresh out of the mould, and were utterly free of blemishes or experience; I was like a young boy on his first day at secondary school, conscious that my sparkling-new pencil case was missing the requisite band insignias, amorous messages or pictures of cocks, which all the older, far cooler boys seemed to have.

One of the lures was the perfect replica of a small trout. I thought, given this was a trout lake, that was a fair choice. The second was a luminescent-looking perch, like the fish had spent its days swimming around nuclear fallout before finally making its way to my tackle box. I couldn't imagine what had drawn me towards that one; it looked hideous.

John eyed them both up before giving something of a damning verdict: 'Well, I wouldn't go with that perch, Will, not right away anyway, and the pike won't recognize that as a rainbow trout either. They've never seen a rainbow trout under two pounds in this place.'

I hadn't even made my first cast and I was already on the back foot. John, perhaps sensing I felt a little downcast, revisited the trout. 'They might just take it thinking it's a roach though; it is very white and, after all, all you need in this lake is just one take.'

That was good enough for me. I hooked it up to a strong wire trace and took a deep breath. It had taken an awful lot just to get to this point. I cast out well away from the reeds, watched my braided line snake out a little before feeling the lure strike the lake's bottom. John was right; it really was shallow. I began my retrieve, keeping it slow, steady and tight to the bed, as instructed. This was it. I was finally fishing Chew.

Five minutes later I felt the telltale thump and head-shake of a predator. A brief but solid fight brought an impeccable little pike of about 4lb to the edge of the boat. It was a nerve settler, the piscatorial equivalent of a pre-match pep talk, and there was even a small, but satisfactory, tear in the side of my new trout now. Perhaps I was worthy after all?

Soon afterwards a spiteful wind picked up off the Mendip Hills, rocking our boat and biting sharply into my bare hands. Of course, Chew wasn't going to let me have it all my own way. We pulled up our anchor and headed for shelter behind a large, semi-flooded island. 'Blimey, John, there's plenty of boats down here.' A quick head count revealed well over half of all the boats on the lake were also taking refuge, strung out in a long line like the floating buoys of a giant gill net.

I blew some hot air into my hands. 'Don't be fooled. They're not down here just to stay warm,' said John, with a quiet intensity, 'this was where that forty-one-pound giant was caught last week.' He selected a very, very large, fresh-looking mackerel from his bait box and fixed it firmly to a treble hook. 'I know, because I was here.' He cast the mackerel right out into the middle of the channel and tightened down his line till his fat, red-topped float could be seen bouncing happily along the surface.

I settled into a trance-like state: casting my lure, retrieving, focusing in on the play of the line through the water, and arching my neck occasionally to check our floats were still in place. A curious sensation came over me. It was a feeling that comes along with such infrequency that it feels like a sort of temporary psychosis, yet it strikes with such undeniable force that it is impossible to ignore.

As sure as King Canute knew he could not really turn the tides, I became convinced the pike were coming on to feed.

'We're going to get a fish here, John,' I said, venturing to vocalize my forecast, in spite of the lack of any discernible evidence. It was a gut instinct, a primeval intuition long since buried beneath several thousand generations of comfortable living and comfort eating, but I was utterly convinced I was right.

One of the men on the string of boats suddenly stood bolt upright with a rod buckling in his hand. I knew it.

We watched as his boat partner threw a massive black net from port to starboard, like a man wrestling with some giant sail on an ocean-going clipper. The angler started to pump the fish towards him; the tide was turning against this pike; soon it was subdued somewhere down by the engine block. They shook hands. It was a good one, at least 20lb in weight.

'My float is doing something funny.' Instantly, I snapped my gaze from the drama unfolding in the other boat. John was staring out at his float, which was now beginning to wheel.

When I was sixteen I learnt how big pike can often feed in spells. I remember that day clearly, my legs whirring as I ran away from the riverbank and back towards Grandad's bungalow. Behind me, submerged in a net, I had left a pike. A proper one, not a small jack or an emaciated summer fish, but a fat female that almost tore my rod into the deep alongside my smelt dead bait. The fish in itself was remarkable, but of far greater significance was the other, even bigger, pike that lay in the net right beside it.

In just ten minutes I had smashed my personal best, twice. I was in pike-fishing nirvana and I prayed Grandma had film in her camera as I exploded into the kitchen.

Grandma took my photo with both fish. 'Well done, boy!' shouted Grandad, giving me the thumbs-up I'd hoped for. He was off to play carpet bowls, he said; fishing in the bleak mid-winter wasn't really his thing.

I knew that was a special day. Over 30lb of pike in just two casts. Sometimes I feel I've been paying for that piece of good fortune ever since.

John's float started kiting hard to the left. This really was it.

'You take it . . .' John pulled the rod from its rest and handed it down to me in an act of extraordinary generosity. 'Really, are you sure?' I stuttered, and we had a brief and ridiculously British standoff, at the absolutely critical moment.

'Yes! Go for it, Will!' he eventually shouted, imploring me to take up the rod.

I didn't need to be asked for a third time. I reeled up the slack line, sank the tip and swept the rod upwards.

But there was nothing. No riposte. No bone-churning heavyweight thump. Just air and slack. I reeled down once more and gave it another slam, but it was useless. The pike had already let go.

'That was the big mackerel bait, wasn't it?' I asked, half hoping John might answer in the negative, or just assure me it was possible a trout could have chewed the bait from the hook. 'Yes, Will.'

My chance had been and gone. As plausible as it is that a 40lb pike might feed on a tiny chironomid, there was no way a small fish was ever squeezing a 1lb mackerel bait down its gullet. As quickly as the feeding spell had been triggered, the big pike turned themselves off once more.

There was excited chatter among the boats as we pulled into the docks that sunset. A Chew employee placed a thick boot on the side of our boat as we drifted into the melee. 'There were seven thirties out today, lads!' he revealed gleefully. 'How did you guys get on?'

The van's windscreen wipers squealed as I fought with the drizzle on the drive back home. I wonder how big that fish really was? I'll never know now of course, but I felt oddly calm.

When I was a boy I recall Grandad telling me a story about a great fish he once hooked that ran with an unstoppable force until it emptied his reel of a hundred metres of line and eventually broke free, leaving his rod hanging limp like a washing line cracked in a storm.

I asked him to recall this anecdote many times, both because I loved the idea of the mysterious giant in our waters, but also because I was unable to process how he could recall such a tale of calamity and yet appear so at peace. Perhaps in the retelling his demeanour would one day buckle, betraying his true feelings of raw hurt and resentment; but, of course, it never did.

Grandad, I realize now, was simply enriched by the experience of angling. His inner tranquillity came from a confidence emboldened by the knowledge that when it comes to hooking a big fish, a degree of loss is simply inevitable. It was not something to resent or regret; it was simply an acceptable part of what it meant to be a true fisherman, and a better person.

I would return to Chew if I ever get the chance again, but for all the ticketing process, the beefed-up tackle, circumstance and ceremony, could I reasonably say my day today had brought me more pleasure than the pike I had caught in the canal? Perhaps anglers' success is not determined only by the sheer size of the fish they catch, but the manner of, and pleasure to be had from, the pursuit and chase.

It had taken me over twenty years to learn the wisdom Grandad was once trying to impart, but I'd understood in the end. I would turn my attentions to fish of smaller proportions for the rest of this fishing year, and leave the giants for another time and place.

It was almost the close of the winter of '92 before I caught my first pike. As is often the way with these things, the fight of my fears was over before it began.

My spinner approached a hole within a cluster of reeds and a small pike materialized hot on its heels. I hastened my retrieve, and the fish, believing its meal was about to escape, near launched itself out of the water to engulf the lure.

Of all the pike I have caught, it was by far the easiest to land. I hooked it less than a foot from the bank and simply sprinted backwards, tearing the fish clean from the water and almost getting run over by a passing car in the process.

Unfortunately, behind the wheel was my Year Four primary school teacher, Mrs Hills. I could tell I was in for a massive rollicking by the steam coming from her brakes and ears, so I quickly scooped up my pike and sprinted off before she could even lay a hand on her car door handle.

It didn't occur to me then that this fish was merely a juvenile, or that I had been extremely lucky not to lose it or snap my line with my terrible antics. As far as I was concerned I now had living, breathing proof that Dad and Grandad were not always right. Pike were extremely hard to catch but I did have the strength to do it on my own.

In a quiet, teacher-free corner of the Creek I slipped my little pike back into the shallows. I couldn't possibly have realized it at the time, but, as it kicked its tail to disappear once and for all, it was taking a vital piece of my childhood down into the murk with it.

A Never-Ending Golden Sun

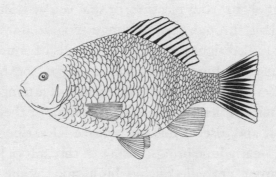

Summer will end soon enough,
and childhood as well.
George R. R. Martin, *A Game of Thrones* (1996)

Early June in Britain has a definite smell. It's not quite the sharp relief that you might associate with the first shoots of spring; a sliced crab apple that's fallen straight off the tree, maybe, or a sudden rain shower on crisp grass, perhaps. But it isn't anything like the sweaty oppression of a hot summer's day either, which hovers somewhere between a damp gym sock and an overripe banana.

Early June is much more subtle than that. It's a gradual sweetening of the air, an almost honey-like scent that creeps out across the land and rolls out a yellowing haze in its wake. It is experienced especially well at dawn by the side of a pond, when it can feel like the whole country is being gently dusted with a caramelized sugar crust simply for your pleasure, or that you've been viewing the land through a pair of ginger-coloured stockings that are pulled tight right across the balls of your eyes.

When early June is on form it brings the humans warily to their gardens, to cook meat and attempt some ice in their drinks, and also calls bees out of their hives to gather and discuss making a move. Don't be fooled, though – early June brings a sense of threat too. It is not yet summer, and all that has built since winter could quite easily be swept aside in a solitary night of single-digit temperatures, or a week of sullen rain. It is a risk that only doubles if someone is foolish enough to remark: 'What wonderful weather we've been having recently.'

For me, and anglers like me, early June exists as a hidden fifth season. It's not always found in early June; it can actually be any time from May, or even as early as late April, if we have had an exceptionally warm spring. Throwing our increasingly irrelevant Gregorian calendar aside, it is more accurate to place this season somewhere between the point the bluebells pass their best, and the seven days of proper sun we call summer. It brings trout to the surface to feed voraciously on the first of the serious fly hatches, a time known as 'duffer's fortnight', where even the most novice of anglers could seemingly catch a fish with a bent pin, but it is early morning on a certain type of water targeting a certain type of fish that defines the hidden season for some of us.

If you are lucky enough to catch this bridging spell at its climax then it is as close to climatic perfection as I think it is possible to experience as a fisherman. To achieve true flawlessness, though, is to time these rarefied atmospherics with your presence beside a lily-choked and tree-lined pool, at the exact point of sunrise. Obviously you will need a rod, loaded with light line and a bright float. Preferably there will also be a billowing steam peeling off the water's surface, and, once you have made your first cast, great plumes of pinhead-sized bubbles will surround your patch of water in a fizzing carpet.

If there is an angling scene that better represents the quintessence of this unsung time of year then I am yet to see it, but the fish that leads the charge doesn't just show itself to anyone. You have to be willing to search.

It was the start of the summer holidays from school, my first in secondary education, and Grandad was searching furiously at the back end of his living room. His arse had just nearly knocked the television over.

'Yes! I've got it!' he shouted in triumph. While lifting an old Polaroid cleanly from the labyrinth of VHS cassettes and family albums, he resembled an immense old walrus emerging from the water with a fresh fish in its teeth.

It was a black-and-white photo showing a solid-looking young man kicking a rugby ball. His shoulders are leaning back, his spine is straight, and the ball has just been thumped so hard it is leaving his toe as nothing more than an egg-shaped blur.

Grandad restored his breath. 'There, Will.' He presents me with the image while inhaling, this time for dramatic effect. 'The perfect kick. You'll never see it done better than that.' He thumbs the photo to make his point. 'That. Is how you do it, my boy.'

I grip it in my hands.

It's him in the picture, isn't it? Of course it's him.

Things hadn't gone too well at my new school. The endless evenings of fishing after lessons were over for a start – homework and a long journey to and from the gates had made sure of that – plus, after seven years of climbing the year groups at the local village primary school, I had found myself unceremoniously dumped back at the very bottom of the pecking order. It wasn't like Wisbech Grammar was all that bad. I was bullied, but not terribly so; it was the brand of schoolboy cruelty that had you tying a coin into the knot of your tie, to stop it being pulled so tight it was impossible to undo, rather than the threat of actual bodily harm. But having any sort of fear of attending school was new to me, and I didn't like it at all.

This was the start of adult life, though, where the first lesson you learn is that your free time will be leased back to you only once you've earned it, and that your future now depends on your ranking within an extremely narrow field of disciplines.

In lieu of stellar grades – I was no academic – I was to be judged by my ability to hit a cricket ball and take a full-contact rugby tackle. The problem was I was terrible at both rugby and cricket. We had played neither at my primary school, bar the very occasional game with a soft ball, or tag rugby, where the worst thing that could happen is that your mate grabs your shorts, and not your tag, and you end up exposing yourself to the class.

Unfortunately there really isn't much room for fishing in the arena of competitive team sports, especially those played by adolescent boys. Sure, there is a match-angling scene, but mostly this still boils down to individuals performing against other individuals, and no one – I repeat, no one – has pictures of the latest match-angling stars plastered across their bedroom walls. Anglers just aren't idols or icons for your normal teenager. My obsession with John Wilson suddenly seemed very childish and, to be frank, a bit embarrassing.

My recent progression as an angler was an irrelevance to my new classmates, of course. No one cared how good my casting was getting or that I had recently broken my perch personal best. Instead, my fishing became my escape route, the secret place I could vanish into to hide from my struggles at school. Later angling would actually offer me something of a pathway out of my problems, but that was all to come and in the first year of the new school I simply had no choice but to play the sports they instructed me to play.

I couldn't even catch a cricket ball, let alone throw it. They were rock-hard and frightening, much like the teachers and older kids who pushed past me in the corridor, and, as such, I tried to avoid them, all of them, at any cost.

'You're a bit of a loner, aren't you?' remarked one of my peers, after yet another lunchtime of dodging the other pupils in the first year. I felt hot tears puddling in my eyes and quickly looked away. 'No.' You're just all dickheads, I wish I could've said.

Dad and I were sat together in the Rose Tavern pub at the end of the school year. He was a massive real-ale nerd so going to pubs was hardly something new. Even as a twelve-year-old I had seen the inside of most of the decent pubs in our area, especially if they graced the hallowed pages of the *CAMRA Good Beer Guide,* but it was a rare occurrence to be alone with him and without the rest of the family. I was finally sat in the inner sanctum, the actual bar and not just the 'Family Fun Zone'. In with the real men, who drank by the pint, smoked and swore, I thought for a moment that Dad might even buy me a beer, but really I knew the real reason why I was here. I had just experienced the sporting equivalent of being tarred, feathered and marched around the market square naked. It was time for a fatherly pep talk. He slid an orange juice across the table towards me. 'It will get better, give it time, Will.' I felt too sick to even drink it. He had to 'give it time' at his school, he explained, and it wasn't easy for him either, at first.

'It actually took me right till sixth form before I really started enjoying it,' he attempted, jovially. Sixth form! Was Dad absolutely out of his mind? That was six years away! I looked at the orange juice in front of me and wished my whole life would go away.

My first rugby season had been a complete and utter disaster. It began with quite possibly the most anonymous performance in rugby union history, where the one touch of the ball I had was the moment it collided with my face, and split open my nose, and ended, even more dramatically, when one of the teachers used my limp form to demonstrate the dump tackle and shattered my collarbone in the process.

Sadly, my collarbone had re-fused just in time for the cricket season, but, unlike the X-Men, it had not mutated into anything that might have given me superpowers or even just a better throw. The year's crowning glory, truly the fly on this absolute turd of a term, had occurred just an hour before Dad's morale-boosting speech in the pub.

The Under-12 first-team cricketers were a man down, and as I had volunteered to do the scoring in the ludicrously misguided parental belief that 'it's all about taking part', I was drafted in as the eleventh player.

I spent our opponents' innings just trying to avoid the ball, a feat I achieved well by virtue of the fact my team wanted me nowhere near the ball either, but when it came to our turn to bat my luck ran clean out.

Wickets tumbled with regularity from almost the moment our batsmen began their run chase. They had a bowler with an arm like Hercules, who, quite remarkably, also appeared to have grown some facial hair. I could only assume this man-boy was part of some witness protection programme, sent to terrorize the Under-12 cricket scene in relative anonymity.

Stumps exploded into puffs of sawdust and all too soon I found I was strapping myself into every single piece of protective equipment the school owned. I was sure I was going to die at the crease, and, ten minutes later, I realized I had.

All I needed to do for our team to escape the debacle with a draw was to bat for three balls. Three balls. The first fizzed past my head. I didn't even see it. Hercules glowered at me. 'He isn't moving,' I heard an ignoramus shout from within my own team, who, I noted, had helpfully gathered in a ten-man semi-circle around the boundary rope, as if they were witnessing an execution by stoning.

The second ball swung away, just inches from shattering my fingers or, worse, my stumps. Everyone groaned. Hands were placed on heads on both sides. Just one more left, I thought to myself. I looked to my dad, off work for the game, but never really a sporting man either. He tried to give me an encouraging thumb's-up look from behind his glasses and improbably thick hair, but his face betrayed his true feelings: I was in deep shit. With sad inevitability, the third and final ball crumpled my wicket.

You could've heard my teammates on Mars as I trudged off the pitch. 'Fucking useless Millard, we should never have sent him out there.' A darkness descended. I scooped up my bag and headed for Dad's car and the Rose Tavern pub, without speaking a single word till I was wedged in the triple sanctuary of a Toby mug, a fruit machine and my dad.

'They totally blamed me, Dad. You heard what they said. How can I show my face in school after that?' I was ranting at my juice. 'I hate this place. I hate this school. I hate everything about it. All of my primary school friends went to Downham, I just don't understand why I'm here in this place with these blazers and rules and teachers and tests . . . and terrible sports . . . and not . . . not with all my friends.' I started to cry, properly this time.

Dad put a hand on my shoulder. 'If you still hate it at the end of next year we'll move you out. I promise.' I sniffed hard and plunged my wet face into his shirt. 'Give it time,' he said again. I could tell it was hurting him too, but I didn't care.

'But what about rugby season next year, Dad?' I shouted. 'They'll kill me!'

He looked at me with glassy brown eyes, and said nothing.

The reason for Grandad's sudden expedition to the land that time forgot was that he had spoken to my dad and believed the solution to all of my problems was behind his television set.

'All you need to do is study this picture and you'll be able to kick penalties from the centre spot.' He slapped me so forcefully between the shoulder blades I felt the tremor in my stick-thin legs, like two albino chipolatas.

There was no way that this was what Dad had advised Grandad to do. He had come up with this solution all on his own.

'You've got all summer before the start of the rugby season. Just give it some beef, boy!'

I looked up at him, hoping he could see through to the lost child within. There was a pause as he stooped to meet my gaze, understanding dawning perhaps?

'You can even take it home and study it if you like?' He gave me a chummy wink and another slap on the back.

I didn't take it home. I had eight weeks before I had to be back at that school and I intended to spend it all forgetting the place ever existed. That meant two things: fishing, and really big carp.

By my final year of primary school the memory of the first pike had faded. I had a clutch of close friends from the village whom I fished with and, together with our bikes and the timetable of the Norfolk Green bus, we were pushing further than ever before. Bigger drains for bigger fish, stronger rods, thicker lines and the greater levels of patience required to sit through the shoals of roach and perch for something really special.

With them I caught my first zander, our first proper pike, my first ever chub, all by strapping rods to the crossbars of our bikes and pedalling as far as our legs could carry us in a single day. We were the kings of the Fens, bound only by the parental rule that we must be home by nightfall, and by the end of our time together in school our angling ambitions were inevitably extending beyond what we could feasibly catch from our home waters. We wanted more, and we weren't alone.

From the late 1970s onwards anglers nationwide were draining from Britain's rivers and canals and taking their tackle to well-stocked and exceptionally well-polished commercially motivated fisheries. Overwhelmingly, the explosive popularity of one single species had driven the change: the king carp. It had first been introduced from Asia as food for monks during the Middle Ages, and selective breeding had seen the proliferation of a heavier, hardier and highly varied cyprinid species that combined a readiness to feed with a heart-stoppingly powerful fight from even the smallest specimens. There was hardly a pond in the UK that they couldn't be stocked in, and, with astronomic annual weight gain possible from a new wave of protein-rich baits, targeting the species passed from the specialist and into the hands of the everyman.

Images of these giant fish, with their magnificent scale patterns, implausibly broad guts and thick, rounded mouths, screamed from the front page of every fishing magazine and tackle shop in the country. Even John Wilson was far from immune to carp fever: he built a carp lake in his own back garden, and soon released a video titled *Oliver's First Carp*, in which a boy exactly our age caught a single fish that weighed more than our entire annual catch from the Creek.

That was enough for us; and what remained of that summer was spent begging our parents to drive us out to our closest commercial carp lake.

I have hardly ever felt as ill-prepared as the day we

eventually arrived on the banks at Wood Lakes in Stow-bridge. This wasn't fishing as we knew it: it was war. Row upon row of stiff, carbon-fibre rods sat on tripods backed onto hi-tech bite alarms, like a battery of anti-aircraft missiles, and behind each rig sat a grizzled-looking angler dressed head to toe in camouflage gear. Even the baits were unrecognizable: brightly coloured balls called boilies that looked more like sweets than an edible fish attractant, but, my God, these set-ups were effective. Every so often a bite alarm would scream off and one of the men would lift nonchalantly into the sort of fish that would have had us talking for months.

We stood in silence and watched the carnage. It was all we could do. Our rods, cobbled-together collection of tackle and Mum-made foil-wrapped sandwiches were pathetic in comparison.

When we eventually did attempt to fish we hid away in the far corner of the lake, and took to plundering our way through the shoal of tiny perch that lived there. It had to be tiny perch, didn't it? Despite all the fish we had caught together in months past we were now thrown to the minnows of our adolescence. That one morning in the company of the kings of carp had proven we were still just little boys after all, and I wasn't actually the king of anything. Things just got worse from that point. I would be even more aware of my shortcomings the fol-lowing summer, thanks to cricket at my new school, but of even greater concern that year was the discovery that I was no longer surrounded by my friends. In big boys' school I was just another fluff-faced squeaky-voiced competitor lining up in a bizarre, hormone-driven race without rules or a discernible finishing line. Quite quickly, catching a big carp became the embodiment of my teenage frustrations. It was my fantasy fish, the one creature capable of bridging the gap between my shortcomings as an angler and my teenage aspirations, and meant so much more than just ticking off another species in the Wilson *Encyclopedia*. For me, it *was* puberty.

If only I knew then what I know now I might not have been so eager to commit myself fully to commercial carp fishing at such a young age.

My friends and I were very late to the party. It was the early 1990s by the time we graced the banks of Wood Lakes, by which point the nature of commercial carp fishing had been refined to such an extent that it felt like the whole fishscape might well have spilled off the back of the same truck.

Identikit lakes, fish and fishermen spread out across the land, reducing the sport to catching as big, or as much, with as little effort as humanly possible. Well-maintained fishing platforms replaced wild holes in the reeds, flattened roads led direct to well-manicured banks, and, in many places, fishing swims were dragged entirely clean of debris, detritus or any other snags that could result in a lost carp, and a spoiled day.

For the most part, any native wildlife that could be seen to have any detrimental impact on carp growth in the carp pond was actively discouraged or ruthlessly controlled. At the fisheries that could afford them otter-proof fences were erected, cormorants – 'the black death' – were managed, or just shot, and so-called 'nuisance' fish species – bream, roach, rudd and tench – were netted en masse and removed altogether. The key to success is to ensure the customer's hook baits always have the very best chance of working their way to the lips of a specimen carp, and specimen carp only.

Chris Yates, an angling legend and staunch traditionalist, who famously broke the British carp record in 1980 on an antique rod and single grain of corn, wrote a scathing attack on the direction of the sport in his brilliant 1997 book *The Secret Carp*: 'this standardization has gone beyond a joke. Not only do the majority of carp anglers have to fish with at least three identical rods and reels, they must also have the complete product range of whoever happens to be the most fashionable tackle and bait manufacturers of the day. And of course they also require waters that can accommodate this multi-rodded, heavily equipped regimental approach. So the lakes have become standardized as well. Ultimately even the fish have become standardized with all specimens entered onto graphs which show growth ratios, condition factors, identification marks, colour variations, dietary habits, intelligence ratings, dress sense, musical appreciation and knowledge of world history.'

He's being disingenuous of course, but only slightly. Carp fishing today has arguably gone even further down the standardization road. On one side are the big fish venues with lightly stocked, but named and well-known, carp giants that might grace the bank several times in a season, and on the other are fish-filled carp factories that provide constant rod-bending action all year round.

Thirty years ago a fishing catch totalling 100lb or more would have been big news, but this season a six-hour match was won by an angler who banked an astonishing 1,500lb of carp. His haul amounted to 350 fish at a catch rate of one carp a minute. With the top three competitors also catching in excess of 1,000lb of fish each as well, it amounted to over 1,900 carp out of that one lake in a single August afternoon.

Given the Environment Agency recommends that natural fisheries can only hold 200 pounds of fish per acre to remain healthy, it is clear something is very definitely, very seriously, wrong. No fisherman is that good. Fishing in this way places fish, and fish welfare, as firmly secondary to the demands of the angler. In the worst-case scenario, the fish in these oxygen-depleted and unnatural environments must eat the food we offer them just to survive. It's little more than *Battle Royale* or *The Hunger Games* of carp, fishing reduced to a game of numbers based wholly on a single species.

It sounds awful, it really does, but for the past twenty years I've absolutely lapped it up. This is, in part, because not all commercial fisheries are quite that bad, but also because they can be an enormous amount of fun. I get the attraction, I really do. When you haven't got much spare time to indulge in a hobby that has a tendency to be a slow burn on the best of days, sometimes you just want to catch, but this overpowering magnetism of the commercial lake has fundamentally altered fishing as we know it, and not for the better: for the majority of anglers today, there is simply no longer any alternative to the commercial.

I had learnt from the Canal & River Trust that many of our once great waterways have fallen into a state of neglect purely through a total lack of angling interest, but I also recalled John Ellis's comment that all the youth seek these days are thrills from bigger and bigger carp; and this, I discovered, doesn't necessarily keep them in our sport for life.

This season's rod licence sales show there is a huge lack of young people coming to fishing; worse yet, junior licences are down a massive 50 per cent in just the last five years. The only growing branch of the sport today is among pensioners, the sorts of people who had grown up around massive canal matches and the understated pleasures to be had from dangling a worm in wild rivers and streams.

In building up to the carp lakes through the small perch, roach and pike of my local river, I had already received a gradual apprenticeship in the essential techniques I needed, but I also formed a critically important, and deeply intense, connection to my natural environment. It just isn't the same if you jump straight into the sport and catch a big lump from a stocked pit at the very first time of asking. There's no question that carp fishing is extremely exciting, but the buzz wears thin if that's all you ever experience and catching something is guaranteed. It's hard to imagine many young people sticking with fishing once that box has been ticked multiple times, and I can't see them reverting to the subtle pleasures to be had from plundering small fry from a river either, especially once they've been hooked on the power of the carp.

You can't blame the owners of the commercial fisheries. It's just business after all, and many have since taken serious steps to set up in a manner that is better for the carp, but these waters shouldn't be to the exclusion of all other fishing styles and species. It is down to us, as a fishing community, to take responsibility for protecting the integrity of our sport by choosing to be more diverse with our angling. After all, shouldn't fishing represent the exception, the foil, the buffer, to a modern world already filled with uniformity, instant gratification, clickbait buzzes and shrinking attention spans? Angling, by its very nature, is a random, often chaotic, collection of environments, species, methods and possibilities that afford the fisherman the opportunity to get utterly lost for a lifetime or more. You can't always win, but that doesn't mean you necessarily lose.

'Whatever next? Rods that reel the fish in for you, or devices that cast your bait into the perfect spot?' I didn't want to tell Grandad about the electronic bait boat I'd seen during my latest trip to Wood Lakes – it quite literally did cast that man's bait into the perfect spot. 'It's taking the skill out of fishing,' he droned on and on.

By the end of the summer after that fateful first year at secondary school my fishing friends from the village had drifted away. We had caught a handful of small carp between us, and had swapped our river tackle and maggots for our own series of identical rods and bags of boilies, but the polarizing demands of our new schools in different towns had come between us in the end. We were all on different paths now, and I missed them a great deal.

The biggest new challenge on my horizon was found within the new commercial carp fishery that had just opened, ironically, at the end of Grandad's garden. I knew beyond doubt that I needed those carp more than ever now. Besides, it seemed more than just mere coincidence that big carp were available a stone's throw from Grandad's lobelias. This was my chance to fill the void left by friends and sporting failures, and it felt like it was being handed to me on a plate. I told Grandad we had to go. He just laughed. So I went on my own.

It took a couple of weeks down there before it happened. I was fishing a bunch of maggots tight to the back of a purpose-built island feature when my rod was, quite literally, ripped clean off its rests and into the lake.

I picked it up by its disappearing butt and began a fight like no other. The reel screamed and the rod hooped to breaking point as it tried in vain to cushion a thunderous opening run. It was far and away the biggest fish I had ever been connected to at the time, a fish I had long dreamt of and a fight I had spent long hours practising for and considering. But now it was all happening I felt a sense of near-paralysing fear, both at what the fish might do to my tackle and what it would do to my vulnerable emotional state if it managed to escape.

Eventually the great carp wallowed, hippo-like, directly under the rod tip. It was as if I was watching Wilson on a video of my childhood, laughing along and reaching for the net, but it wasn't him, it was me. I leant forward, waist-high in the lake with water seeping down deep into the fibres of my Umbro tracksuit bottoms, and folded the fish deep into my memory for all time.

I had caught a mirror carp, so named after the set of shining reflective scales that adorn its flanks. It tipped my scales at a hefty 12lb, not massive by carp standards, but the restorative properties that fish had for my self-belief were worth a thousand centuries in cricket or a winning goal in the ninety-third minute. If I could emulate my fishing hero, then what else couldn't I achieve? I was euphoric that night and, in a rush of blood to the head, asked Mum, our household's cricketing impresario, if I could join the village cricket club.

From now on I would seek only bigger and bigger challenges, and I would take them head-on. The capture of the mirror carp had bolstered my sense of self-belief to such an extent that I could almost imagine its immaculate scales were to be worn as plates in my own suit of armour. No one was going to make me feel scared or hopeless ever again; and I was going to get better at sport, even if it did kill me.

In spring, I returned from a long period of filming in the jungles of New Guinea to find blissful sunshine bathing the nation. Finally, the horror rains of the endless winter had passed and the new season had brought some superb fishing weather.

I had wanted to catch crucians from the outset of this challenge. Mostly because I thought they were among the most beautiful fish swimming in our waters – I still do – but I also hoped it would be a really good way of exploring the unsung traditional still waters of the nation. The sorts of places you might see in the paintings of the English Romantics, very Constable-esque, I imagined, but I also felt, after the drubbing at the hands of both the pike and the perch, that this was a fish I actually had a fairly good chance with. I had caught a fair few crucians while out carp fishing, including one real beauty almost 3lb in weight, so surely with just a few tweaks to my tactics, and perhaps a bit of research, a whopper was well within my reach?

I, along with many others, believed that the crucian was native to Britain. Its pocket-sized and dignified appearance was surely more in keeping with these fair isles than the brutish king carp? However, I soon discovered that was not the case at all. The most recent DNA analysis of a sample in Norfolk can only place the crucian here in the medieval period, around the same time as all the other carp species. I forgave myself for my mistake – the analysis was only a couple of years old and was hardly official. Even Alwyne Wheeler, fish expert and former curator of the Natural History Museum's fish department, had believed they were native, stating as much in his paper published in the year 2000, but there was still no way of getting round the cold, hard, present-day facts: this fish was introduced.

Its being so much smaller than the king carp has led to suggestions that the crucian might have been brought here from the east as something of an ornamental species, a splash of colour in the noble's pond, but it is hard to find precise references to support the supposition. What we do know is that carp as a whole were a much sought-after food item in the Middle Ages: perhaps a multitude of carp species were actually ordered to create something of a smorgasbord for those with a piscatorial palate? Carp was no food for the peasantry though – maintained by monks and consumed by monarchs, carp were both luxury food items and status enhancers, favoured, in particular, by the House of Tudor. Who knows? Perhaps the rotund King Henry VIII was chewing down on his umpteenth crucian while considering executing another wife? He certainly had a partiality for the carp species, and practically every other freshwater fish in Britain. Susanne Groom, in her book *At the King's Table: Royal Dining through the Ages*, describes a magnificent starter course served to Henry

VIII that naturally included carp, but also herring, cod, lampreys, pike, salmon, whiting, haddock, plaice, bream, porpoise, seal, trout, crabs, lobsters, custard, tart, fritters and fruit, and that doesn't even touch on the man's penchant for whale meat, black pudding and swans. It was curious, I thought, how all the other fish species to grace the tables and plates of the palace were so well distinguished and explicitly referenced, yet when it came to the carp, everything from goldfish, to commons, to crucians, fell under the same generic 'carp' banner. I glossed over this detail at the time, but it was actually a sign of things to come.

I thumbed through the Wilson *Encyclopedia* to the crucian section. I noted his description of the unusual 'upturned mouth (without barbels)' and tendency to 'shoal according to their size'; but it wasn't until I came to cast my eye on the listed British record size that I stopped in my tracks. Something wasn't right.

5lb 10.5oz.

There was no way that could possibly be accurate. I knew for a fact that there was no verified crucian catch in Britain in excess of 5lb as, after I caught my three-pounder, I had checked the record books and discovered that the record back then was only around 4.5lb, but I just couldn't imagine Wilson making such an elementary mistake either. I was going to need some help.

Peter Rolfe runs a wonderful website dedicated wholly to the species (http://www.crucians.org) and after a friendly exchange of emails I tapped the digits of his number into the receiver and a gravelly, almost Shake-spearean voice soon answered the phone.

'The sooner we drop "carp" from "crucian carp" the better,' he growled.

Peter Rolfe has been dedicated to the preservation of the crucian for the past forty years. He is a bona fide hero for the species (even receiving the Fred J. Taylor Award for Environmental Stewardship in acknowledge-ment of his work), but I doubt he'd ever wear such a title.

'People think the fish is related to the king carp, when they hear that "carp" moniker, when of course it isn't. It's related to the goldfish.' I scribbled furiously as he spoke. It was all news to me. 'The bigger carp species out-compete crucians for territory and food, so that's bad for one, but also they interbreed with them with tre-mendous ease, as does the very similar brown goldfish. As commercial fisheries and the stocking of king carp became popular everywhere, well, the humble crucian didn't really stand much of a chance.'

In my twelve-year-old haste to pivot on the scaly backs of king carp and hop into the world of 'real' men, I didn't once stop to consider what the consequences of such a wholesale stocking programme might be. By the end of the 1990s it had become abundantly clear that the crucian was actually in very real trouble indeed. 'It hadn't seemed so bad at first, I suppose it was just that they had become less popular,' continued Peter, 'but once we realized just how many fish that we thought were crucians were in fact cross-breeds with goldfish or common carp, well, we realized the situation was somewhat dire.'

Peter was putting it delicately. If the crucian wasn't marching to the brink of extinction in this country, it was certainly gearing up for the walk. It was a paradox of sorts, our obsession with the king carp speeding the decline of a different species of carp, but it was pretty easy to see why things had gone so wrong for the crucian: it was small enough to be ignored. Little wonder it preferred the hidden season: as a fish of Britain it was once dangerously close to vanishing altogether.

The Wilson *Encyclopedia* puts a crucian mega-specimen at over 3lb: that is chump change for the king carp, really, a very average-sized fish; and with an angling population hooked on the bigger-is-better mantra the crucian was almost predestined for trouble. The odds were stacked further against the fish as their traditional habitat – small, rural pools – began to disappear nationwide through drought, pollution and shifting agricultural practices. The crucians might have stood something of a chance in an environment where a disappearing waterway would at least make local news – in small pools in our parks or urban ponds, for instance – but unfortunately the well-intentioned communities here have a tendency to unwittingly liberate their pet goldfish directly into the crucian gene pool. With that, it seemed, to Peter and his friends at least, the crucians' fate was sealed.

Then came a quite unexpected turn in their fortunes.

In 1997 the British Record Fish Committee hit the 'reset' button on the whole crucian record list. Following the cross-breeding revelations it was felt the record as it stood was essentially redundant: no one could be sure if the leading fish were pure crucians or just cross-breed hybrids with goldfish and common carp. Clear rules were set out to help the layperson identify the fish – between thirty-two and thirty-four scales along the lateral line, a lack of barbels around the mouth, a large convex dorsal fin – and a new fishing challenge was laid down to an army of anglers apparently itching for something new.

One year later, the capture of a truly enormous 4lb 2oz pure crucian lit up the angling press, and the wider fishing public, surprisingly, switched on to this diminutive fish wholesale. Perhaps the king-carp-shaped blinkers were gradually being lifted as the new millennium approached, but, either way, as the tragic plight of the fish made the national press, the call to do much more to save the crucian reached an unprecedented level.

'Things were quite suddenly much more optimistic for the crucian.' Peter warmed at the thought. 'The word has since spread and many more people are interested in fishing for them these days. Really, I'm chuffed it's all happening.'

The Wilson *Encyclopedia* had hit the shelves, and my Grandad's own Henry VIII-esque stomach, in 1995. Wilson, like the rest of us, simply didn't realize these 'carp' were all separate species with a truly extraordinary ability to cross-breed.

'There is a lot of misinformation out there about the fish still. Ponds and fisheries claiming to hold the crucian when really they don't, and also fish breeders who think they are selling pure crucians when in fact they are goldfish or common-carp hybrids. You can see online, people still think they are catching near-record crucians when, in fact, they are all just cross-breeds. The problem is, as soon as you've unwittingly stocked these hybridized fish you stand no chance of maintaining a healthy pure-crucian population.'

I put down the receiver and immediately ordered a copy of Peter's superb book *Crock of Gold*, which is, to date, the only book dedicated solely to the crucian carp, but I had an awful feeling. If the entire nation, and many of our top anglers, had been so easily duped with cross-bred fish, then what was to say every crucian I'd ever caught was not an imposter too?

Days later, with Peter's book spread across my thighs, my fingers hovered nervously over several digital folders filled with photos of fish. Gradually, I began clicking my way through my catches past.

The princely brace from a recent visit to a farm pond were clearly just brown goldfish; they looked like crucians but the scale count was way over. I went back further. The surprise two-pounder from a Newport commercial in the depths of winter. Urgh. It was glaringly obvious now: the dorsal was the wrong shape and the – almost grossly – disproportionate fantail marked it out clearly as another goldfish cross. This was looking bad. Armed with the truth in Peter's book I was starting to feel pretty foolish. I clicked through to the folder containing my personal-best crucian, the 3lb fish, a real beauty: a Wilson mega-specimen none the less. Staring proudly down the lens in the twilight, I'm holding what I knew now could only be a clear crucian–common-carp cross. I even sent the image to Peter Rolfe to be sure. His capitalization of the word 'not' before the words 'a crucian' was the final thumping nail in my specimen-crucian-carp coffin.

I continued, searching, almost desperately, for something to cling to, but as fish after fish failed to make the grade it slowly became clear that in all my years of carp fishing there was probably only one occasion when I caught a pure crucian. I was eleven years old, fishing a holiday pond somewhere in the rolling farmland of the south-west because I had been told by the owner that it held a mirror carp. The surprise crucian had taken a fancy to the piece of sunken bread flake I had freelined unwittingly into its path, but, back then, I couldn't have been more underwhelmed.

I can remember it now, this little golden fish in my palm, all friendly curves and smoothened fins, that I decided couldn't possibly be a proper carp. It was small and somehow fraudulent, more suited to a gold-fish bowl than a fishing pond. Mutton dressed as mutton. I plopped it back in and re-cast, harder and further, hoping pure brute power would bring me closer to my own Shangri-La: my first king carp, just like the ones in all the magazines.

I hadn't even bothered to photograph that fish, and here I was, over twenty years later, pleading the details of that distant memory to materialize into a barbel-less fish, with a convex dorsal fin, and thirty-two to thirty-four scales along its lateral line. It probably only weighed around 6oz, but that crucian, I realized now, was my new personal best.

In that moment my whole record-breaking challenge had been turned right on its head. It was like someone had fired a rocket into my front room. I slapped the laptop closed, more astonished than disappointed. This was absolutely extraordinary. All this time. All those carp. Not one of them actually a crucian. I laughed out loud and sent Lottie, my cat, charging out of the catflap in fright.

This was far bigger than me and some record chase. Not for one moment did I actually ever think I would end up chasing a species with the pure objective of simply catching one for potentially the very first time as an adult, let alone a fish that had survived such an epic threat to its very existence.

I fell in love with the thought.

As I type, the crucian record at 4lb 10oz is held jointly by two anglers: Stephen Frapwell and Michael James, who caught the same fish in early May 2015 from the crucian mecca, Johnson's Lake in Surrey. I had been very kindly invited by Peter to fish the crucian ponds he had developed with his own hands, but they observed the close season until 16 June. I couldn't wait till then. It wasn't simply just aesthetically pleasing to be bankside at this time of year: all my research pointed to the fact that the bigger crucians came out then too. They were fit to burst with spawn by early June, preferring to deposit their loads before the king carp, and, according to Peter, just after the roach, perch and rudd. This year June had arrived with unseasonably high temperatures, and the king carp in my local lakes were already beginning to splash the shallows and deposit their loads; if I was going to smash my personal best I needed to act right now.

Utilizing the fisheries database on Peter's crucian website I narrowed down the potential waters to those that had either recently broken records or had only just been pipped at the post, then I hit the phones. Back in May 2003, Little Moulsham Pit near Yateley had given up a 4lb 9oz fish to Martin Bowler. It was tricky to get a ticket and there were few details online. A call to the Yateley angling centre revealed it was now a syndicate carp lake owned by a man named Alan Cooper, who ran a groundbait company. Eventually I got through to Alan, but the news was bad. 'They've all been eaten by cormorants, mate,' came his flat reply, 'it's too expensive to restock them and it'll take twenty years before a crucian ever gets to that size again. That's twenty years of running the gauntlet with the cormorants and even at record size they can still be eaten. Big carp are a much better bet for me, everyone is a carp fisherman these days. I'm afraid it's where the sensible money is.' Over in Pembrokeshire, I was very excited to learn that Holgan's Farm claimed to house potential record-breaking crucians, in a bespoke crucian lake, but a phone call there brought another rebuff. They had opted to stock brown goldfish and the resultant 'crucians' today were almost certainly hybrids. Realistically that only left me with two other places: one a real wild card, the Leather Lake, on the Verulam Angling Club ticket, which had produced a – at the time – record-equalling fish of 4lb 9oz five years previously; and the other the home of the current record, Johnson's Lake, which is looked after by Godalming Angling Society.

I was in a very tight spot. Membership to both those clubs would set me back over £200. Perhaps if I lived closer it might be worth considering at a real stretch, but just for a day's fishing out of my home in South Wales it was, quite simply, an insane amount to spend. I'd learnt my lesson the hard way that winter on Chew and my funds just weren't going to stretch.

I emailed both clubs and explained my case. A week later the wonderful people at Verulam got in touch to grant me permission to fish the Leather Lake, asking only that I let the bailiff know when I intended to fish, but sadly I didn't hear anything back from Godalming. Life at the top of the crucian tree is probably tough – you can't be granting permission to every Tom, Dick and Harry with a hard-luck story. There was some very good news though. Johnson's Lake was actually closed till 16 June anyway, to give the fish a deserved break, but right next door was Harris Lake, which was available to the public on a day ticket and stocked with the same group of crucians as Johnson's (which I later discovered, to my immense surprise, were all originally taken from the monsters past of Little Moulsham, an afterlife of sorts for this exceptionally strong strain of fish). A call to the on-site tackle shop revealed the lake had emerged, perhaps unsurprisingly, as the odds-on favourite to best the fish in Johnson's, and with favourable conditions and a larger stamp of crucians coming out earlier in the week I needed to get down there sharpish. I cancelled all my work plans for the next day and set the alarm for 2 a.m.

I had a chance.

Just before 5 a.m. the sun was rising on the most beautiful lake I have ever had the fortune to visit. Found the other side of a glistening trout stream seemingly fit to burst with Canada geese and their young, the Leather Lake unfolded from a thicket like something out of a dream.

It looked almost like the water had been poured into a divot in a fantasy forest, such was the density of the trees and greenery pressing into the water and spilling out of the sides of the small, shrub-tufted islands. It felt to me that if you simply were to pull the plug and drain the lake water, the rest of that forest would still be there underneath, just waiting to heave up from the lakebed.

The dawn added to the whimsy. Reflected in the gin-clear water it cast something of a week-old-bruise purplish haze across the place, and one inviting-looking corner was so choked with lily-pads that it wouldn't have felt out of place in a Beatrix Potter book. Indeed, I could very well imagine the hapless frog, Jeremy Fisher, punting his way through the whole scene in search of his next minnow.

But it was the noise of the birdlife that set this place apart from anything else I'd ever experienced. There was a riotous, cacophonous clamour coming from all sides of this avian amphitheatre. I don't think it was simply that I was up at a ridiculous hour – I have been fishing at silly-o'clock many times in the past, but I have never ever heard birdsong quite like this in Britain. For at least an hour it was absolutely astonishing and caused the whole lake to crackle with the sort of electricity usually reserved for major sporting events. This was a gathering of feathered souls participating in a massive collective experience, and I felt utterly privileged to witness it. This was their performance though – I was merely an uninvited audience member, and shuffled round the junglified banks with my head down in deferential silence.

I settled myself into a spot hemmed in by a weeping willow and a semi-submerged tree branch. I had seen a few bubbles, not a mass of action by any means, but certainly better than nothing. Plumbing the depth revealed it was significantly deep at the margins, a healthy five foot or so, but also that the entire swim was chock full of weed. A long tendril of green blanket snared on my line as I retrieved, like the clasping arm of a mighty kraken or sea serpent. On inspection, the tendril was erupting with tiny bloodworm that leapt from the fresh air and back into their lake water home as I tried to free it. It was a wonderful sign of the health of the place, but not so good for my chances of catching. These were naturally fed fish that didn't need the carpet of synthetic bait I was proffering. Here the ethos seems to be to stock light and let nature do the rest. There was no question it had worked, as, alongside the record crucian, the lake had once housed a legendary leather carp, a variant on the mirror that has hardly any scales, which had risen to be among the largest leathers in the UK.

I put down a couple of doormat-sized patches of freebies to try and tempt the crucians in for breakfast – a few halibut pellets, some sweetcorn, maggot and casters – and float-fished over the top with the lightest kit I dared. Crucians are renowned for being delicate feeders, taking small baits and giving only the slightest indications of their presence – a murmur on the float and tiny plumes of bubbles, so I had heard – but my presumptive experiences with the crucian had taken such a battering recently I had elected to start from the standpoint that I effectively knew nothing.

Great spirals of buzzers and nymphs drifted like

wood smoke across the lake. As the night gave over its hold and allowed day to break, a regal-looking pair of great-crested grebes hunted in the depths beyond my float. Their wonderful russet-coloured plumage fanned water droplets from the upper reaches of their slender white necks every time they emerged from the drink, resembling snowflakes cascading from a furry bordering around the hood of a winter jacket. Clearly, they were having significantly more success with the fish than me.

The birdcalls faded as the dog walkers arrived. All too soon I could hear the M25 droning in the background and all the magic that had briefly held the lake in suspense had gone. It was midnight and Cinderella was back to being a maid with a pumpkin and I was back in the world of man. Nature was supposed to take its rightful place on the seats at the back of the theatre.

It was weird. Like the compression of our natural and wild spaces in this phenomenally over-cultivated and over-populated island had caused the most intensely compacted expression of the resident wildlife in the space of that single hour. I began to pack up my gear.

When I was a child, my favourite joke was:

'Knock-knock.'

'Who's there?'

'Cook.'

'Cook who?'

'That's the first one I've heard this year.'

If I'm blessed with children, the amount of expla-

nation required to describe why that joke is funny will
be as tragic as it is pointless. I remember reading recently
that one in five birds in Britain are now on the Royal
Society for the Protection of Birds Red List. Just in my
lifetime the majority of those have had their natural
habitat reduced by half.

By mid-day I had successfully negotiated my way around
the massive single-storey, three-lane car park that is the
M25 at rush hour, and arrived at a very different place
entirely.

Images of crucians adorned the sign to the Marsh
Farm complex that housed the Harris Lake, as if I were
in any doubt that in the small world of crucian fishing
this place was the celebrity venue.

At first glance, it felt every inch the comfortable commercial: cut grass, a huge on-site tackle shop, neat gravel
paths, and clean toilet blocks with hot water and hand
towels, but down at water level there was more than a
nod to wildlife. Thick flag iris and reeds smothered the
banks between fishing pegs, lending the place an air of
seclusion once you had settled into your spot lakeside.
Numerous mallards cruised the water alongside diving
tufted ducks, and, most wonderfully of all, a breeding
pair of Arctic terns had taken up residence for the
summer. With their long, brilliant-white starburst tail
feathers, black caps and bright-red bills, they danced like
sprites over the water all day long, remarkably fresh
from their recent migration from the Arctic.

All the other anglers had stationed themselves in the deeper water that ran along the opposite bank next to a trainline. The tackle shop had advised that these were very much the hot swims, but, as I'd turned up late, I was going to have to look elsewhere.

I wandered around the lake perimeter before eventually settling into an overgrown corner fed by a stiff breeze. I was feeling confident despite the slim pickings. I quite liked the look of my corner. In truth, I probably would have picked it regardless – it put more space between me and the other anglers on the complex, which I always liked – and within seconds of placing my bag a large fish rolled right at my feet. If that wasn't a good omen, then I didn't know what was.

I had some fairly hi-tech gear with me – flavoured fish pellets and syrupy liquid attractants – but I decided to leave them all in the bag. Instead I mixed up a bucket of blended breadcrumbs, which I balled into the deeper water about three rod lengths out, and fixed up a simple float rod with half a worm as hook bait. This was fishing just as Grandad had taught me: traditional and simple.

I had been forewarned that though the king carp might rock up to your bait and sucker-punch you like a heavyweight champion, the crucian tends to dance around it like a featherweight, throwing the occasional jab, that might just quiver your line, without actually taking the hook. That means you need to be prepared to spend time sat on your hands with your heart in your mouth: waiting for a positive indication that something has happened down there.

Half an hour in, my float tip wobbled. It was so gentle, like a divination rod in the presence of a spirit. The crucians had arrived and were transmitting their presence. Gently, oh so gently. The float tip lifted.

The fight of the crucian isn't anything like the smash-and-grab of the king carp; nor is it jagged like the perch or a sustained pressure like a tench. In the words of the Supremes: it's a game of give and take; a tug of war where your opponent gets randomly weaker and stronger, leaving the hook free to be pulled out at any time.

Gradually I stole line from the fish till I had it in the net.

It was breathtaking. I wrapped my hand around its golden form. The crucian was exactly 2lb, a phenomenal start, and everything about it – scale counts, fin shape, mouth – matched up precisely, but I just couldn't believe the size. It was well above the average for this fish. I had crushed my personal best with my first fish. I looked up to see an even larger crucian roll on the surface above my groundbait. The plan, unbelievably, was working.

I slipped the 2lb fish right back and re-cast feverishly. This place was extraordinary; by rights these are fish that should be the sole preserve of the dedicated specimen fishermen, yet here I was fluking one out after an absence of over twenty years. I felt as cheeky as if I'd borrowed the rod of a proper crucian carper, caught his fish, and then nicked his wallet.

Almost immediately I hooked and landed a second fish. Slightly smaller this time at 1lb 8oz. These crucians are deep-bodied, high-backed fish. They had a totally different feel to the so-called crucians I had caught before. Of course, that is understandable, given what I now know, but holding that first brace of fish, with their wonderfully curved underbellies that so elegantly filled the palm of my hand, it felt as rarefied an experience as cradling a newborn baby. In fact, the Harris crucians were so utterly distinct in feel (and, I realize now, I did need to 'feel' the fish, as photographs simply don't cut it) that it is hard to believe I could ever have mistaken those hybrids of my past for the real thing. The crucian is one of those very few fish that doesn't seem to lose its sheen after capture. If anything, the shape and golden hue are so satisfying, you could fool yourself into thinking the crucian was crafted purely to be held in the human hand.

Other anglers approached. No one else on the lake was catching anything. My late coming had put me right on the fish. Another huge crucian flopped over my carpet of breadcrumbs. 'They are really taking the piss,' laughed an elderly angler, albeit through gritted teeth.

As the afternoon wore on into evening I felt I was going crazy. Not only was my swim fizzing like a jacuzzi, but also massive crucians just kept rolling, one after the other, right next to my float. If that wasn't enough, one specific fish kept swimming forward, projecting its body clean out of the water, and tail walking like a dolphin in repeated nail-straight assaults on my float. To be perfectly honest, it made me feel so self-conscious I started to look over my shoulder to check no one could see what was going on. (Later I read a chapter in Peter's book by a very experienced crucian angler called Peter Wheat. He too had witnessed the performance, and attributes it to one individual fish, commenting: 'I have never known another crucian to activate itself in this way.' I was just glad I hadn't completely lost my marbles.)

My float bobbed and weaved like a crochet needle. The bites were near imperceptible and almost impossible to hit. I was missing twenty indications for every hook-up, and lost several crucians to hook pulls in the fight. It was frustrating, and not purely down to having had just three hours' sleep the previous night. These fish were living up to their reputation of being extremely cute feeders. I took a risk and upscaled the size of my hook and immediately snared another brace of fish, breaking my personal best for the second time that day.

As the evening came on, the intense exhaustion I was feeling, combined with the insane levels of concentration it took to just watch a flickering float in windy conditions, started to puddle my mind. Everything was exacerbated by the total lack of activity elsewhere on the lake, and the constant heady presence of those giant acrobatic crucians, every one a fish of a lifetime, crammed en masse into my corner. It began to have me wondering whether really I was just asleep at my seat and dreaming it all: giant golden hubcaps bouncing around the lake like fluffy sheep over a gate. I would have started counting the fish if I hadn't been sure I'd end up falling in, but, then, was it possible to fall asleep while still in a dream? A mallard croaked to the right of me. I considered striking up a conversation, but then my float started to tremble.

Grandad, truly, would have loved this place. Perhaps I had honoured him in some small way by fishing the lake in the same style I knew he would have adopted had he been here in my stead, but I also knew that, in spite of all the advances in fishing techniques, tackle and bait, I had caught today because I had simply been in the right place at the right time. Sometimes that is all it takes.

The big one dropped at 2lb 5oz. It was like holding on to the moon.

After a not inconsiderable amount of sleep the next day, I rationalized my crucian was no record shaker. It wasn't even a Wilson mega-specimen and, in reality, the British record is exactly double the size of the fish I caught. All sobering food for thought, but, quite honestly, I didn't care. It was still a very good fish and one to be proud of. Besides, how often do you break your personal best three times in a day?

At last light the biggest crucian of the lot had rolled over my float. It was as deep as a breezeblock, dark and ancient-looking, like it had been cut out of a piece of pure teak. It looked to be well in excess of 4lb, perhaps even a five-pounder at a push, but I couldn't be sure. Moments later, the great fish rolled again, this time right next to a particularly nervous-looking tufted duck. It really was huge. I peered on from behind the reeds with an intense longing, a neurotic dog trapped behind a window as a cat plays freely in the front garden. Some fish are just not meant to be caught.

Mum took me to almost every match and training session throughout the first summer of carp. In the company of men I grew up fast and their patience allowed me to learn the game properly and in my own time. By the end of the next summer I had banked numerous double-figure carp and had developed a competitive, aggressive streak that saw me take over as captain of the school cricket team the year after my humiliation.

I hated losing, but I hated cowardice in myself even more, and would absolutely insist I faced the first ball of our innings when the opposition bowlers were at their freshest and the ball was at its hardest.

Grandad came to my match in Upwell one summer's evening. I was annoyed because, being only thirteen years old and playing in a team filled with men, I had been put down at the end of the batting order.

When it was my time to bat, I remember the bowler being told to come off a shorter run and bowl slower. 'Not a chance,' he spat, 'if he wants to play in a men's league he'd better be ready to take it like a man.' Good, I thought. I took my guard, and chinned his first delivery straight back over his head for four runs.

'You little twat.' The bowler strode right into the middle of the wicket with his hands on his hips. I stepped forward too and stared right back at him. Over his shoulder, back on the boundary, I could see Grandad stood up, and the rest of my team going ballistic. I knew that the next ball was going to be short and aimed at my throat, so when it came I made sure I was well on my back foot and hooked him right into the cow field down at deep fine leg.

The only time I have ever seen steam come out of a man's ears is in cartoons and that evening. The next ball was full, straight and right on middle stump. I should have defended it but the adrenaline was coursing through my veins and I knew I was better than him, so I swung at it with everything I had.

The ball hit the meat of my bat and just kept going and going. It bounced only once before it hit the pavilion filled with my teammates, who were, it is fair to say, absolutely losing the plot. I was out caught on the boundary in the very next over, but they all gave me a standing ovation as I walked off.

'They were banging on the windows, son,' said Grandad, his face still bright red with pride. It was an hour later and we were all crammed into the Red Lion pub down the road. The team were spread out across the bar, hammering the fruities and swearing, but Grandad and I were sat alone and quiet at a corner table.

Grandad slid a frothing pint of beer my way. He didn't need to know that it was the capture of that big carp, and not the picture of him kicking the perfect rugby penalty, that had turned things around for me. In fact, nothing more needed to be said. In his eyes, I had made it.

'The fish in this pond all came from just seventeen crucians I purchased from a fish farm over in Essex. They sat them down on the platform at Gillingham station and called me up: "Mr Rolfe, we have your fish."'

Finally, I was putting a face to the gravelly voice of crucian authority. It was late summer by the time I had picked my way to Peter's ponds. I rolled the van through Dorset, over the chalk beds of the River Frome and Nadder, and on into the leafy borders of Wiltshire. There is something of the fairytale about this whole part of the country. The map reveals charmingly titled hamlets – Milkwell, Birdbush, Hammoon, Bugley – and by the time I made it to my eventual destination at Donhead, it felt infinitely more plausible that it would be twinned with Hobbiton of Middle Earth, than in any way conjoined to the same land mass that belches the Regent's Canal out at King's Cross. I should have been arriving on horseback with a staff, not in a van with rods, but none the less I can't tell you the precise location of these ponds. Even if Peter had sworn me to secrecy, which he hadn't, after a couple of blissful hours floating through this landscape I was wonderfully lost.

Peter runs a large tanned hand over a clear plastic box filled with floats. Here was a man who spent most of his summer days outside. Methodically, he tackled up his rod and traditional centre-pin reel; you could tell he had done it so many times before that he didn't really need to think about it any more, so we chatted about his past instead.

He had always fitted his work as an English teacher around his fishing, and had thus been able to spend his spare time visiting a vast roll call of big fish rivers across the south. 'After the big-roach fishing in the Stour turned sour I decided to look into wild-pond fishing, but really there was virtually none to choose from back then.' Peter slid his float to the appropriate depth. The country was being swept by a commercial-fishery fever by the late seventies; the sea-change had been so great that by the time I was wetting a line, the thought that there was once an alternative to the commercial lake hadn't ever really occurred to me. Peter, faced with the same issue but armed with memories of catching crucians from secluded sand pits in Essex in the 1950s, took matters into his own hands. 'I spread out an Ordnance Survey map and saw all of these wonderful blue specks. Forgotten ponds, hidden away on farmland and in remote woods, some of them really ancient too. After that it was just a case of going from farm to farm and asking for permission to stock a few fish.'

I was quite surprised. Throughout my youth I had feared farmers and the way they aggressively defended their rights to their territory. All of my friends had stories of being chased from fields by the shotgun-wielding 'geroff-my-feckin-landers', so the thought of door knocking with a request to fish seemed suicidal. Mind you, I was a BMX-wielding oik, and not a Cambridge University-educated grammar school teacher.

'How do you convince a farmer then, Peter?'

'Light pressure, Will,' he replied, his eyes twinkling. 'Most farmers are conservation-minded at heart. The idea of saving a species has a lot of appeal, and besides . . .' He paused for a moment as he fixed his hook. '. . . I always explained that there was a market for the crucian, if they multiply.'

Peter was almost ready to fish whereas I was still sat on my chair scribbling notes with my pencil. I had instantly recognized him at his door from the warm and wide smile he shared with the man on the jacket of his book, but I had been expecting a schoolmasterly presence, a fiercely intense man who might dole out fifty licks across the back of a chair for a wayward cast. In reality Peter exuded a benevolent brand of charisma, a gentle soul armed with the infinite patience you need to be a really good fisherman, and, I suspect, a thoughtful and caring teacher. With trousers tucked into socks, flat cap and long, playful white hair flowing out the back, there was more than a sense of a man refusing to slow down in his senior years. Peter was clearly exceptionally fit; we couldn't travel together in his car as he had a large, double-handed scythe and a pair of anvil loppers filling the boot, 'just in case we need to do some work on the banks later on'. It was, in fact, while he was swinging his heavy scythe into a rampant mass of brambles that he revealed he was eighty-two years old. I was gob-smacked, and felt guilty for leaning on a fence post prattling on while this octogenarian beat out the earth in front of me. Clearly crucian rearing is something of an elixir of youth, and my goodness was it worth the sweat and blood. Peter's ponds were stunning.

The waterways in the south-west bleed with a life you rarely see elsewhere in Britain, but there was a palpable intensification of nature around Peter's ponds. Tucked away in a patch of trees on a dairy farm, these twin ponds acted like a pair of lungs, heaving their influence from the water and into the trees and fields that framed their banks. Kingfishers, ducks, clusters of lilies, sedges, iris, even an otter were all drawn to the restored water, and it was occasionally hard to focus just on the fishing.

Peter tapped his float, loaded with a chunk of bread-flake for bait, a rod's length out and near a fringing bush. 'I limit it to only about fifteen anglers on these ponds, but most of the time you've pretty much got it to yourself.' He flicked a few tiny fish pellets around his float to draw the crucians in. 'Once I feel we have a surplus of crucians in these ponds, I try to sell them off for around £5 or £6 a pound. It's less than the going rate, but I just want to get the crucians out there.'

I finally got my own rod in, carefully shot down so the float was merely an ultra-sensitive pinprick, and plumbed the depth to perfection to ensure my bait just about kissed the sediment on the pond's bottom. My float immediately dipped and I turned out a tiny thumb-sized perch. I laughed. I was ten years old and back at Wood Lakes again. The next cast brought another, and then another. 'Try some of my bread, Will, it'll keep those pesky perch away.' Peter leant over to reach for a fluffy white roll and his float dipped purposefully, proving conclusively my long-held belief that certain fish will only ever bite when you are distracted.

'Oh! Huh oh!' A youthful delight creased Peter's face as his rod tip danced to the fish's tune. 'I've got one!'

A short fight delivered a perfect little crucian, like a small gold medallion. 'What a lovely little fella,' said Peter, admiring his work before underarming me the bread roll. His float dipped again before I could re-bait. 'I can't believe it!' he laughed as I reached once more for the landing net. 'I promise I put you in the better swim!'

I managed to get my own piece of bread out in the water in front of me and, incredibly, caught a perch on bread. This was something I had previously considered to be impossible, but there was little time for contemplation: Peter was bent into his third and, all too soon, his fourth crucian.

'I really don't understand.' I could sense a tinge of embarrassment in his voice. 'I usually fish your swim. I promise I gave you the more favourable area.' I slipped the net under his fifth. I really didn't mind; in fact, this moment in time meant far more to me than simply a few hours studying this crucian-whisperer.

I was far too shy to say so at the time, but I was right back with Grandad, decades earlier, stood at the Creek, devouring every movement of skilled operation, trying to learn, not simply catch. The student with the master. 'Right,' announced Peter, snapping me out of it, 'you must come here and use my rod.' I settled into his cushioned seat, desperate not to make a mistake or miss my chance, but moments later I was up netting his sixth fish, this time on my rod, in the swim I had only just that moment vacated. 'Oh, I'm so so sorry about this, Will.' Peter's voice trembled with something approaching remorse as I near shook with laughter. His metamorphosis into my grandfather was truly complete. It was destiny, of course. Just as there was never an evening, no matter how shot Grandad's eyesight or reactions became, when he didn't catch more than me, there was never a family cricket match where my dad, who really couldn't play cricket, failed to clean bowl me while I was batting. Some men are simply meant to always be your better, and it is much easier to take their lessons squarely on the chin than ever try to fight it.

The fish were all quite small and Peter was keen to place them in the other pond to improve the stock. Together we carried a white, plastic-handled bucket through a small thicket and over a stile towards the dammed end of the second pond. 'I liked the line in your book, Peter,' I began, hitching up the bucket as Peter gently waded into the shallows, 'that read: "The only unsuccessful fisherman is the one who is not enjoying what he's doing."'

'Ha! Oh yes! I think I may have been making a comment about those that obsess over the weight of their catch, the commercial carp fishers' mentality.' He began to gently hand-place each crucian into the new pond. 'Fishing is a ridiculous pastime anyway of course: "A worm at one end and a fool at the other", as the great essayist Samuel Johnson once wrote, but there has to be so much more interest to it if your enjoyment is going to last through the decades. It's being in beautiful places, like this, and probing the mystery of the depths not for what is, but what might be. If you already know what's in there the catching can simply become a bit, well, stale.' Peter's bucket was empty of fish now, so he upended the remains into the pond with a 'splosh'. '. . . But each to their own.'

That afternoon I spotted a water vole scurrying along the banksides. It was the first I'd seen in over twenty years. It took me a while to place the location of the last one, but on the drive home I nailed down the memory. I was eleven years old, fishing a farm pond near identical to Peter's, also somewhere in the rolling farmland of the south-west. It was when I had caught my very first crucian. Sometimes in fishing, the stars can align in quite curious ways.

'I'm a crucian carp madman.' It was impossible not to like the crucian scientist Dr Carl Sayer. He possessed a wonderful Norfolk twang to his accent, placing him as more combine harvester than petri dish, and spoke of the halcyon days of his youth, rods across the handle-bars, with a melancholic nostalgia I could instantly relate to. If fifty-odd miles of dykes and drains hadn't separated us, I'm sure we would have been good friends when we were tearing around Norfolk in the 1980s.

Dr Sayer and his colleagues have been busy reintroducing crucians and restoring ponds in remote farmlands across Norfolk from their Norwich headquarters. He has kept his work largely secret, in part to keep the landowners onside – 'in case they think we're planning on starting a fishery' – but also because their success in breeding the crucian means theirs are now worth a small fortune. There are some 23,000 ponds on Norfolk farmlands, but the vast majority of them have grown over, dried up, or been smeared into new fields for crops. '"Ghost ponds" is what we call them,' chirped Carl, 'we've actually found beer cans on some of the old sites that date from the 1960s and '70s, clearly the last time there was anyone actually sat there fishing!' The seeds of waterside plants can actually exist in a dormant state for centuries, which means, even if several feet of soil and corn crop have been layered on top of an old pond, a bit of an uncovering job, fresh water and fresh fish can see a 'ghost pond' brimming with wild plant and animal life once more. Isn't nature brilliant when it's given a chance?

'But why should we care about saving the crucian in Britain if it was never a native species?' I asked, somewhat pointedly.

'Who is to say it isn't native, Will?' shot back Carl, bluntly. I stammered something about the DNA analysis that had placed them here somewhere in the Middle Ages. 'True, it did, but that work was based on just one tiny sample of fish.' Carl pressed. 'Since then we've found so many more ponds with crucian populations. We should be pushing for a much wider study of all these newly discovered populations. You can't tell me you can take one study, from one population, and just say: "Well, that's it, the crucian isn't native then."'

He certainly had a point. Carl went on to describe a remarkable theory that hinged on how ancient waterway management during the Roman era, which saw many ancient ponds and oxbow lakes drained to irrigate lands for agriculture, could easily have wiped out the crucian, only for them to be reintroduced at a much later date. 'But that's the problem, isn't it?' he concluded. 'You can't prove absence, can you? You can only prove presence, and it is impossible to get grants to fund these sorts of studies.'

I could see where he was coming from. All that DNA results can really confirm is that that particular sample set were introduced during the Middle Ages, but there was nothing to say that other populations from other ponds might have been here much earlier than that. Dr Sayer's theory jogged my memory of the extraordinary story of the British pool frog. Right through until the 1990s it was generally accepted that the pool frog was native only to mainland Europe (in fact, until the 1970s it was incorrectly classified as merely a subspecies of the edible frog, when in actuality it transpired that it was the edible that was a hybrid of the pool and marsh frog); then, in the Norfolk town of Thetford, a colony of pool frogs was discovered that would electrify amphibian science.

Found in a 'pingo', an ancient pool formed by the melting of subterranean swellings of ice at the end of the last Ice Age, the small colony appeared darker and browner than the classic livid greens sported by the pool frogs of France. That couldn't be, though; the accepted wisdom read that our climate was far too cold for the pool frog to establish itself here naturally. Bone analysis of the Thetford frogs was conducted and, sensationally, it was discovered that these frogs had in fact been here since before the last Ice Age, making their own way from Europe before the close of everyone's favourite freshwater species superhighway: the Doggerland land bridge, which delivered us the pike all those centuries ago. The pool frog was hastily reclassified and, almost overnight, we gained a second native frog species to call our own.

For the crucian, though, until the 'smoking gun' of some conclusive DNA evidence can be unearthed, its plight in Britain remains precarious. 'Why should we care?' might seem a narrow-minded question, but a lot rests on the indigenous status of our wildlife. The classification of what is and what isn't a native may seem ambiguous to say the least. As Richard Kerridge states in his superb book on reptiles and amphibians, *Cold*

Blood, qualification only hinges on proving whether a species 'established itself in a country independent of any human activity, no matter how long ago the arrival occurred', but without it, it is virtually impossible to gain access to government funding and practical protective legislation for a species.

For the pool frog it all came too late. In 1999, the year before the startling results of the bone analysis were published, the last of the Thetford population died in captivity; an avoidable tragedy caused by our somewhat over-zealous ranking of wildlife based on arbitrary status and public popularity.

Whether we like to admit it or not, we inflate the importance of certain species over others all the time. The face has to fit. It has to penetrate the public consciousness and pull at the heartstrings for virtually anything to be done. Take the otter, for example. I love otters, and unlike most fishermen would dearly love to see one in the wild, but their celebrity status and cute looks have seen them garner a massively disproportionate amount of public sympathy and a hugely successful reintroduction, whereas other, less desirable, freshwater species have slid to virtual, or even actual, extinction with little or no protest whatsoever. The pool frog is one example, but what of the orache moth or the large copper butterfly? The slimy burbot fish? The Davall's sedge plant? Or my water vole, with its yellow teeth and *Wind in the Willows* fame, whose numbers have plummeted by 90 per cent in the last twenty years?

I could go on, but my point is that we quite clearly have much bigger environmental issues to worry about than simply whether a species is definitely native. As I write, one in ten of the UK's wildlife species are threatened with extinction and the numbers of our most endangered animals have crashed by two thirds since 1970. I don't mean to unduly anger those specialists who work tirelessly to curb the catastrophic damage caused by invasive species (see the grey squirrel, signal crayfish, American mink and oak processionary moth for further details), but there is absolutely no evidence to suggest that the presence of crucians affects our freshwater environment negatively in any way. According to Dr Sayer and Peter Rolfe, they cause no harm, and coexist with other species in just about the most high-quality environment you can imagine, so can we just get on with protecting them properly, please?

We can be in no doubt today that our crucian populations are absolutely vital to the survival of the wider European crucian species. Over in Europe the aggressive-feeding and exceptionally well-travelled gibel carp, an interloper from Asia, has spread its seed into virtually every major watercourse on the Continent, even making it to the remote eastern reaches of the Baltic Sea. Of course, the gibel can cross-breed with the extraordinarily licentious crucian, and, with that, the purity of the entire continental species is now seriously under threat. However, we have no gibel here and, thanks to the unheralded (as well as unfunded) dedication of Marsh

Farm, Peter Rolfe, Dr Sayer and all their friends, the British crucian has a fighting chance once more, and for that, I believe, we should all be very grateful.

The years passed. I got the knack for carp fishing and fished almost exclusively in commercials until I left school at eighteen. Largely, I fished alone. I was pushing the envelope, fishing for hours and hours in conditions that a man in his late seventies just couldn't take, but even when some of my friends showed an interest in joining me, I largely shunned them. I fully accepted I was obsessed, and that they would just hold me back from my ultimate ambition to catch bigger and, in my eyes, better carp. I would fish on through anything: terrible weather, hunger, tiredness, it just didn't matter to me; there was almost nothing I wouldn't put myself through to get in front of a fish.

Dad had ultimately been right to persuade me to stick with school that afternoon in the pub. I made friends for life there and received grades that I just wouldn't have managed anywhere else. Academically, I realized I needed to be sat on and chained to a desk to achieve, and my ability at sport had improved exponentially. I was extremely fortunate to be in a place where if you showed potential you had all the facilities you needed to improve, and, more than anything, to have loving parents who would do anything they could to nurture an interest in any of their children.

Looking back, though, I just wish the by-product of

all of it hadn't been the development of a competitive, win-at-all-costs impudence that bordered on over-confidence. I realize now it wasn't in fact the winning or the competition I had enjoyed at all, it was the feeling that I belonged somewhere, but in defining success purely through the rigid prism of personal triumph I had totally lost touch with any of the pleasures to be had just from being part of something. The same had become true of my fishing, and as I got older it was inevitable my interest began to wane. After I left school I never played a competitive game of cricket or rugby again.

Perhaps, in its own way that is what crucian fishing is all about. The fish is small and challenging in its own way, but it is the subtle pleasures to be found in the sort of environments it inhabits that bring such a unique joy to this style of fishing. I am indebted to the fish for my having found the traditional British pond before it fully faded from my consciousness. It feels like the blinkers have been lifted from my eyes, but with so many fish records to chase I'm not entirely sure what to do with the rest of my year. Am I really saying that the thought of continuing for something really big is now a pointless endeavour? Of course I'm not, but the spirit of crucian fishing can only influence me to look for more than just a big fish as I continue this quest. Like my grandad before me, I'm a fisherman for life now, and have learnt those who pursue size, and size alone, can never expect their interest in this pastime to see them all the way to the grave.

Early June came and went with no record-shaking fish. Then, utterly against the grain, the biggest crucian of the year was landed from a secret pond hidden away somewhere in leafy Shropshire in the middle of August. It weighed almost 4lb and was accompanied by another brace of fish of over 3lb. Ed Matthews, a hooded chap with a broad smile, had hand-stocked and reared the fish just seven years earlier. 'I was overwhelmed,' he gushed in the pages of the *Angling Times*, 'I stocked these crucians when they were around one inch long and cared for them for so many years, just hoping one day that they'd weigh over 3lbs . . . now it's got me wondering just how big they could go.' Perhaps the hidden season is no longer the time to target the record shakers, or perhaps it is just that the hidden season means much more. I'll leave it to you to find out.

The Fish Everyone Hates

It is easy to see, in the mind's eye, a salmon
resting behind a rock, a trout sipping down an
insect between two trails of green weed, a
chub or barbel swaying in the current where
the willow branches dip. With the eel, the best
I could do was say to myself, 'I know you're
down there somewhere.'

Tom Fort, *The Book of Eels* (2002)

The world lacks love for eels.

The bed of the Creek was absolutely paved with them.
It didn't seem to matter if you tried a big bunch of lobworms or the tiniest of maggots from the tub, if you
rested any bait on the deck for any stretch of time it

wouldn't be long before the float started to give you the telltale tap-tap-tap of an eel making its enquiries.

Such a subtle touch for such a grotesquely powerful fish, but the twisting, pounding fight was not an event to be celebrated; in fact, hooking an eel was categorically, unequivocally and absolutely – a disaster.

If you managed to get it out of the water before it severed your nylon with its teeth it would reward your effort by quickly coiling itself up in a ball against your line, creating a tangle of Rubik's cube difficulty and thoroughly coating you, your tackle, your net and anything else in your proximity in a thick layer of ectoplasmic snot that would linger for days. To actually unhook and release the eel, which has long since taken your bait, hook and half a foot of your line into the depths of its tubular intestinal tract, took such an extreme level of luck and skill it was nearly always better for everyone to just snap the line and hope the hook worked its way out of the fish by itself. A thoroughly upsetting and dispiriting event that left us fishing almost exclusively in the upper layers of the river as children on the Creek.

The eel, like the perch, had a funny habit of following me around throughout my childhood. I continued to catch them in the Creek in spite of my best efforts, and even managed to catch a freshwater eel while out sea fishing off a set of rocks in West Wales. It was my first-ever fish from the sea but it was not a sea fish. I was furious, and quite ignorant of just how unusual a catch that was.

The eels were all the same size: never longer than a bootlace or in excess of 1lb in weight. Small, rapacious creatures that my friends and I didn't really even count as fish. Then, one sultry summer afternoon in the heart of the school holidays, my fishing friend Paul Woods screamed his BMX into my backyard and announced there were eels the 'size of snakes' in his neighbour's back garden, and that they were 'feeding on cat food'.

Paul had a wonderful gift for telling tall tales and attracting trouble. There was the 20lb carp he caught at Wood Lakes when none of us were around, the rope bungee jump in his back garden that nearly killed us all, and then his extraordinary pyrotechnic skills that saw a home-made rocket simultaneously blast all the glass clean out of a neighbouring greenhouse and kill every single fish in their koi carp pond. I didn't know whether to expect nothing or everything, but I jumped on my bike all the same, picking up the third of our angling triumvirate, Lee Wales, from his house on the way back over to Paul's.

We threw a handful of cat food into the Creek and watched. 'That's it, young man,' croaked Paul's elderly neighbour, 'they'll all come out now.' Lee made a highly exaggerated and very sarcastic eye roll and I had to pinch the inside of my arm to stop myself from laughing out loud, but just minutes later all three of us were stood in stupefied silence.

They were everywhere. I looked at Paul. Paul looked at Lee. Lee looked at me. Like those twenty-foot-long handkerchiefs produced from a magician's sleeve, the eels had kept going and going until the mud was simply alive with writhing bodies. It was the snakepit in *Raiders of the Lost Ark*, plenty enough to turn the stomach of lesser mortals, but we were the fishing gods and these creatures were desecrating our temple. We sprinted for the rods, fixed the biggest hook we owned on the strongest line we had, and deployed a single piece of cat food deep into the centre of the twisted masses.

A darkly marked python bee-lined for my bait, angled its neck, and swallowed. As I struck, the shoal scattered to the darkness and my serpent hauled back hard on the hook. Any thoughts of a prolonged fight were banished: I was using my sea rod with a line like steel-wire and my reel drag was bolted down so tightly it would take a spanner to loosen. In short, this fish was coming out by hook or by crook.

The beast landed on the grass and we leapt on it with all three pairs of our hands. We were never going to keep this eel, but since we had now caught and subdued it, it seemed somehow wasteful to just put it back straight away. It was magnificent. Thick and black as the ace of spades, it probably only weighed 2lb but it was double the size of any eel we had ever seen before. We needed to at least try to do something different to celebrate the catch.

For some inexplicable reason I decided to place my thumb in the eel's mouth.

I remember being momentarily surprised to learn the

eel's teeth felt a bit like sandpaper before a brand of pure, crushing pain consumed my digit. It pulsated from my thumb, travelled up my arm, and exploded out of the roof of my skull with a scream.

Lee and Paul jumped back in fright and the eel, realizing it was partially free, went into something of a crocodilian death roll, comfortably twisting my arm around in its socket and leaving me with the very real fear that it would soon tear my thumb clean off. As its tail met water it showed mercy to me, released its teeth and back-paddled into the murk to tell all its friends about the idiot boy it had just encountered.

Eels are the absolute opposite of the carp, in physicality, feeding habits, popularity, everything, and now I hated them more than ever, but then, one day, I baited the bottom of the river and didn't catch one. I tried the next day and failed again. I spoke to my friends; no one had caught one in weeks. It was utterly bizarre, but the eels of the Fens seemingly disappeared overnight.

There's something about the shape of the snake that makes us stand up and take notice. We are actually hardwired to pay greater attention to the snake than the frame of any other animal. Surprisingly, the fear of snakes is not actually innate. According to findings published in the *Journal of Experimental Child Psychology* we are only born with the ability to quickly detect, and immediately respond to, the serpentine form, but the phobia itself is a culturally conditioned response. The two aren't mutually exclusive of course: the fact that we are so reactive to snakes makes the adoption of a negative emotional response so much easier, regardless of whether the animal in question is actually dangerous or not. Bad news for the eel then.

The eel does itself no further favours in the public-relations department by conjoining its superficial likeness to the snake with what Wilson describes as a 'slippery body... covered in a heavy coating of protective mucus... and strong jaws lined with microscopic whisker-like teeth'.

It is unfortunate that the eel's appearance has brought it such loathing. If you can look beyond its aesthetics there is truly a wondrous fish in waiting. The eel can live comfortably for over eighty years, with some reports of fish passing over a hundred; they can also increase or decrease the size of their eyes, jaw and head, and change colour, to suit their surroundings; and, when required, the eel can even survive out of water by absorbing all the oxygen it requires through its skin. The dorsal and anal fins are fused seamlessly with the caudal fin, framing the eel's entire body in one continuous paddle, which allows the eel to swim backwards just as strongly as it can forwards; plus they are born as hermaphrodites with the ability to adjust their sexual organs to suit the demands of their locale. Impressive stuff in itself, but none of this can come even close to matching the greatest feat of the eel.

Most eel species live entirely at sea – giant congers

with breezeblock heads, and colourful and sharp-toothed morays that slither across tropical reefs – but there are also sixteen freshwater species to be discovered right across Europe, southern and eastern Africa, North America, parts of Asia, and the South Pacific. Every year, hundreds of thousands of these freshwater eels undertake an extraordinarily perilous quest to reach their breeding grounds, with the most obscure, and certainly the most remote, reserved for our own eel species: *Anguilla anguilla*, the European eel. If the following tale of endurance doesn't make your eyes glisten and chest swell with new respect for the eel, then truly: you have no heart.

When the time is right, nothing can get between the adult European eel and its desire to reproduce. Wilson notes, in a rare moment of encyclopedic ebullience, that the eel's snout 'becomes more pointed, the eyes glass over, and the body's fat content increases in readiness for the monumental journey ahead . . . Even eels living in tiny ponds or pits miles from the nearest river system find running water and travel downstream.' Their determination to breed is the stuff of legend. Fishing author Fred Buller writes of a night in Cumbria when he witnessed 'a stream of eels' that 'were not halted by my walking among them'. I too remember once encountering an eel in the middle of a cricket pitch just after rainfall, head down and thrusting forward to flowing water some half a mile away. I wanted to pop him in my worm bucket and take him there myself, but this fish needed no help, and was soon gone, at a far greater pace than your average outfielding farmer might make in pursuit of a cricket ball.

It quickly became clear, to those who cared to look, that the freshwater eels were all heading out to sea. Even the philosopher Aristotle was moved to record in the fourth century BC how the eel would suddenly become hell-bent on making it to salt water, but for centuries no one had a clue where they went once they were there, or, indeed, why.

Tom Fort superbly breaks down the origins of the eel in what is surely the seminal eel text of our time: *The Book of Eels*. He highlights how it was actually not until the seventeenth century that an Italian naturalist, Francesco Redi, correctly hypothesized that the eggs of the eel were laid at sea; before that, the best guess was that eels were formed from mud, but Francesco was a long time dead before any evidence was unearthed to support his theory. In 1897, another Italian, the celebrated biologist Giovanni Grassi, was the first ever to net a sperm-carrying eel and then went one better by capturing and identifying the youngest eels ever recorded: gentle, transparent fish only a few centimetres long, known henceforth as 'thin-heads'.

Grassi's seminal capture was made off the coast of Sicily in the Strait of Messina, a turbulent spot where giant tides and severe up-swelling currents frequently dragged unusual deep-sea creatures towards the clutches of man. It might have seemed a leap of faith to then assume that the breeding place of European eels had been found along with the thin-heads, but Grassi had the weight of Italian pride bearing down on his shoulders, and as he watched his captive samples metamorphosize into elvers, the final juvenile stage of the eel before adulthood, he rushed to announce that he had dispelled 'the great mystery which has hitherto surrounded the reproduction and development of the Common eel', and claimed *Anguilla anguilla* for his country. That's where the case could have been closed; then a young Dane rocked up and spoiled everything.

Sadly for Grassi, and the people of Italy, it transpired that the young eels of Messina were actually fully grown thin-heads. He couldn't possibly have known at the time – these were still the first correctly identified thin-heads after all – but the thin-head only metamorphosizes into the elver after up to three years of drifting eastwards on the Atlantic Gulf Stream. The results in Grassi's aquarium had been such an instant success because he had collected his thin-heads right on their home straight: they were absolutely primed to begin their new lives in fresh water.

In 1904 the Great Dane, Johannes Schmidt, a botanist by trade, was merely expanding his knowledge of land plants and researching the spawning grounds of cod, when a young-fish trawl happened to bring a 7.5cm thin-head to the net. The problem for Grassi was that Schmidt and his Danish research vessel weren't in Messina; in fact, they were nowhere near. Schmidt was

2,000 miles away, trawling a net off the North Atlantic's Faroe Islands.

By 1922, Schmidt had declared in a Royal Society paper that 'all the eels of Western Europe come from the Atlantic', having successfully, and somewhat sensationally, narrowed his search down to a 700-mile-wide patch of sea located off the eastern coasts of Florida and Bermuda. Simply, Schmidt had gathered along a southern line that produced gradually smaller thin-heads until he captured the smallest thin-heads ever recorded, a positively larval five millimetres in length.

Grassi was blown clean out of the water. Schmidt's research vessel was hovering above the abyssal recesses of the Sargasso Sea when it snared its minute prize. Could there be a more fitting circle of ocean to untangle the enigmatic web that surrounded the origin story of the eel? Perhaps only the Bermuda Triangle can conjure up a greater sense of mystery; little wonder then that the borders of these twin obscurities overlap. Contrary to popular belief the Sargasso is not chock-full of the brand of tentacular monster that once dragged pioneering explorers and their boats to a grisly oblivion. Sargassum weed might occasionally exhibit itself on the surface in vast golden clods but the sea itself is relatively benign, fenced in on all sides by currents that swirl in perpetual motion around its great oval perimeter, as waves of long-distance runners might around an athletics track. It leaves the centre of the sea calm, quiet and, relative to the rest of the Atlantic, quite devoid of life.

Quite why every eel from across Europe, North Africa and America chooses this spot to spawn is anyone's guess, but that is merely the tip of the iceberg when it comes to what we are still waiting to discover about the eel.

After the adult eels have mated, the baby eels hatch from fertilized eggs as the tiny, willow-leaf-shaped thin-head larvae of Schmidt and Grassi's obsession. The second wave of the eel's mass migration can then begin again, as the adults, finally relieved of their life's burdens, pass away into a three-mile abyss, where their bodies are gratefully feasted on by the type of globular scavengers that lie in the endless black.

I wish I'd known about all of this when I was a child. That each eel I held in my hand had virtually no peer in the whole world of freshwater fish. I would have shown them the deference and respect they deserved. I'm pretty sure I could even have grown to love them.

We might not always have had a grip on the specifics of the eel's life cycle, but humans have certainly tracked their movements for about as long as we've been hunter-gatherers. Eels have been harvested in their masses as far back as 6000 BC and eel traps and spears have been discovered on the banks of Northern Ireland's Lough Neagh that date right back to the Stone Age. There was scarcely a watercourse in the UK where eels couldn't be found in plentiful supply. From the River Thames to the Scottish lochs, the major drawcard of the eel was simply its pure unadulterated abundance.

The eel was the fish of the everyman, as, unlike the carp, anyone could employ virtually any method to catch it and near guarantee protein for the table. Izaak Walton wrote in his 1653 *magnum opus*, *The Compleat Angler*, that in one Staffordshire pond he noticed: 'such small eels abound so much, that many of the poorer sort of people that inhabit near to it, take such Eels out of this mere with sieves or sheets; and make a kind of eel-cake with them, and eat it like as bread'. They were so plentiful you didn't even need to worry about salting their meat for another day: simply re-cast the lines or reload the traps and haul in all the eels you need afresh. In October 1257 Henry III celebrated St Edward's Day with 15,000 eels, and in 1697 the north-eastern Italian fishery of Comacchio took three quarters of a million fish in a single night; earlier still, the annual tithe of eels paid under the terms of King Edgar's charter of 970 saw just twenty fishermen hand over some 60,000 eels every year; a truly mind-boggling figure from a time before the deployment of industrial fishing techniques.

The fact is, eels were available in serious numbers for a very long time, and there was real money to be made, especially from elvers. This immature adolescent eel is a thing of real beauty. Its translucence makes its dark eyes and black spinal column stand out against the rest of its body, almost as if it has been comically electrocuted as part of a child's cartoon, but when a mass of elvers are held together in your hand their bodies blend collectively into piles of immaculate silver-white threads, as if pulled from a royal wedding dress. Given their appearance it is perhaps little surprise they were termed 'white gold', especially when elver prices can peak at as much as £500 per kilo on the French and Japanese markets. I once met an elver fisherman who used to illegally fish the estuary of the River Taff, 'before they put the barrage over the river and ruined it', who claimed he could make £5,000 in half an hour of work back in the 1970s. He was hardly an exception though: around the corner in the prolific Severn estuary it was apparently possible to make as much as £100,000 in a season; in fact the head of running elvers in the Severn was once so great they held an annual competition to eat a pint of elvers in the quickest time, and would regularly spread any surplus catch right across the fields to fertilize the soil.

The value of the eel had something of a role to play in the life of my grandad too. He might have lived out his senior years in the Fens but he was a Bedford boy born and bred, and plundered the rivers around his home with great proficiency. He hadn't been called up to the frontline during the Second World War owing to his skill as an engineer, but it can hardly be said that the threat of imminent invasion by the Nazis softened his ability to recognize a clear economic opportunity.

Grandad wrote a self-published book detailing many of his exploits, but sadly there is only one copy of *Bedford, My Bedford* by Ken Millard in circulation. He hadn't quite mastered the art of saving his work to the computer, so he'd just type out a page of memoirs and then print it straight away. This is a great shame as I think it is only myself, Dad and his second cousin Christine (whom he press-ganged into editing his material) who have actually been able to read his masterpiece, and thus the world will never know of the time he once watched the town brass band sink into the river during an ill-advised attempt at a floating bandstand, or the time his father forced the local school to promote him up the classes with the wonderfully illiterate and vaguely threatening: 'just because this boy has a hole in his pants, he is still going to get an education', or even how he narrowly avoided being court-martialled for what I can only gather from the chapter marked 'Home Guard' was a heady mixture of utter fecklessness, heavy drinking and a total disregard for any figure of authority. The end of that section climaxes in a particularly entertaining story that involves a pub, a dentist's chair, a narrowly avoided night-long exercise in a ditch, and the revealing, yet clearly quite accurate, words: 'we were very poor soldiers'.

The chapter marked 'Fishing' recounts a story I had heard many times before. Wartime restrictions around the coasts meant fresh fish were extremely scarce, so when Grandad approached the local fishmonger to ask if he would like some eels, it came as no surprise that the answer came back: 'As many as you can supply.' Every Friday night thenceforth Grandad and his mates were to be seen creeping off around the local gardens in search of lobworms before fixing up to six rods behind the Clapham Club in the dark.

'Many a night the six rods would be dipping in the river,' he writes, 'making a very hectic time difficult because the hooks had to be removed under a covering blanket and in a black-out as any flashing light would bring the local copper.' Yes. My grandad was out fishing during the Blitz, a period of time when virtually every other person in Britain was hiding in the darkness within sprinting distance of the local air-raid shelter due to the very real fear of German planes bombing anything illuminated. 'Our best haul was twenty-two fish,' he proudly recounts, 'which to us at one and ninepence a pound was very acceptable.' Sadly his days of illicit eeling were to come to a premature end, not at the hands of the police, the Home Guard or, dare I say, the Nazis. No, much worse than that. 'A number of the local ladies soon discovered that if they waited in Clapham Road they could stop us and buy our eels before we got to the fishmonger's. It became so bad that the competition between these ladies meant that they would wait nearer and nearer to Clapham, so in the end we had to stop', presumably before he started Bedford's first eel riot. 'Enterprise is very difficult,' he laments, at the chapter's close.

Comfortably the largest of the freshwater eel species are the longfins found in Australia and New Zealand. Some specimens Down Under have been reliably recorded at almost five feet in length, and with other, less reliable accounts of eight-feet-long 100lb eels seen dragging cows into the depths, it is fair to say the crown for the world's biggest eel is unlikely to ever leave the southern hemisphere. Meanwhile, here in the UK, the long-standing eel record stands at a comparatively small, but none the less very impressive, 11lb 2oz. It was caught by Steve Terry in 1978 from a lake in Hampshire, but there have long been rumours of unclaimed record breakers which have enough clout behind them to very reasonably suggest that Terry's record is breakable.

In 2013 an 11lb 8oz beast snared on sausage meat failed its verification checks for not having an independent witness; three years prior to that, a purported 13lb 1oz record fish also slipped through its angler's hands for the same reason, but the most famous close call arose in 2005, when another 13lb monster was caught by a man known as 'Norman the plumber'. His bait might have been intended for a big carp, but the rules and regulations of his fishery guaranteed a lifetime ban for anyone seen to be publicizing record breakers from any species. Despite a number of witnesses to the fish, and its immense weight, no photos were ever released to the public and the giant eel was not mentioned again.

I was heartened to learn that my childhood home had turned up some of the most legendary eels in British history. The Fens are rightfully steeped in eel folklore, as, prior to the drainage work beginning in 1630, the entire landscape was flooded bar a couple of hillocks occupied by small hamlets, and eel fishing was a massive part of the economy. Indeed, so esteemed was the eel, our local city, Ely, took its name from them, and to this very day it holds an annual festival dedicated purely to the fish. The eel-hunting market was monopolized by a band of lawless hunter-gatherers known as the Fen Tigers, who ruthlessly opposed the drainage schemes and took to destroying the newly constructed sluices, justifiably concluding that they would devastate their eel-catching, reed-cutting and duck-hunting practices.

I was fortunate enough to once meet the last of the Fen Tigers. Ernie James lived with his wife in a house right out on the Welney Washes, nestled in a remote spot between the prolific Delph and Old Bedford rivers. He trapped eels well into his nineties and built the most amazing willow eel traps with his hands, one of which he gave to my dad, who was his doctor right until the day he passed away at the princely age of ninety-nine. I was only a child when I met Ernie, and, sadly, I never had the chance to ask him about really big fenland eels. If I had I would've asked him if it really could've been possible that the River Ouse once produced a 36lb giant, or if Izaak Walton's Peterborough eel of almost two yards in length was plausible, but, most of all, I'd want to ask him about an immense eel supposedly caught from a dyke not two miles from my house back in the nineteenth century. Witnessed by a man of the cloth and reputed to be some six feet in length, it seems from the realms of pure fantasy, but then what would a man of God stand to gain from lying about such things? Stranger things have happened in these parts, after all.

Ernie and his friends once trapped a 34lb sturgeon in the Welmore Sluice, a critically endangered armour-plated fish that numbers fewer than 1,000 in Europe and which has long since been extinct in the United Kingdom. Unfortunately, for the fish at least, it was taken to the markets of London and fetched such a good price that the men of the village all skipped out of work and went on the beers for a week. You'd now have a better chance of harvesting poo from a rocking horse than ever seeing a repeat capture of such a fish in the wild.

Okay, so I might not be able to conclusively prove there were once record breakers in the Fens, but one thing I do know beyond doubt is that there were very big eels to be found here, as, against all the odds, the fenscape had already gifted me my own giant.

I was nine years old when I had my first afternoon fishing with Grandad and Dad on the big river. Popham's Eau flowed sluggishly down to the tidal Ouse and out towards the sea at King's Lynn. It was the river where Grandad spent most of his time; it was close to his bungalow and contained large heads of bream and massive roach, if you knew how to catch them. I was keen to impress, but having been used to fishing the Creek, at no more than ten metres across and a few feet in depth, I was really struggling to cast my heavier, deeper tackle without help from Dad. Late in the day I managed one serviceable cast on my own and the float dipped with purpose.

The fight tested my tackle to its absolute limit. I knew nothing of playing big fish, and this was far and away the biggest fish I'd ever hooked, so I simply wrenched as hard as I could and refused to give the fish any chance of running. The eel eventually erupted on the surface, projecting its long, muscular body out of the water like the arm of a giant octopus. We struggled to get it into the net as the eel was thicker than my wrist and as long as my arms, and when we tried to weigh it the fish thrashed so violently we were forced to take pity on it and quickly release it back to its domain.

Grandad estimated it was around 5lb in weight, which made it my first bona-fide Wilson mega-specimen. I smelt my net afterwards; the eel slime resembled freshly sliced cucumbers. I didn't wash it out for weeks, and carried the webbing as a badge of honour.

As Wilson had prescribed, this eel had packed on the last of its weight and was on its great journey out to the sea. It didn't have far to go at least: Popham's Eau spewed out into the great estuarine mudflats of the Wash not fifteen miles from where we were sat. It's a memory I haven't considered in a very long time indeed. It was well over twenty years ago now and an absolute one-off, a shock that only fishing can produce, but as is customary with such moments in life they either stick with you for ever or they lose their momentum and fade into the background. I soon went back to deriding eels.

I could consider heading back to the rivers of my youth in search of that eel – it is possible it's still alive and it would've accrued a great weight in such a time – but realistically there would not be a repeat capture of that fish; what's left of him was probably digested and excreted somewhere in the Sargasso many, many years ago. Catching another big one was going to be a tough undertaking. I had been warned that serious eeling took a lifetime of study. This was a marginal branch of fishing where only the utterly committed found success. I joined the 'Eel fishing' Facebook group and found one expert advising an enthusiast not to give up on his potential water 'till you've fished at least 10 nights without a fish, and even then don't totally discount it'.

I could've been in real trouble, but I had an ace hidden up my sleeve: I knew exactly where I was going to look for my big eel.

I flicked back through my notebook, right back to when this all began at the start of last winter. There, scrawled in my shorthand, were the following words: 'Leicester Line. Roadside service station. 8lb 2oz, 6lb 14oz'. I knew that would come in useful, I just knew it.

I emailed John Ellis of the Canal & River Trust for more information and he graciously returned my message with specifics. It still wasn't going to be easy: the Leicester Line Canal is some thirty-five miles long, and it spills into the Grand Union Canal and the River Soar at either end, but the numerous locks offered a real chance of eel entrapment at least, and the massive weights of those two fish suggested they may have gone sedentary in that patch for a number of years.

The key to finding any record-breaking eel in the

United Kingdom is the discovery of a landlocked fish. The sorts of water where either escape to the Sargasso is impossible or the supply of food is so undeniably consistent that the eel decides to hunker down for an extended stay. Most specimen-eel hunters head to large commercial lakes, where carp fishermen have piled in baits and unknowingly supplemented the growth of a giant; in fact, out of the fifty biggest eels of all time only two have come from canals. I wasn't going to let that put me off though; after all, the larger of the captured eel pair was only 3lb off the British record. When it came to canals I strongly suspected it was the lack of anglers that had failed to deliver a record, and not the lack of potentially record-breaking fish.

In truth, though, I knew my focus had shifted from the pursuit of rod-caught records. I just didn't have that burning desire any more. Don't get me wrong, it would still have been very nice, but I felt that I was finally in a place where the experience of fishing meant more to me than anything else and I didn't want to spoil that by now tearing off to the nearest big-water commercial to fish for eels with a legion of carp anglers. The canal eels felt like a gift, an opportunity to fish somewhere unusual, where I knew the chance of encountering another angler was virtually zero; pure guerrilla fishing for a pair of fish who have almost certainly never been caught on rod or line. Either one would be a massive achievement, comfortably smashing my personal best right out of the water: really, what wasn't there to get very excited about?

I began to make plans. This was uncharted territory for me: to say I was a novice big-eel angler was a gross understatement – I didn't have the first idea what I was doing and scoured internet forums, books and specialist websites for the best advice on tackle, location, bait and fish care. Wilson writes that 'thundery weather finds them particularly active', a fact borne out by almost every single expert on the subject. I needed a serious downpour, preferably a storm, right now, in the middle of summer.

It felt weird hoping for rain, especially since I had been so comfortably outmanoeuvred by bad weather earlier in the year. We were experiencing the most extraordinary period of good weather as summer heaved on in its finery, a few days of sprinkling showers here and there, but nothing more than a blessing, and the whole nation was basking in a sort of collective euphoria.

I felt a little guilty, but these big eels demanded a near biblical event: Old Testament rain of the sort that brings the pagans to the hills and leaves a disgustingly sticky night in its tail. Weeks dragged into months and I began to worry that it might not actually happen at all, then one day I woke up, checked the forecast and saw cloud icons blacker than Satan's arsehole spreading right out across Britain.

I should have been delighted but I had one very serious problem: the storm was due to hit the Leicester Line the day before my twin sister's wedding. I spread out the map. It wasn't all bad: the fishing spot was pretty much slap bang in the centre of the country, and as Anna was getting wed out east I could just about justify the diversion. However, this was no daytime sortie. There was absolutely no question but that the big eels were at their most voracious in darkness – why else would Grandad have risked arrest? But I absolutely had to be at the wedding venue the following afternoon for a family barbecue, which meant leaving bright-eyed and bushy-tailed first thing in the morning and not turning up looking like I'd been on a night-long eel-bender the day before the seminal event of my beloved sister's life.

There was another major consideration: the stench. If I caught a giant eel I knew I was going to end up looking like the Creature from the Black Lagoon, and even if by some miracle I didn't, the bait I intended to use was firmly from the drawer marked 'stinkiest imaginable'.

Specimen-eel fisherman Matt Johnson in *Eel Fishing for Beginners* makes the case quite clear: 'I will prebait for several weeks, on a regular basis, using a mixture of old fish, maggots, chopped worms and, if allowed, chicken offal,' he notes, before coming to his senses and adding the following caveat: 'Please check with your fishing club before baiting up with chicken intestines, as I do not want to be held responsible for your expulsion from the club for breaking the rules.'

If I had been able to act alone I might just have got away with it, made up some excuse about getting a last-minute job in a sewerage system, and palmed it all off as an unavoidable inconvenience, with: 'Hey, guys! I'm at the wedding now so just direct me to the showers and I'll be down in a jiffy!' However, for a couple of years now my life has been intractably intertwined with another. I didn't quite know how I was going to tell my girlfriend, Emma, that we had to leave for Anna's wedding a day early so I could fish for giant eels, but I knew how it was going to go down.

I did some more virtual pre-baiting of my own and quickly discovered there was some sort of hotel located in the very set of roadside services I needed to be at to fish for the eel. Perfect. I could just imagine Emma having a bit of a pampering session there before the eve of the wedding as, Lord knows, she wasn't going to be interested in the eeling. If I played my cards correctly I might even be able to convince her that this was actually a really great idea, a way of breaking up the long journey ahead of the weekend's festivities.

An internet search revealed a very reasonable early-bird price of just £46.75 for a room, but just as I was about to punch my credit card number into the booking form I foolishly read a couple of reviews on the establishment. One, on motorwayservices.com, gave the hotel a two-burger rating out of a possible five, worrying both for being a low score and for the fact that the place couldn't even score well on a rating system inspired by fast food.

I wish I could tell you I closed the computer down and saved my money. I wish I could tell you I picked a different, more reasonable fish from my list of options. I wish I could tell you I didn't check that the lorry park was actually right next to the canal, so ideally located for the fishing, but the memory of *Bedford, My Bedford* by Ken Millard burnt brightly. I asked myself, quite honestly, what would Grandad do?

And then I booked the hotel.

All I can think about is eels and all I can see is eels.

The storm hits on the drive over and the lightning streaks across the sky like livid white eels. Small sea-through eels streak in watery lines down my windscreen before the giant pair of rubber eels sweep them aside. I follow a thin white eel on my satnav and funnel my car along the thickest and greatest eel in the land: the M1.

The services turned out to be the wrong side of the motorway, but I discovered a little flyover behind the hotel that led into the sort of seedy-looking darkened layby where you wouldn't want to inadvertently flash your lights around. A squeeze under a fence line, a scramble through a furrow fit for a badger, and I'm shipped onto thick grass and the water's side.

My London perch water stretched all the way from King's Cross to Birmingham on the Grand Union Canal, a distance of some 137 miles, but shortly after leaving Northampton a single arm separates from the main route and heads in a new direction up through

Leicester. It was along here that I'd found myself, in the dusk, somewhere below the Watford Gap locks.

Down by the canal all was calm. Nightfall was approaching fast and the tiny pipistrelle bats had taken to the Persian blue skies to hunt insects. They danced silently like blackened flakes of ash during a forest fire, their calm animation serving only to emphasize just how quiet the canal actually was. The water, frankly, was disturbingly still.

It couldn't be more different to the section of the Grand Union I experienced in London. There the banks were filled with people and commerce and the clear water revealed a sub-aquan dumping ground jostling for space among the city's waste. It wasn't pretty, but there was an elemental honesty to the place. Here, there was something of an unsettling air.

Two rows of hazel and sycamore trees, and a heavily grassed towpath with blackthorn, elderberry and patches of giant hogweed, were all lovely enough, but the driving rush of the M1 in the background, the white lights from the cars and screeching brake pads, the constant pounding of air, like herds of wildebeest trapped in a ravine, stopped it from truly feeling like a breathing space.

When you encounter green patches in densely populated areas there is something exciting about it, like you've discovered a small and unlikely victory for nature, a place where urban tension can be released, where the citified world can take stock and just 'be' for a little while. But when the scenario is reversed, when human waste collides with the countryside, it feels like an assault. Human hands built this canal, but the presence of water is usually good company for the wild, however it is formed. The M1, however, struck right through this place like a great grey spear.

The whole place felt as if it was in a state of limbo, like this pair of opposing forces were simply getting through the uncomfortable pleasantries before each moved on with its life, two manmade cousins forced together for Christmas, one brash, right on and relevant, the other sloping towards retirement with stories to tell if the other would only listen. I'm sure if I had walked a mile up- or downstream I would have reached a point where the M1 curled a satisfactory distance from the water and the atmosphere would instantly have lifted, but then the monster eels wouldn't be there, would they?

Bricked on either bank and filled with a fudgy brown water that resembled something the greedy Augustus Gloop may have entered in the children's book *Charlie and the Chocolate Factory*, the canal possessed a regimented symmetry that made it quite hard to find features where my water serpent might actually feed. Eventually I identified two potential areas that differed from the rest. One was a step into the canal on the opposite bank, cut deliberately to about the size of half a tennis court. It was designed to allow boats to pass each other, but its position off the main flow, and the accompaniment of overhanging trees, made it prime real estate for an ambush, or, failing that, at least the sort of area where I could imagine insects or carrion would get held up for the eel to feast upon. The second spot was further along and on my bank. It was a small instep in the brickwork about thirty metres from the first lock gate for the Watford Gap, where a series of seven gates have lifted canal boats over the sixteen metres of elevation known as the 'Leicester summit' from as far back as 1814. I couldn't fish any closer to the gates of the locks as, understandably, the Canal & River Trust didn't want anglers getting themselves or their tackle in the way of the working machinery. Still, I could imagine an eel might patrol out from those giant wooden doors, moulding its body tight to the canal walls till it found that little deviation in the brick, and then hopefully landed upon my feed.

The shade came on fast and the recce drew to its natural close. I cursed myself for not bringing a few bits of bait to drop into my spots to tempt some fish in early. A single white security light flickered into life above the locks. It cast an uneasy paleness over the place, like pallor mortis shortly after death; just perfect, I felt, for those that slither from their holes to gorge on the dead. I returned to the van as a plume of silver fish scattered across the canal's surface like shards of broken glass from a mirror. The predators had arrived.

*

The more I learnt of the eels' plight the more I grew to respect their resilience. Given the sort of dark and nasty places they turn up in, it's all too easy to transfer the characteristics of their bleak dwellings onto the animal itself. To do so is an injustice. When an eel appears in a storm drain, sewer or horse trough, it is a display of its extraordinary tenacity and iron will to survive and not necessarily an indication of preference. Never judge an animal purely by where it is forced to rest its head.

'So, I erm.'

I haven't felt this guilty in a very long time. Probably not since I grassed my sister up to my parents for putting orange juice in my shoes when we were ten.

The hotel where I'm going to have to leave Emma is too depressing for words. It's the sort of place you would come to cheat on your partner, not turn up together for a romantic overnight stay. If anything, the reviews on TripAdvisor were generous. Quite what levels of depravity you would have to reach to get less than a two-burger rating doesn't bear thinking about.

Nicotine-coloured walls blend seamlessly with a floor that's more stain than carpet. The whole place smells like the smoking area in a factory and it appears that the last guests had opted to have a massive fight with a full cafetière right before they left.

Emma peels the net curtains back from the glass. 'So this is my view for the night.' We gaze silently at the petrol station forecourt out front. A large man fills his lorry with one hand and inhales a Ginsters Cornish pasty into his face with the other.

'I feel, to be honest with you, like the biggest bastard in the world.' I look earnestly into Emma's eyes.

If I'd thought this ham-fisted attempt at emotional revelation might elicit some sympathy then I was barking up the wrong tree entirely. 'There's probably a dead body in here,' she says bluntly, flicking the blind shut and turning sharply, which is lucky as she doesn't notice the enormous black blowfly wafting up from the window frame. I attempt a stiff grin and widen my body frame out to conceal the uninvited guest.

'Come on, it isn't so bad,' I proffer, knowing it's actually worse than bad.

'Will. This is the sort of place in the films where women get murdered while they are left alone in a motel.' She climbed onto the bed.

'What, while their boyfriends are all off eel fishing?' I retort, while dying a little inside. 'Don't be so ridiculous.'

I consider, very seriously, just jacking the whole night in and heading off. But where could we possibly go now? The wedding doesn't start till lunchtime tomorrow and we are hours from home.

Liminality. 'The quality of ambiguity or disorientation that occurs in the middle stage of rituals, when participants no longer hold their pre-ritual status but have not yet begun the transition to the status they will hold when the ritual is complete.' It feels quite fitting that I am attempting this feat from a service station, the symbol of being neither here nor there, where no one wants to be, but a stop you simply have to take if you want to make it to your destination eventually. In the services we are a metaphorical stream of eels, pausing to sniff the water, to feed, confirm the direction of our target and leave at the earliest available opportunity. I have extended our stay here purely for my own purposes; what, I wonder, does that say about me? I sensibly opt to keep my navel-gazing to myself.

'Look, love, why don't you just come out with me?' I try, as a last resort, while knowing really how reluctant Emma is to fish at the best of times, and that a canal towpath at night could well be the final nail in the coffin of the chances of me ever luring her into my hobby. 'It'll be fun!' I add, somewhat weakly.

'No.'

She thumps the remote and sends the television crackling into life. 'I'm just going to sit here and do a facemask for tomorrow. See, I told you there were flies.'

The giant fly settles above the head of the bed as I creep out of the door and accede to Emma's demand to lock it securely behind me.

I left school, went to university and entered the real world with little idea of how I was going to pay for the ticket on the door. I wanted to travel, so I worked as a barman and slept on a mattress before getting one of those month-long English language teaching qualifications that gives you access to the planet and a classroom of people who are sadly expecting an actual teacher. That introduced me to a small school in the Indonesian half of New Guinea and from that moment forward something of a spell was cast over me and my future. Nothing was ever really the same again.

This wild, natural fortress had repelled outsiders like me for centuries, but in recent decades a gradual easing of borders had revealed some of the most fascinating tribal communities on earth. Spread out across the most bizarre set of geographical extremes that included the largest mountain range in Oceania, Asia's most intact primary rainforest, and the largest swamplands south of Borneo, I discovered that these people had maintained pathways and networks of intertribal trade for almost the entirety of their 45,000-year history. These were the longest-running trade routes in human history and they were virtually unreported, but as the modern world pressed into New Guinea at pace they were in danger of fading into the background without record.

I took it on myself to try and walk as many of these routes as I could, documenting the experiences of those local people who could still remember them, and then released my evidence onto the world, evidence, I felt, that elevated these people beyond the stereotype of them as backward, cannibalistic savages and firmly into the realms of what they deserved: recognition as a highly functioning, highly complex, co-operative society.

The world wasn't really interested though. I spent the best part of the next decade of my life applying for small grants, researching, and going on ever more dangerous expeditions on the island. I had some successes, making the first record of the foot-only salt trade in the far west of the island and mapping almost the entire length of a 1,000-kilometre section of trade route stretching out to the southern coasts, and for many years that was just enough. I was living my dream and felt uniquely privileged to be following my own path in life. Sure, I had no money, and my work only interested the most fanatical of geographers, but I had enough to get by and, besides, I passionately believed in what I was doing. I supplemented my income away from the island by slowly going up the rungs in the world of documentary television, flitting from being a runner in London to working as a researcher in Cardiff, and generally felt quite happy with my lot, but as the years passed a creeping anxiety began to seep into my soul.

In the beginning it felt a bit like the first time you get scared climbing trees as a child. You've done it hundreds and hundreds of times without a care in the world and then suddenly the fear grips you, usually when you are right at the top of some oaken giant with no obvious safe path back down. You realize you are mortal, that what you are doing is reckless, that if you fall you could seriously hurt yourself, or even die, but you are hopelessly addicted to the buzz and thrill of pushing forever forward so you don't get down, you just sort of sit there, helplessly.

My moment came when I was lost somewhere deep in West Papua, the Indonesian side of New Guinea. I had dragged my friend and medic Callum with me and we were now without food having barely escaped a maiden white-water descent with our lives. I had made a terrible error of judgement that had led us not onto an ancient trade route, but down into a vast, uninhabited, 400-mile square of thick forest that it would take us weeks to escape from. I lost two and a half stone, and we walked out with our lives, but Callum and I would never work together again and I left behind something vital of myself that I never quite recovered.

I had gone almost as far as I could with my expeditionary career, probing towards my own breaking point and plumbing the pits of a very real, very visceral, fear of death, but I couldn't seem to escape my hard-wired desire to push even further. Leading expeditions was my full-time job by the end of my twenties, and I didn't feel qualified to do anything else. I pressed onwards and downwards into ever more dangerous territory: the Pennine Way alone in a tent in minus 10°C temperatures, the first solo descent of the river that marks the war-torn border of Sierra Leone and Liberia, alone and afraid, but blinkered to the damage I was doing to myself and everyone who cared about me. I had a recurring nightmare during that time in which I was an animal being hunted by an unseen but very deadly predator. I would put distance between me and my pursuer and almost slip free, only to suddenly discover I didn't know how to run any more and instantly find myself back in front of its fangs. Its hot, smelly breath would pound the backs of my calves and I knew I was seconds from death, and then I would awake covered in my own sweat.

A hundred million years ago the first freshwater eels left their sea home and were also settling in to a new way of life somewhere off the coast of Indonesia.

We still don't know exactly how the eel reproduces and an eel egg has still never been found. We don't know the nature of the adult eel's extraordinary navigational skills or why the European eel doesn't just join the American eel in making the much shorter hop to the American continent from their shared breeding sea. We have yet to witness an adult eel actually die from the exertion of spawning, and, despite thousands of assaults on the Sargasso, a breeding adult eel is yet to be recovered. According to Tom Fort, there has only ever been one record of an adult eel being found in the open Atlantic: it was semi-digested and in the stomach of a sperm whale somewhere off the Azores. We may not know any of these things for sure, but there is one thing we do know: during my twenties the eel experienced a catastrophic decline in its numbers.

By 2010 the Environment Agency had recorded a 95 per cent decline in the European eel. In keeping with the astonishingly one-sided ratio of questions over answers whenever the eel is involved, it still isn't clear precisely what is driving eels towards early extinction. One factor could be illegal fishing and the over-exploitation of the elvers; the eel, after all, is one of the only fish to face such abuse of their young; but another possibility involves the spread of a particularly nasty nemotode worm that feeds parasitically on their swim-bladders. Then there is the increased use of hydroelectric dams and their thwarting of eel migration, and surely there can be no question that climate change, which has warmed the Arctic ice cap and slowed the Gulf Stream, has hampered the procession of thin-heads to these shores. The truth is, it is probably a mixture of all of these factors, but actually getting a firm grip on how to reverse the crash is proving extremely difficult.

Export bans and tighter restrictions on fishing have helped, as have restocking programmes, but the benefits are only found locally in those places that care enough about the eel to invest in its future; elsewhere, the out-look is still very bleak indeed. My entire childhood was spent trying to avoid the attentions of the eel; then, for almost twenty years, I didn't catch a single one. I felt deep shame at having taken this fish for granted.

I shuffle along the towpath in the pitch black, glad of the half-light recce. Everything changes after dark. Things move around and obstacles emerge from nowhere. I want to limit the use of my torch, to allow my eyes the time to adjust naturally, but also to slip through here without disturbing the eels, or any other animals that could be watching from the shadows for that matter.

The elemental vulnerability of spending time in the dark alone can quickly bring a deep sense of paranoia with it. A fear of the dark is something we dismiss as adults as being somehow childish, but ask yourself this: how much time do you actually spend in the true dark? When the light switch isn't within reach and you have only your own mind for company? Total darkness was for a long time a CIA-approved 'enhanced interrogation technique', and those who have experienced interrogation in Guantánamo Bay claimed it to be the most feared torture method; proof that there is not much worse than being forced to retreat into your own mind to find out what fears feed down there.

I was used to hiding in the dark. On expeditions, especially as I started to go solo, I would pride myself on my ability to conceal my camp. I felt far more fear of the random acts of people than I ever did of the more predictable behaviours of the wild animals that roam the forest floor. When night fell I would retreat well away from any paths or watercourses and pull myself into the densest foliage I could find. One night in West Africa I remember being near paralysed with fear as a pair of poachers hunted the banks of the river I was following. I could see their torches, scanning the bushes like a searchlight from a prison, and was absolutely convinced they were about to discover me. They came so close I could see the whites of their eyes and teeth and smell the pile of dead and dying primates they had gathered in a sack, but I remained undiscovered.

This canal might not be Conrad's 'heart of darkness' – it's just a towpath in the Midlands after all – but it still has the ability to really scare. Here I have nowhere to go and nowhere to hide. There is no shelter, just one way in and one way out, and I'm perching myself right on the main thoroughfare, where anything could pass: a person, a badger, a fox, perhaps even a ghost.

I'm glad of the moon then. It is almost full. So bright and lumpen in appearance, like it has been drawn by a child or moulded out of porridge, but it means my way is lit comfortably enough, and I'm able to shuffle my feet along the path to my chosen spot without too much emotional upset.

I take a deep restorative breath and my heart rate starts to drop. A beautifully soft ethereal smoke drifts off the fields and a pair of spectral-looking moths flutter past, using the canal's unnatural break in the treeline as an unencumbered passage. I wonder if they will make it past the squadron of pipistrelle bats though.

In West Papua and West Africa, any break in the wilderness provided by rivers was always a relief from the intense claustrophobia of the forest. If I could, I would always use them to expedite my passage on a particular bearing, and many of the coolest things I've ever seen have been thanks to them. Rivers have a magnetism for people and wildlife – it was one of the reasons I continued to love them so much – but if you were potential prey you knew your life was out of your hands every time you opted for this clear path through the forest. It was why I spent so much of my projects hiding.

I peel the lid off my bait bucket. In keeping with all

I've learnt about the particularities of the eel's nose a putrid cloud fills the air with the smell of microwaved vomit. The bait is suitably horrendous then, pellets soaked in fish oils for over a year and dead fish from the depths of the freezer: a lamprey, a smelt, a small joey mackerel. I'll fix their heads to large single hooks and throw a generous handful of dead maggots over the top. I set up two bite alarms paired with stiff carp rods and strong lines. Who really is to say what could come to my baits out here in these under-fished passages? Whispered rumours of giant catfish, hulking canal pike and record-shaking perch brush shoulders with monstrous eels, snapping turtles and at least one truly massive python. The canal systems of Britain might have been made by man but they have long since been reclaimed by nature, both natural and discarded, so it pays to be prepared for anything.

It is surprisingly hard to sever the head of the lamprey from its body. I use a knife and the plastic top of the bait bucket and stick to my dour butchery till I have successfully parted tendons and spine. It oozes blood and oil, the perfect chum for the eel, a connoisseur of the gruesome. The dark feels right for this work, but I try and keep my mind focused on the task at hand and steer well away from the grim acts that may, or may not, take place in these hedged lands after dark.

I underarm the lamprey head out into the dark and listen as the line fizzes satisfactorily from my reel. By some miracle it lands with a splash somewhere in the far bank hole and I feel the lead meet a solid bed. It is sat right on the fringe of the bushes. Perfect.

Ten minutes later, with both traps laid, I flick my bite alarms on. Momentarily they light up, just to let me know the battery is charged and they are ready to go, before settling into the night's watch. I too settle. Keeping my profile low to the moonlight, I pull the hood of my sweater over my head and hunch forward over the water like a gargoyle.

When I was a child I was warned that the eel was known as 'the Devil's fish' and that if you lay them out in a cross shape they will remain that way until they die. Later in life I learnt that they are actually just an unusually sensitive fish. They are armed with thousands of sensors along their bodies that aid them when hunting in the murk, and I discovered it was actually possible to crash their nervous system by simply tipping them up and running a finger along their lengths. It made unhooking them a much more straightforward task, as they simply fell into something of a trance. The crucifix stuff was a nonsense, of course. The eels had simply been subdued, and stupid people had just seen what they had always wanted to see, but the power of suggestion can't be underestimated. Night fishing to exorcise freshwater snakes from brown water certainly sounds like fiendish work.

The alarm on the lamprey lets out a single bleep and my adrenal glands eject their load. Something is out there. Something is stirring in the dark. I hover over the rod. 'Do it again,' I whisper, and the alarm obliges with another bleep. Do I strike? Do I not strike? The mind swims with what it could be: something with a pulse for certain – the canal is far too still and the lamprey far too dead for it to be anything else.

It bleeps again. One more time and I'm definitely going to hit it. The giant could be out there right now, just mouthing the bait. I don't want to snatch it from its jaws before the hook is in place. Perhaps it's just a small perch though? Pulled in by the fishy scent. Or maybe it's a crayfish gently stripping the severed head from the hook? I wouldn't be too surprised if they were in here – they seem to be everywhere else – in which case I should definitely reel in and check the head.

The rod settles again, and this is where madness lies. Do I reel up and check the bait is still there or leave it out in what I know is the perfect spot? Do I risk disturbing a swim with a feeding fish for an unnecessary investigation? What if I can't cast it back into that perfect spot again? But what if I'm now fishing on a bare hook? I'll never ever catch and all this time is wasted. I sit back down and reposition my hood. 'What the hell am I doing down here?' I say, to no one in particular, suddenly feeling very restless and quite scared. An intense feeling of disquiet enters the pit of my stomach. 'I don't like it here,' I whisper through gritted teeth. In fact, I don't like it here at all.

When I was younger I used to believe in ghosts. In fact, I was so convinced the house I grew up in was haunted I once persuaded Paul and Lee to come over and stake the place out for a night. It was a disaster though, and the worst thing we captured was Anna smashing our carefully laid cotton trip lines and shouting 'woooooo' down my tape recorder at the top of her voice in the middle of the night. I did have one very odd experience when I was twelve though. The family were all staying in an old fisherman's cottage in Little Haven and my brother Tom and I were sharing a bunkbed in one of the back rooms. In the middle of the night I woke to see the shadow of a boy hanging over me on the top bunk. I assumed it was Tom and told him to go straight back to bed, slightly surprised he had managed to climb the ladder without me waking, especially since he was only five years old and pretty clumsy on his feet. The shadow simply waved at me, before noiselessly drifting away from view. Shaken up a little I flicked on the light switch and discovered Tom was sleeping soundly and I had been staring at a wall no more than a foot from my face the entire time.

Weird things seem to happen around water and those associated with it, but in all the years I've spent fishing in the dark alone I've only experienced a handful of occasions when I've felt genuinely unsettled. Certainly this night eel fishing on the canal is one of them, but there is also one pond in the Vale of Glamorgan that I simply will not fish in the dark no matter how much you pay me – as soon as the sun falls behind the trees I am out of there like a whippet from a trap and so is almost every other angler I know.

The best, and certainly the most convincing, of all stories of the paranormal are the ones where 'the weird' catches you utterly unaware though, when you aren't already in an anxious state and primed to elevate a suggestion into a full-blown apparition. One autumnal evening I was walking home along a stretch of Cardiff's River Taff with Emma when we both heard the distinct sound of a cycle bell right behind us. It was no great surprise given we were on a route frequently taken by cyclists, so without even breaking our conversation, we took to walking in single file as the bike rushed past. Except there was no bike. Just the hair-raising sensation of having something pass right through your body that isn't really there at all. We stopped, looked up and down both banks, waited for a few moments, and concluded there was not another single living soul for hundreds of metres.

As I said, though, I don't believe in ghosts. The inner machinations of our complex brains and their multitude of ways of interpreting the world on our behalf seem to me to be both deeply fallible and something that we are only just beginning to understand. However, I do absolutely believe people who say they have seen ghosts. In their mind's eye they definitely have, in which case they are telling the truth. I just don't necessarily think what they believe they've seen is evidence of the undead.

Still, the paranormal naturally appeals to the fisherman in me. Not necessarily the idea of things that go bump in the night per se, but more the idea that if anyone spends enough time really focusing on the world, and I mean really intensely focusing, they will naturally begin to notice things that deviate from the norm. Fishing by its very nature is prying into the unknown, dropping a line into a largely unseen world and trying to make a connection. Certainly, the best fishermen I know have something of a supernatural instinct about them. They can literally feel the presence of a fish and will go on to catch with such an enviable sense of inevitability it is almost as if they have arrived from a realm in the future where they have already seen the precise location of every fish on earth. It must be sublime.

Yes, if pressed, I would say I am an open-minded sceptic, but I recognize we are still a very long way from fully understanding ourselves, and nearly completely ignorant of that mysterious other part of the world that operates all around us, in spite of us, and not because of us.

The red light on the alarm lights up once more in the black. It is like something from a fantasy novel, the crimson eye of a demon approaching me in a tunnel. So I can conclude that the head of the lamprey is definitely intact then, unless a fish has simply swum into my line. One more bleep, but still no full-blooded run. The first hour alone on the canal has been a bit like being buried alive in a coffin, a sensory deprivation chamber that has left my nerves shredded and my wits screaming at me to switch on my torch, but once I committed to denying myself that indulgence my body tapped back into a set of skills deep within us all.

The animals start to creep out of their holes since it has become clear I am not a threat. The featherweight rustles of rodents disturb the leaf litter, those miniature tigers emerging to hunt the night-crawling insects, worms, bugs and spiders, followed up by larger crashes and intermittent barks and moans from the brush behind me. Disturbing, but actually just a family of foxes burrowing their way through the thin wooded strip between this canal and the M1. The fox is one of the great mammals of our time. Adaptive and loathed, just like the eel. I didn't see an urban fox till I first moved to London, and could scarcely reconcile the mange-filled and greying creature before me with the snatched glimpses I had had of the fenland fox, back implausibly arched as it leapt over another fence line and vanished. The mammalian expression of the wild as we know it today is a plucky *Vulpes vulpes* strolling through the Marble Arch with an entire KFC chicken carcass trapped between its teeth.

Every sound is amplified when your eyesight is dimmed. The movement of mammals is thunderous, like pressing your ear to a metallic track as a train approaches, and the rolling fish of the canal resemble a whale breaching right at my toes. I know that can't be, that this is just my body over-compensating for the loss of one of its primary senses and that the still water itself is acting as an amplifier, but it's a compelling idea. This is precisely where monster legends originate from of course: I see an eel and report a Nessie, I hear a tabby cat and report a panther, I smell a badger and report Big Foot.

A large rat slips into the canal and sends shockwaves out across the water's surface. They detonate on the brickwork bank like a bouncing bomb so I use a finger-tip to check the line is still running under tension to the bait. I can feel the pulse of my heart and the gentle give and take of the water. All is in place still. The torch stays off, the baits remain out, and I keep still.

Another hour passes and I realize my eyesight has not departed me: it has just taken longer than my other senses to come to the party. As brain and eye eventually pull together I am prised from the blanket of pure darkness and into the multi-textured world of the colour black. Against the bushes on my bank the coal black is so uniform it lends the whole scene a one-dimensional effect, as if the bushes are simply the stuck-on backdrop to a shadow puppet theatre, but where the moonlight casts a silver-tipped black on the scene my adjusted eye is able to pick out textures: the outline of the branches, the frame of a crow's nest, the denser hollows in the shrubbery that taper into a fine inky black at the water's edge.

One of the hollows pierces right through the bush and into a wide field behind. It billows with mist and stirs in a playful candyfloss fashion, as if the whole scene were being whipped up with a giant invisible spoon. A large ancient oak tree stands out proud and solid in the field's centre and its long, loving arms reach out to offer shelter to several dozen sheep. As the traffic on the motorway fades I begin to hear their bleats offering both them and me reassurance. The championship rounds of the night are pulling in. This is real darkness.

My most recent trip to the forests of New Guinea was just one month before. I had been living with a remote forest people known as the Korowai, as part of a series for the BBC. The Korowai are rightfully famed for their abilities as hunter-gatherers but also for their extraordinary houses, built high on stilts, clear of the forest floor, well away from the floods, mosquitoes and white devils that live down there. It was my second trip out in a long-running project that intends to follow their turbulent lives over the course of a year. The old men I befriended requested I bring a lamp on my return. Instantaneous light. After food security, shelter and clothes it is the next thing on the list before money. I lay in that treehouse every night, silently watching as the lamp I had brought was switched on and off, on and off, and on, again.

Having light at the flick of a switch is such a luxury that denying yourself it when you do have it feels quite self-indulgent; however, I know that one press of that button will expunge all I can see now in an instant. It will leave me in a puddle of artificial light with the pitch black waiting just outside the reach of the bulb. It's actually far more frightening than just being in the dark, where I can at least see the shadows. It will take another hour of waiting for my night vision to be restored if I turn on my torch now.

The bleep of the alarm thumps through the night air like a lump hammer through a breezeblock. My soul leaps clear of my body in fright and I have to race it to the far rod, but just as my world is about to conjoin into one clean strike the line, once again, falls dead. I curse the black as my striking hand shakes. I'm being taunted by unseen forces.

I remember from my research that the best of the big-eel fishing is to be had two hours before midnight, and two hours after dawn. I check my watch and note that this last take has happened on the stroke of the witching hour and decide that if nothing happens on the lamprey line in another half an hour then I must reel it in. Having not given the crayfish a single thought prior to nightfall, I have long since convinced myself that the canal is absolutely crawling with them and that they've definitely relieved me of at least one bait. By the time the half-hour is up I've descended further into my own mind and reel in both my lines, fully expecting to find them utterly barren at the hands of the thieving crustacean.

The baits on both are unmolested. It was the wrong call. I re-bait and re-cast, but I suspect I may well have blown it now.

After 1 a.m. there is a palpable shift in atmosphere. It feels like someone has drawn a shroud over the entire canal, that a switch has been flicked and all of the life that was, no longer is. The foxes have gone with the rodents, splashes, moths and bats and in their stead the dank smell of the canal fills my nostrils. It is a stagnant aroma, like an old fishtank long after the death of its residents. Even the grass beneath my feet has expelled the last heat from the day now and I begin to feel a creeping chill through the rubber soles of my boots. It is definitely a lot colder and I know the time for catching has passed. My lines hang still and limp, the water makes no noise. I close my eyes and can feel sleep trying to take me.

I don't know if I've got what you need to take up solo night fishing. In my heart I know I'm just not hardcore enough. There have been other times on the bank when I have thought of going home late at night, but I've always eked every last moment of fishing out of an experience, no matter how cold, wet, hungry or uncom-fortable I might feel. There is always the chance of that one take which turns around a session, and the list of last-gasp fish I've caught in the dead of night stand as a testament to the lingering angler.

However, it was precisely that 'never say die' attitude that eventually led me into so much trouble as an exped-ition leader. Sometimes my determination tips over into blind stupidity. There is nothing to catch here now and I know it.

Robert Macfarlane once drew the conclusion that 'those who travel to mountain tops are half in love with them-selves, and half in love with oblivion'. The same is probably true of most modern-day adventurers.

By the end of my twenties I had taken things to the point where I had burnt through relationships, jobs, finances and expedition partners with frightening efficiency. My last girlfriend had walked out on me with the epitaph that I had taken my life to the point 'that no one can ever reasonably go with you'. She was right. My myopic desire to confirm my theories thinly masked a burning desire to prove myself. To whom, I'm still not even sure.

I eventually found rock bottom on the jungle-choked river that splits Sierra Leone and Liberia. My hammock was laid in the leaf litter, enveloping me, entombing me, as *Plasmodium falciparum* malaria pumped its way around my bloodstream and into my cerebral cortex.

My parents and close friends had all been to great lengths to vocalize their fears for my well-being throughout that decade. I remembered then how Grandad had been the only person who said I would be all right, but years later Grandma told me that he too was terrified. He just hadn't wanted to say it to my face.

I fished much less through that decade, but Grandad had persevered in going out to the bank. He started missing takes as he moved into his mid-eighties and all too soon his eyesight began to seriously trouble him. However, he did manage to snare another giant eel from Popham's Eau. Later he reported back to me how his line had been halfway across the river before he had even noticed the float was missing. It became a serious worry for us all. He was slowing down on a big river that was no place for an old man to fish alone. Dad was convinced he would fall in and drown one day, but he absolutely would not be stopped.

The last time we fished Popham's Eau together he fell three times, once on the way to the bank and twice on the way home. The final time he fell I remember shouldering his great weight and how he had looked at me with these great sad brown eyes that I had never seen on him before. The legendary Irish boxer Barry McGuigan, a man whom I knew Grandad admired, once remarked how 'boxers are the *first to know* when to quit and the *last to admit it*'. That was the moment we both knew the game was up. Wordlessly I carried on home, and didn't speak a word about what had happened to anyone, least of all to Grandad. He never returned to Popham's Eau, and I never wanted to see the place again either.

Grandad, the greatest of all the great eels in my life, was sliding towards the abyss of the Sargasso, having lived a fantastic and full life. Whereas I was simply at risk of ending mine prematurely, an adolescent elver who had chosen a stupidly dangerous path that would consume him without hesitation unless something changed.

I crawled out of the West African forest on my hands and knees and came home. With little idea of what I would do next I quit solo expeditions and moved in with Anna and her boyfriend, James, back in the Fens, back where I needed to be. I picked up my rods and started fishing again, targeting the only fish I could remember how to.

It was while carp fishing that I found eels again. The familiar tap-tap-tap and back-winding resistance in the fight, the struggle to net and unhook, were throwbacks to times past, but for the first time in my angling life I felt the utter euphoria of being covered in their slime. The eel was back and now so was I.

A spring of clear water had opened up ahead of me as I pulled into my thirties. It was leading me towards the coast and I knew what I needed to do.

I pick the reel off the rests and wind both rods in. I don't need to be like this any more. I shouldn't have allowed the old selfish me to bring Emma out here but I'm so grateful to the eel for the lesson. Everyone is allowed a relapse.

We made it to Anna and James's wedding the very next afternoon and I don't believe I smelt too bad. Maybe I had had a chance on the canal that night, but I doubted I would ever return to test the theory.

The Great Game

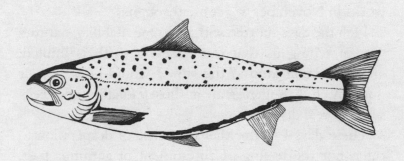

Home is a trial, domestic chores a torment, life
is dust and ashes until you take up a fishing rod.
Wales was my answer to this problem.
Paul Boote and Jeremy Wade, *Somewhere
Down the Crazy River* (1992)

I never really liked autumn when I was a child. It was
always a tense time. The year was running out, the
fishing was getting harder, and September always meant
back to school.

When I was inside, staring at the white iron bars that
framed the school radiators, I used to wonder what on
earth had just happened to August. It was the only
month of the year when we weren't interned for at least

some of the time in classrooms and when it started it felt like it would go on for ever. Then the last Bank Holiday weekend would flash past and I was back here, locked in until Christmas with only the prospect of a few fireworks in November to get me through.

I felt the days shorten with quiet inevitability; nature's way of telling us that our time on earth is limited, another circuit around the sun. I would blow hot air onto my chilly fingers, stare at those radiators, and feel a sense of real disquiet.

These days I feel neither the sense of desperation to catch nor the feeling of entrapment of autumns past. The river crackles with tension, and the fish can feed exceptionally hard during this period if you can get a break in the weather. After a long, late summer, and the blank night with the eel, I started to catch really well again. For two nights running I ended up in the water in my pants: the first instance was on a remote Forestry Commission lake where a robust, double-figure wild carp snagged me up in a rotting bed of lilies, and I had to fetch it, and the second was a tussle with a big barbel which ran my line into a rocky snare and refused to lift its head until I had made my way downstream of its lie. I fished the magisterial River Wye with Dad, getting him onto his first big brace of chub, as happy for him as if I had caught the fish myself, and landed a pair of picture-perfect grayling trotting a fat float loaded with maggots through fast water above Cardiff.

My slate is wiped clean in August and it has long since

become my second spring, responsible for delivering me more fresh starts than any other time of the year; and some of the biggest fish of my life.

The week after I had wrestled with my first eel for twenty years my life took a major turn. I had been visiting my friend, and occasional boss, Steve at his cottage down on the Gower coast in South Wales. We had supposed to go on a fishing trip, but, having nearly lost the family car in the turning tides around Port Eynon, we wisely decided to call it a day. I thought that was pretty much it in terms of the weekend's dramas, but then he slid a large manila envelope my way across his garden table.

In it was a thick document with a colourful picture of a mask-wearing man stood waist deep in azure blue seas on the cover. The photo caption told me this was an indigenous shark caller from the island of New Britain in Papua New Guinea, and the title told me this was a pitching document for a new BBC series.

While I had been embroiled in my existential (and malarial) crisis in Sierra Leone, Steve, who runs an independent documentary company in Cardiff, together with my director friends Jamie and Will, had pitched me as a presenter to BBC Two. *Hunters of the South Seas* was set in the South Pacific and would see me live cheek by jowl with the last subsistence hunter-gatherers of the sea. Sensationally, BBC Two had agreed to let us all make it together.

'Is this for real, mate?' I asked nervously. He laughed,

and forced a beer into my hand. Not one season after I had quit expeditions, and just two years after I had sworn I would never work another day in the world of television, I was sat, in Cardiff, penning my name against a primetime project. After a decade of juggling my careers in both adventure and television it seemed the hand of fate had finally found a way of meeting my passions in the middle. I couldn't have been happier.

Well, actually, I probably could have. I needed to move back to Cardiff immediately to start researching potential communities and locations, and, in my haste to get settled, I signed for quite possibly the loneliest single man's flat in history.

The hallway was unlit, the windows were cracked, and every appliance, from the fridge to the oven, had a major fault. When I flicked on the lights for my first evening alone the switch simply crumbled backwards into a giant cavity in the wall. I called the landlord immediately but found his mobile to be strangely 'out of service' since the rapid collection of my deposit and non-refundable two months' advance rent.

Fishing provided a release. My new place was in a supposedly rough part of town known as Riverside, but if you can look beyond the concrete, graffiti and grit, there was a wonderful stretch of the River Taff to discover.

The Taff flows for just forty-five miles from its high source in the Brecon Beacons to the sea at Cardiff's Tiger Bay. It is one of the steepest and shortest descents of any river in Wales but it packs in the features along its length. There's world-class trout fishing in its upper reaches and some of the biggest chub and barbel in Britain towards its mouth, but hardly anyone ever seems to fish it.

I had lived in Cardiff for a couple of years before but had only thought to fish the Taff once. I found it a difficult and wild river, met at a time when I was interested in neither. I caught one stringy roach and turned my gaze back to the carp ponds, but now I was back, and, living alone, it felt like the time was right to give the river more effort.

The Taff was nothing like the rivers and drains of the Fens. My home waters were slow and sluggish, man-made receptors used to keep the fields from sinking under water. The Creek was almost completely static and the only times the big drains ever moved were if someone had cranked open the sluice gates at Denver. The Taff stirred under its own immense gravitational pull. When it rained on the hills the water would flow with a rabid intention towards the coasts, swelling and raging with an angry brown foam that boiled with litter, streamer weed and sometimes even entire trees.

Thinking I could rock up and fish this river effectively because I had experience in the Fens was like believing I could look after a wild wolf because I had once owned an Airedale terrier. It took many weeks just to learn the basics, and months more before I would even come close to catching a reasonable fish.

The first lesson was that using the same tackle and tactics every day was a definite no-no. Different fish came on in different conditions, and the River Taff was a living, breathing ecosystem that changed its moods continually. Sometimes you would need a heavy single bait rolling along the deck and other days you could get away with light float tackle and a steady trickle of grubs. There were days you could wade out across crystal-clear waters and trundle a bait right along the middle of the river, and others when one misplaced foot would see you swept to the north coast of Somerset. Through trial and error I eventually discovered there was nearly always somewhere you could cast a line, though, and, in spite of the Taff's reputation for being devoid of life after decades of industrial punishment, I found there were some fantastic fish just waiting to be caught.

I can pinpoint the precise moment fishing the Taff became more than just a distraction from my hovel of a flat. It was early autumn, but the river's water was still warm and I was able to wade in barefoot. I cast a large golden spinner towards a weeping willow tree on the far bank. My mind was utterly blank, locked in the trance-like state that only spinning produces, when an explosion, something like a silvery pipe-bomb, bowed my rod and electro-shocked my soul.

I heard it once said by a crinkly old angler that just as a watched kettle never boils, an over-considered fish never bites. I didn't even realize there were salmon in the Taff, but by the time my brain had processed the cause of the assault the fish had thrown the hook and vanished. I cast again, and again, and again, till my arms ached and darkness fell all around me, but I couldn't seem to raise the fish for another round.

It was a big salmon, of that I was in no doubt: returned from the sea to spawn and recovering its strength somewhere out in a hidden hole just off the main flow. My spinner had invaded its personal space. It hadn't snapped at my spinner to feed on it, like a pike or a perch might — the take had been violent, GBH on the line. I just hadn't been prepared.

I was back every night through that season but the salmon proved to be exceptionally elusive. My lack of success wasn't down to an absence of fish: every time the river rose a conveyor belt of fresh sea-run salmon moved upstream and into the holes outside the city park. I knew they were there because they always declared their position in the last hour of light, leaping clean of the river and flaying their silver sides with water. Perhaps it was just an effort to blast irritating sea lice from their bodies, but it was hard not to feel like I was being ridiculed.

Carp fishing had made me soft. After weeks of effort my fingers and thumbs had blistered and calloused into layers of hardened skin on my casting hand. I hadn't wanted to catch a fish this badly since the winter of '92 and that first pike. This was way beyond a simple distraction now. I had to catch that fish.

*

The American humorist Ian Frazier noted how 'casting for steelhead is like calling God on the telephone, and it rings and rings and rings, hundreds of rings, a thousand rings, and you listen to each ring as if an answer might come at any moment, but no answer comes, and no answer comes, and then on the 1,001st ring, or the 1,047th ring, God loses his patience and picks up the phone and yells, "WHAT THE HELL ARE YOU CALLING ME FOR?" in a voice the size of the canyon.'

It took me until the final week of the game-fishing season to finally make the salmon's acquaintance. The trees had turned a golden brown and the horse chestnuts had swelled and dropped their load, but my reel roared forward once again. I was up to my knees in water, my rod bowed to the river king.

The take had come from nowhere. Salmon have this ability to materialize, not like eels from the mud, but like some shape-shifting spirit blessed with the ability to metamorphosize from mineral to animal at will. The salmon may happily take the form of a rock for hours, even days, before deciding to emerge as a mighty fish and collide with your world with all the brute force of an articulated lorry meeting a wall.

On a city canal you will be noticed – runners have to go around you and pedestrians will take a passing interest in you as a curio – but in a big city river anglers are absorbed within its width like just another shopping trolley or abandoned car. As I fought tooth and nail with the fish the urban world swirled all around me like flakes in a snow-globe. A family chatted above the banks, a man threw a dog a stick, an ambulance screamed over a distant bridge and no one noticed my salmon pounding the rod and rocking the world beneath my feet. It isn't that city folk don't care, they just don't believe in their wildlife.

Eventually I beached the fish and placed my hands across its sides. When you have to wait for something you really want, and have fantasized about it each day to such an extent that you feel like you must have experienced it in a previous life, sometimes when it happens for real it can all feel a little anticlimactic, that the thrill of the chase was truly greater than the capture itself. That was never the case with my first salmon: it was like I had been trapped in a dream where I had been reaching and reaching for something that I could almost touch, only for it to slip from my grasp at the last moment, but here, now, I had woken to discover the very object of my desires had been lying in my hands all along.

The fish was beautiful. I cradled it in my arms and took in its thickened, muscular body, its dark, paddle-like tail and its kype, an elongated and upturned lower jaw that resembles the tip of a billhook. It was a mature male fish, a 'cock', but it wasn't the brilliant silver of an adult salmon just hours out of the sea. It had quite some colour to it: a hood of brown along its top and black spots that met with a dark silvery side. I had almost mistaken it for a giant brown trout at first glance.

Its smoked appearance was a sure sign that this fish

had spent some weeks waiting to move upstream. I didn't mind that at all. I was new to the salmon game and immune to the strange angler's belief that a fish progressively loses its value with each day spent away from salt water. This was my fish, my first salmon, and I gripped it tenderly as it recovered in the shallows.

My friend Fred had been with me that day and took a couple of pictures on his phone, and so it was, later that evening, that I was able to post the picture on Facebook and change the trajectory of my life for the second time that season.

As was standard with my Facebook friends the typical commentary sidestepped the magnificence of the fish and focused entirely on some irrelevant detail, in this case the shortness of the pair of shorts I was wearing, but the picture did catch the eye of a girl I had long admired but hadn't dared approach.

Emma and I had been friends since we worked together the last time I lived in the city. She was beautiful, smart and funny, and lived in the most delightful pool imaginable. But it was an impossibly difficult cast away, tangled right up in the complex branches of other relationships with far cooler guys who probably thought fishing was for nerds. I didn't think I stood a chance.

She messaged me saying it was good to see that I was back in Cardiff, and that the fish was pretty great, but advising me I needed to purchase some new shorts. Then she asked me out for a drink. I overcast my finest lure right into the trees in my excitement to reply. Far too much punctuation and an over-liberal use of the caps lock button made me appear more than a little desperate in my message, and then I foolishly gushed: 'I live in a right dump in Riverside these days so any excuse to get out of the flat is gratefully received.'

Incredibly, she considered my lure anyway. I mean, it was my finest, after all.

Sixty-five years earlier the life of a young man with a shock of black hair was slowing to a standstill. The other figures grinding and spinning in the dance hall were blending gently into the background, leaving behind just one striking, confident young lady.

Ken Millard was aware that this was like a moment in a romantic film, so it was possible it couldn't actually be real. He straightened his tie, turned to his mates, and announced: 'That's the girl I'm going to marry.'

Dad recently found Grandad's diary from that year. It was a small, pocket-sized book with a black leather cover that detailed his everyday comings and goings. He was hardly going to pour his emotions into his prose, Grandad wasn't that kind of man, but it was clear the shift in his behaviour after he met Grandma was seismic. The heavy-drinking, rugby-playing, cinema-going dance hall wag all but disappeared overnight, to be replaced by a man wholly and fully dedicated to his new relationship.

Nadine. He wrote her name in excitable large lettering with a dramatic use of space on the page; hers was a name that mattered. He eased right off the fishing as the diary filled up with the details of their various dates and trips out on his motorcycle. This was more than just a man in love; Grandad had found a new way of life through Grandma and it was obvious he was fantastically happy.

Grandma squeezed a teabag with her fingers and topped up my mug with a more than generous measure of milk. 'I had lost my previous boyfriend in World War Two. He was a pilot returning to the airbase near Ripon when his aircraft became lost up in the mist on the Yorkshire Moors. I found out about the accident through the matron; it was all in the papers before anyone had told me. She just asked: "Have you read the news?"' Grandma placed my tea on her coffee table. She still had the newspaper clipping somewhere, she said. Grandma was extraordinarily resilient. Years passed, the pain eased, and then Grandad swept her off her feet in the dance hall.

'They were wonderful times,' she smiled.

I had seen pictures of Grandma when she was young. She had striking dark hair, hazel eyes and an impish grin that stuck with her for life. 'I was training to be a nurse and living in the nurses' lodgings. The girls would all watch for him out of the window and shout: "He's here!" Then in he would sweep on his bike with his long coat and black helmet. I would wear a canary-yellow swimming cap, just in case any rain would spoil my hair, and off we would go on all kinds of adventures.'

Grandad's trips out with Grandma became fewer and

further between as their relationship became increasingly more serious. They were saving coins for the day Grandad could write in his diary with the biggest letters he dared: 'Got Engaged!'

They were soon married, but it was fair to say that some members of Grandma's family were unsure about the suitability of my grandad for her hand. He was considered a coarse fish, as well as a coarse fisherman.

For 200 years fishing books had been written with a wonderful breadth and simplicity: no class divide, no alienating language, no suggestion of a hierarchy of rank, just the idea that angling involved a set of skills that anyone could learn to catch all species of fish. There were no discernible divisions in angling literature, and as a result very few obvious divisions in angling.

Things changed dramatically with the arrival of the twentieth century. As the fishing author Jack Hargreaves notes: 'The salmon and trout were raised to piscine peerage and the rest were called by the new name of "coarse fish". By the years between the wars the assumption that gentlemen went fly-fishing while ordinary men confined themselves to cork and quill was so well established that nobody would have believed the idea to be scarcely more than a generation old. The two tribes developed their separate private mysteries, and fishing books were pretty well divided into two classes – *Where My Fly Has Fallen* (cream-laid in handsome boards), and *Gentles and Groundbait* (paperbacked).'

The prevailing wisdom dictated that 'coarse' fish were rougher, dirtier and easier to catch, to be targeted by the great unwashed public using their crude tactics, whereas the 'game' fish, by contrast, were much more exclusive. It all came down to little more than the presence of a small rayless fin found behind the dorsal. This, the 'adipose' fin, carried the weight of an elitist fantasy on its fleshy form, marking these fish, the salmon, the sea trout, the grayling, as the target of the more distinguished sportsmen. The sheer volume of writing since the world wars has only served to progress this prejudice. Quite honestly, I can count on one hand how many recent fishing books care to mention the fallacy behind the origins of the 'coarse' and 'game' classification. An utterly standard reading occurs in the opening pages of Jeremy Paxman's *Fish, Fishing and the Meaning of Life*, where he highlights the sense of superiority of 'the grander British rivers and clubs' in describing the game fish as 'wilder, freer and harder to catch', before touting 'fly fishing' as the advanced version of the sport because it is 'more dainty, more predicated upon observation of the natural world, requiring greater precision and skill'. Warming to his theme Paxman concludes: 'The numinous properties of fly fishing are held to embody some Platonic ideal of fishing.'

Paxman, I believe, must have his tongue slightly in his cheek, but, really, the 'Platonic ideal of fishing'? As any serious angler of any discipline will tell you, there is just as much skill and precision required in any aspect of fishing you choose to master. The lure anglers who can flick their trap to within an inch of an overhanging branch have equivalent finesse to the fly casters who can drop a fly on a handkerchief; the pole fishermen, who tie their rig to such a level of precision that it becomes virtually invisible to its quarry, pay the same attention to detail as the fastidious fly tier; and the trotting special-ists, who can weave their float perfectly around obstacles and catch fish from a hundred feet away, utilize the same watercraft as the very best of the crack fly-anglers. In actuality, I have yet to meet any successful angler, of any discipline, who has not spent some several thousand hours reading the water and learning to interpret the habits and routines of whichever fish they hope to trap. As far as I can tell this game vs coarse snobbery is designed to catch the fisherman and not the fish: a care-fully crafted sales pitch to boost egos and lighten wallets, as, make absolutely no mistake, when it comes to fresh-water angling there is no division of the sport that can end up costing you more money than a few weeks on the fly.

Fish don't recognize the size of your bank balance; nor do they care who you are or where you're from, a fact borne out by the vast numbers of celebrities who go fishing precisely to feel a sense of anonymity. Just as game fishing does indeed attract a high percentage of the more well-heeled members of society, there is noth-ing to stop that very same class of person enjoying an afternoon drowning maggots down the local carp pond.

Equally, for every salmon fisher dropping a rapper's bankroll on a helicopter fishing trip to Russia's Kamchatka peninsula, or a weekend fishing the Junction pool at Kelso, there are hundreds more catching salmon on cheap season tickets up and down the country, especially on urban rivers like the Clyde and my own Taff in Wales. We are all equal before the fish and yet this sense of a divide has successfully bored its way deep into our collective angling consciousness. It serves to do our sport absolutely no favours.

Of course, I was immune to all this nonsense as a child. I just did whatever Grandad told me to do, and as the only exposure I had to angling literature was the inclusively penned Wilson *Encyclopedia*, I had no reason to suspect there was any sort of divide in the sport. Age and experience narrow the mind. It wasn't long into my teenage years when I began to notice a divide between 'us and them'. None of the magazines I ever bought (*Angler's Mail*, *Angling Times*, *Improve Your Coarse Fishing*, *Carp Talk*, etc.) ever mentioned fly-fishing, and when I did eventually locate the game-fishing publications I discovered they were in a different part of the newsagent's altogether, apparently more comfortable rubbing shoulders with copies of *Tatler* and *Horse and Hound* than they were *Auto Trader* and *Guns and Ammo*.

Against my better judgement I began to buy into the prejudice. Fly-fishing and fly-fishermen really were fundamentally different to Grandad and me and, as we had no real chance to fly-fish in the Fens anyway, it wasn't exactly hard to buy in to the idea. On the one occasion we did actually try it, during a family holiday to Scotland, it became pretty clear that we were both spectacularly awful at it anyway, and when you've spent most of your life getting good at one particular aspect of fishing it is extremely hard to go back to being terrible again. To our great discredit, the fly rods were quickly binned.

My dad, however, did have what it took to stick at it. His work had mostly kept him away from the bank with Grandad and me, but fishing wasn't really his thing when I was a child anyway. By the time I was able to take myself fishing Dad had extended his hobbies beyond birdwatching and butterfly collecting to include scuba diving, a sport where he really could enter the fishes' world and examine them at first hand. He loved to dive, and gave me a great many tips on finding fish, particularly the specific sorts of structure favoured by the perch, but around the same time my carp fishing was at its peak he had been forced to hang up his tanks. A fish-shaped void was left behind, and given he had recently moved north to the trout rivers of the Yorkshire Dales, it made sense that he finally learnt how to fly-fish properly.

Fly-fishing made sense to Dad. He understood a lot more than most about the trout's invertebrate prey, and there was something about the surgical accuracy of the cast and meticulous preparation of the artificial fly that I think appealed to his diligence as a doctor, but the fact that game fishing was never taken seriously by Grandad would definitely have appealed too. Grandad was impossible to beat at any of the sports he played or followed. Even if you weren't interested in having a competition with him, from dominoes to bowls, to rugby union and Test match cricket, or the FA cup draw on the television, you could not avoid being dragged into some sort of gentleman's wager, which he would, with unerring inevitability, win.

Dad had tried to distinguish himself before. Grandma once told me he had taken up table tennis at school purely because it was a sport Grandad didn't play. Grandad, who was also in the room at the time, laughed so hard that you could see his great golden molars shaking in their root canals, before regaling us both with a protracted and highly detailed story of a table tennis triumph that had seen him smoke the entire opposition in a county-wide Bedfordshire tournament. Grandad had, at least, the self-awareness not to let on to his teenage son about his latent talents at the time. Fly-fishing, though, was something he had genuinely shied away from. I am certain if I had ever pressed him for a reason he would have trotted out the idea of fly-fishing being a sport for a certain type of person, from a certain type of background, but I knew from our Scotland trip that in reality Grandad simply wasn't very good at it. In our family, Dad became the master of the fly.

It feels right to me to have the salmon making its appearance in these pages after the eel. Both of them are undeniably magnificent travellers, but, I'm afraid to say, in terms of raw underdog spirit the eel has to trump the salmon. However, the eel will simply never move people in the same way as the salmon. The 'King of Fish' has achieved an enduring status in our collective imaginations, spawning hundreds of pieces of literature and featuring in innumerable documentaries, films, poems and folk stories. There is scarcely another freshwater creature on earth that has had such an impact on world culture: the salmon, quite simply, is one of the most instantly recognizable and well-known fish that ever there was.

Most have heard of the legendary Pacific salmon run of North America, where millions of returning chum, pink, chinook and coho salmon come back from the sea to spawn in salmon 'redds', those small nests dug by female fish into pebbly patches of gravel; but few realize this mass replenishment of salmon numbers also feeds thousands of bears, wolves and birds, and that, in death, the release of nitrogen from the salmon's rotting body is so great that it sustains some 12,000 square miles of Canada's Great Bear Forest. Indeed, in the peak years of the run, when numbers of salmon are at their highest, scientists have found spruce trees where 80 per cent of their nitrogen is provided by the fish alone.

In the UK, if you head to a weir on any of our Atlantic salmon rivers in early autumn, you stand a very good chance of experiencing the seminal salmonoid event of our own returning running fish. It was this season at the

Blackweir on the River Taff where it last happened for me, and, although it might have lacked the sheer strength in numbers of a Pacific run, at least the action didn't take place deep in some montane wilderness; in fact I was staring at the turbulent waters on the corner of Bute Park with a mother and child, a city boy in a suit, a cyclist in lycra and a man in a turban.

Such is the wonder of urban wildlife. We were bound not by action on a silver screen taking place hundreds of miles from home, but by the silvery flash we all witnessed just minutes from our own doors and offices. The salmon's task was formidable, seemingly impossible, but this fish had already fought ridiculous odds just to make it back here. It leapt forward and we started to cheer.

Attacking the fast water head on it slid down the weir's face again and again. We counted over a dozen fails. The Blackweir is a horrible obstacle, a steep tongue of smoothened concrete, a hangover from an age when we needed to harness our waters for industrial production, and with the river nearly in spate the sheer volume of water spilling down the ramp threatened to utterly overwhelm this fish.

Surely the salmon was running out of steam on its umpteenth attempt? Human naivety. The fish had simply been plotting its course, working out the weaknesses, the faults and lines of least resistance. With each move calculated and carefully tested, it was time for the final push.

Once more it emerged and our excitement threatened to overspill. Fists, palms and brollies belted the iron bridge we had gathered upon. A mighty leap brought a skittering zig-zag run that closed the distance to the top lip of the weir. An arching sweep, so uniform it could've been drawn with a compass, placed our fish directly below the top pool, and a simple dip and flick of the tail propelled it neatly up and over the lip. Noiselessly it continued into the next stage of its life. We let out a collective sigh of relief and drifted our separate ways.

As Michael Wigan describes in his 2013 book *The Salmon*, both the Pacific and Atlantic salmon are facing multi-pronged threats today. Man's lack of foresight in the construction of weirs and, in particular, monstrous dams, as well as unregulated salmon netting, poaching, pollution, and the same manmade climate change that thwarts the eel's navigation, is overpowering the salmon species. On the West Coast of the States, the *Scientific American* claims, salmon numbers are down by as much as 99.9 per cent since European settlement began, and, industrial pollution had all but wiped out the salmon on Britain's Taff, Tyne and Clyde rivers by the 1980s. If you thought that farming salmon in pens might provide an easy solution to the industrial-scale harvest of the wild population, then I am afraid the unfortunate plague of parasitic sea lice released as a by-product of that practice has put paid to that. In 2012 the Royal Society estimated that a shocking 39 per cent of wild Atlantic salmon were dying from this parasite alone. They simply attach themselves to the wild fish as they pass the pens, tear into their flesh, and slaughter them in their thousands.

It might seem yet another boorish example of man's commercial ambition trumping that of a lowly fish, but it is worth bearing in mind that the value of recreational salmon fishing to the economy is hardly chump change. In Canada every single freshwater rod-caught salmon is estimated to be worth over £700, and in Scotland salmon fishing represents almost 3,000 local jobs and generates some £120 million a year. Big money by any marker, but when you also consider that salmon fishing is taking place in some of the most remote and rural areas on earth, where money and secure local employment are increasingly hard to come by, then the value of this fish really cannot be overstated. For many, salmon fishing is a vital lifeline in a world of diminishing opportunities.

Without question, commercial salmon harvesting and intensive salmon farming practices need to be curbed and regulated. New dams and weirs should have fish ladders built into their designs as a mandatory part of any construction agreement, or, better yet, they should be torn down altogether. The United States has dismantled over 150 dams since the turn of the century, to no small benefit for the salmon, and on my home river the simple acts of deconstructing weirs and thoughtful restocking have made the Taff salmon the most resurgent population in England and Wales put together. The banks of Scotland's River Tweed, which contains the largest salmon population in Europe, have been protected from cattle and sheep overgrazing by fencing along the river's length. This has allowed the river to mature more naturally and has resulted in some of the largest catch returns in recent history. Even in the absolute worst-case scenarios nature has an unerring way of filling a vacuum when it is given the chance. In my lifetime the salmon of both the Tyne and the Clyde have also made a comeback on rivers that were salmon-free deserts in their industrial heyday.

Having hatched and successfully completed the transformation from small salmon parr to finger-sized salmon smolt (a feat that is only achieved by one fish in every ten), the young fish then enters salt water for the first time. Here it must avoid a phalanx of marine predators, everything from grey seals to skates, sharks and seabirds, while making its way north to the great pelagic feeding grounds off Greenland and the Faroe Islands. If the smolt successfully runs the 3,000-kilometre gauntlet, without being killed, then it can expect to seriously pile on the pounds. Protein banquets of shrimps, sand eels, fish fry and krill funnel into the extreme parts of the northern Atlantic, allowing the salmon to fatten up over a period of up to four years. They can reach weights in excess of 50lb, several hundred times bigger than their size on leaving the rivers, but eventually a hormonal release will call them back across the ocean. All the way home to the very rivers that once gave them life.

Scientists believe that the remarkable journey could

involve a mix of celestial navigation, magnetic fields, ocean currents and even chemical memory. Some salmon have even been known to locate the precise pool they were birthed in. Truly extraordinary behaviour that is without parallel in the animal kingdom; just last week I couldn't even find my way back to a house I'd lived in for over a year.

The sheer bloody-mindedness of the breeding salmon cannot be underestimated. Not only will they surmount all manner of obstacles to achieve their goal, but once they return to fresh water they will not eat another thing. The homecoming adult salmon is entirely reliant on the seafood reserves it built up in the north, so much so that the stomach actually begins to disintegrate to allow the fish to pack in more eggs or sperm for breeding. The suicide pact has been made: from that point on it's breed and die. Which prompts the question: if they don't feed, just how do you convince them to take a bait?

Wilson comments in the *Encyclopedia* that a salmon 'instinctively' snaps at 'worms, spinners and particularly shrimps', but when it comes to the purist, tactics begin and end with the artificial fly.

There is a blistering array of painstakingly designed and hand-tied flies, crafted from natural furs, silks and cottons to imitate everything from tiny nymphs right up to palm-sized baitfish, but, whatever you choose, fly-fishing is unique in that the weight of the cast comes from your line and not your end tackle. It means your chance of catching a fish of any description relies heavily on your ability to cast well.

The perfect fly cast begins with you gradually releasing line from a reel while making false casts overhead, extending the line, and your fly, out across the river incrementally, without ever losing a metronomic rhythm to your casting arm. Sounds hard, but all being well, you release your line in the final cast and watch it unfurl like the striking arm of a darts player, hitting a bull's-eye on the far bank and sweeping your fly upstream towards the fish in a single, beautiful arc.

In other forms of fishing you may well be able to glean a lot from the armchair, but the fly cast is so much more about 'the feel' than it is about careful study. The best fly casters I've ever met struggle to articulate what makes them so good at the sport: they sort of stammer through a few platitudes, and might even offer to cradle your arms from behind as you try, but it never really works. The fact is that, much like throwing a dart at a board, when you are learning to cast and finally get it right, it feels so fluid and natural that you will wonder just how you managed to get it so badly wrong for the previous 4,000 attempts. That's the thing with fly-fishing. It feels utterly improbable, from the weird casting technique to the fact that you are trying to convince a fish that a piece of fluff is worth having, but when it all comes together, the thrill is almost without parallel in angling.

I could cast well enough on a short rod and had spent some time fly-fishing with Dad on several occasions. My best trout on the fly might have been a 6lb humpbacked Franken-fish from a stocked pond, but I had experienced what it was like to 'get it right' on a river on a couple of occasions. An evening fly-fishing above the town bridge at Pontypridd allowed me to borrow the feeling of what it must be like to actually be quite good at fly-fishing, when your cast and choice of fly come together at just the time the fish really decide to feed en masse, and earlier that same season, while I was flicking a fly armed with a small golden bead, a large brown trout had done me a huge favour from deep within a concrete pipe nestled in front of Merthyr Tydfil's central bus station. In both instances I had been fishing under the wing of truly skilled operators, though, lifelong fly-fishermen who instinctively knew the habits of the trout. When it came to casting for salmon I was completely in the dark.

Bill Currie notes in *Days and Nights of Game Fishing* that 'trout fishing is much more reasonable, more logical and in every way a more delicate art . . . It would perhaps be better if I gave no explanation for wanting so much to fish for salmon.' Although trout fishing might sometimes be very hard, at least you know the fish must eventually come on to feed. Salmon fishing is absolutely ridiculous from the outset, so when Dad called to invite me onto his annual trip to Scotland, that gave me pause for thought, but, then, I've never turned down a fishing trip, so . . .

There are over 300 salmon rivers to discover in Scotland and my dad, alongside a small group of his fly-fishing friends, had visited a fair few of the most legendary rivers. Lately, however, they had gone fairly static at one location, the River Findhorn, where, if they were to be believed, they had discovered something of a sweet spot, at which the quality of fishing, natural surroundings and après-fishing verged on perfection.

My salmon from the Taff was caught on coarse tactics, and although I was mightily pleased with the capture, I had to admit I was curious to try and catch one as a purist would. More than anything, though, I wanted to learn why my dad was so enthused about salmon fishing in particular. Whatever it was, it went far beyond an adolescent desire to find something other than table tennis that Grandad couldn't do; the way he spoke of the Findhorn was as if he had had some sort of a spiritual awakening. Believe me, from a man armed with the brand of analytical mind that my dad had it was quite something to hear.

For the last couple of years he had returned from the Findhorn with beautiful stories and pictures, and although he would be the first to admit that salmon fishing could never fill the void in his life left by scuba diving, it was clear that in the Findhorn he had found something which ran it pretty close.

With no spinning tackle, no coarse tactics – in fact, no rod, line or tackle to call my own – I hopped into the van and began the very long journey towards salmon fishing's tweed-covered heart. I considered the chances of a record-breaking salmon as I made my way north.

Wilson notes the salmon-fishing record stands at a whopping 64lb, but this entry in the *Encyclopedia* does little to conjure up any of the sentiment or the story behind this remarkable fish or the woman who landed it.

Etched into my memory is a faded sepia image of Miss Georgina Ballantine. She is wearing all tweed, a wrap-round jacket partnered with a long woollen skirt, and is leaning up against her rods with what might appear to be a practised nonchalance. Her spare hand is casually placed in a pocket, but her expression, the slight angle inwards of her head, her lips, pressed together but almost upturned, in something of a Mona Lisa smile, seem to me to be screaming: 'Go on then, lads, come and have a go if you think you're hard enough.' Lying on the floor, just in front of her, is the longest-standing record in British angling history.

The image was taken on 7 October 1922, the date she landed the 64lb fish from the Glendelvine stretch of the River Tay. Georgina was simply the gillie's daughter, drafted into the trip at short notice as the local laird had pulled out with a headache, but that trip was to be life-changing.

She later gave a wonderful account of the fish's capture in a letter to her rod builder and friend, Mick Glover, in which she describes the 'Homeric battle', where her reel 'screeched as it had never screeched before', and mentions how at one stage she became so desperate she suggested pelting the fish with stones to get it to move closer to her boat. Her father, one of the finest rods in

Scotland, gave her a stiff rebuke: 'Na, na, will try nane o' thae capers.'

After two hours and five minutes she finally landed the fish, feverishly recalling: 'What eloquence could do justice to such a moment in one's life, better left to be imagined ... two hours and five minutes of nerve-wracking anxiety, thrilling excitement and good stiff work.' Her arms were so swollen afterwards that they took two weeks to recover.

Of all the things written about this fish, Bruce Sandison, a writer and longtime contributor to *Trout and Salmon* and *The Scotsman*, reveals perhaps the most telling story of the woman. 'When Georgina's salmon was displayed in the window of P. D. Malloch's shop in Perth, she stood at the back of the crowd who had gathered to admire it. Two elderly men were particularly overawed by the size of the salmon and Georgina heard them talking: one said to the other, "A woman? Nae woman ever took a fish like that oot of the water, mon. I would need a horse, a block and tackle, tae tak a fish like that oot. A woman. That's a lee anyway." She said, "I had a quiet chuckle up my sleeve and ran to catch the bus."'

How cool is she? What strength of character! What modesty! What reticence and patience, in the face of such intolerance. Female anglers are just as good as men – many are far better – yet fewer than a quarter of licences purchased each year are bought by women, and I can count on one hand the women I see regularly on the banks I fish.

Of course, attitudes have progressed markedly since Georgina's time, but I still believe there is a lingering prejudice that angling is a man's game. This falsehood, based on much the same narrow-minded thinking that led to the game and coarse divide, seems to play to the idea that as fishing requires countless hours in the cold, handling smelly baits, and, very occasionally, smellier fish, it is not something that would be attractive to women. Well, let me be the first to say that if this is all fishing boiled down to then it wouldn't be attractive to me either. I don't actually like having hands and fingernails that stink like the Seven Seas, nor do I enjoy being frozen solid to my fishing seat, and I'm not exactly 'loving it' when a bream or eel decides to coat me in its mucus, but have you ever stopped to consider that perhaps the barrier to more women in the sport, as well as young people and anyone else who might like to try one day, is the appalling job we do of presenting fishing as an appealing way to spend your time? Perhaps instead of allowing the focus to settle on the aspects of fishing that even we don't enjoy, we should be promoting what it is we all love about getting outside with a rod and reel. Better still, take a friend fishing, get them onto a fish, and then see how they feel. More than that, even if fishing is occasionally cold, smelly and boring, who is anyone to tell someone else what they can or can't do, or what they are supposed, or supposed not, to like? I do believe there are some male anglers still out there who place an unhealthy amount of their ego and, dare I say, manhood, on their ability to catch fish. This minority, and they are a minority, might very well be threatened by the idea that a woman could come along and catch a bigger fish than them, but ultimately it is of far greater importance that fishing as a sport is allowed to progress in spite of these Neanderthals and their opinions; the very future of angling could very well depend on it.

Long before I had reached the Scottish Borders I had deduced the chances of me breaking Georgina's British Atlantic salmon record were practically zero. Even if I overlook my novice's knowledge of salmon fishing, and that is a very big 'if' indeed, the Findhorn has never really been a renowned big-fish river. The Scottish crown probably still rests with the Tay, with the very occasional big fish cropping up on the Tweed, but there has been nothing substantiated on any British river that has ever come close to touching that fantastic 1922 fish.

I was easy with that, though: some records are not meant to be broken.

I left my vehicle at Mum and Dad's place in the Yorkshire Dales so Dad and I could make our way up into Scotland together. We were travelling on a Sunday, which Dad explained was the traditional 'no-fishing day' as it was when all the anglers turned around from the fishing marks, or 'beats'. There really was no rush then, which was fortunate as the A9 above Perth is a treat to savour, or, as Dad put it: 'This is where it starts to get really good.'

The further you press up into Scotland's far north the more you feel you are shedding the trappings of the rest of our densely populated island. It was cold and dry as the snow-dusted Cairngorms loomed large over our car. The hilltops had a scrubby, stripped look to them: iced at their summits, with bilberry, heather and sheep clinging to the slopes. The valleys were cut by clear rivers, the flow hefting hard over clean stones and exposing gravel beds. They looked low. 'Ignore that, just enjoy the scenery,' scolded Dad. It was like being thirteen years old again. We plunged on into a large forest and a trio of plump-looking red deer scattered behind a curtain of Scots pines.

The fishing cottage finally emerged after a final eighteen miles of real wilderness. A classic highland landscape strewn with lochs, lavender, gorse, more pine, larch, and a patch of birch trees with blistering white trunks. The satnav simply read 'road'.

I had it in my head that Dad's trips up here were something of a wilderness survival epic. That the lodgings would be one-roomed, mud-earth-floored, bothy-cum-bunkhouse affairs, where they were probably forced to forage to survive. In fact, the multi-roomed house contained several bathrooms and bedrooms, a large kitchen, an expertly tended garden and no fewer than three boxes of luxury Scottish shortbread awaiting our arrival. Dad's friend Dave had arrived ahead of us and was already in the process of unloading enough rations to last us for several weeks more than required. Dad, misinterpreting my wide-eyed astonishment as one of concern, sought to comfort me: 'Don't worry, Will. We will have food in the pub on at least one of the nights and Nigel will soon be here with his wife's homemade lasagne.' I wondered, seriously, whether I would still fit in my waders at the end of my time in Scotland.

Dave was far and away the most experienced salmon angler I had ever met. He organized the trips to Scotland and had a wealth of knowledge; as such, I hung on his words, and his words weren't that great. 'They took seventy-seven fish last April, a new Findhorn record,' he began positively.

'So where were they when we were here in March?' chirped in Dad with a chuckle.

'Still all at sea,' answered Dave solemnly, 'but the conditions are even worse for us now. We are going to have to work really hard for our fish.'

I couldn't quite believe it; having begun this adventure with it absolutely shelling it down and facing up to flooded rivers, it was now too dry.

'They just can't move. The salmon are either waiting to enter the river or they are stuck in the pools and going into a dormant state.' Dave glanced outside at the crisp weather and clear skies with more than just a furrow in his brow. 'We need two foot of water from somewhere.' Praying for rain in Scotland. I'd seen it all.

At daybreak I shuffled my feet through leaves that crunched as if they had been baked in salt overnight. It hadn't rained but I did have a raging headache. Nigel had arrived after dark, barrelling through the doors with irrepressible energy, his wife's lasagne and a fantastically rural Lincolnshire accent on hand. As is typical on virtually any holiday exclusively for adults, we got over-excited at the prospect of the coming days, overdid it on the wine, and then decided an impromptu blind tasting of all the single malts we had brought with us was a brilliant idea. I had comfortably lost the game to my more experienced company and was now feeling decidedly rough. Luckily, though, the Findhorn was poised to provide perfect distraction. In front of a fishing hut that wouldn't have looked out of place in backwoods Alaska, the river swept my hangover away with all her majesty.

I'm not basing this on any knowledge of course, but the Tweed always sounded a bit twee to me. Prolific for sure, and very pretty, but its Borders location made it all feel a little too accessible and easy. The Findhorn, however, purely by name alone, conjured up images of a craggy and mysterious waterway, a place frequented by trolls and witches, where you might even still find an army of Iron Age Picts, casually barbecuing a deer and entirely unaware that Hadrian's Wall had been turned into a tourist attraction.

In actuality the Findhorn was all of these things and more. It cut a deep cleft in the side of a heavily forested ravine and the size of the stones scattered on the outside of the bend acted as a testament to the sheer violence the river could wreak. The carpet of moss and lichen on practically every tree in view lent the place a magical green hue. It hummed with wildlife, and confident-looking chaffinch and robin took scraps of bread practically from our fingertips. I sipped at a fortifying cup of tea and noted a community of toads swirling in the pools below my feet. Further down, mustelid prints on virtually every exposed patch of sand signalled that there was a very healthy population of otters in residence.

The river was impossible to ignore. It meandered under a compelling black-tea curtain of colour in the deeper pools and broke into a forceful white in the shallows and rapid tops, clattering over the rocks with a hollow, rolling sound like a bottle of champagne might, if you threw it down a flight of stairs. I shuddered at the thought of what it must look like in high water and was warned to be very careful if I headed upstream into the gorge – downpours brought instant changes to the Findhorn's water levels, blasting the gorge with water and claiming the lives of unsuspecting wading anglers in times past.

Our gillie, George, a very friendly old Scotsman who wore a traditional tweed cap and smart-looking tie, had offered to help me learn to Spey cast. It was a new but necessary discipline. The salmon rod required the use of two hands on the cork grip and was much longer and heavier than I was used to. The lines were much thicker too, and, as I would have to cast some distance at times, it was best that I learn how to execute the cast correctly.

The Spey cast, so named after the wide Scottish river, provided the salmon angler with a far more powerful cast than what could be achieved on standard trout-fishing gear; critically, the method also kept most of your line in motion in front of you, meaning that you could cast a considerable distance even with obstacles, such as trees and bushes, directly over your shoulders.

I carefully taped up the joints of the rod Dad had lent me for the trip – apparently the jolting shock of the Spey cast had enough beef to occasionally rip rod sections apart. I doubted I'd generate enough power to achieve that feat, but I enjoyed playing along as if I could. I had tried to Spey cast once before, on the River Wye. A friend of a friend had a regular rod up there, and, unable to make it one evening, it got offered out to us. I leapt at the chance, but, unfortunately, I found Spey casting about as subtle as fishing with a giant broom handle and ship's rope. Angling success revolves around confidence, and, as I had none, we quickly gave up and went to the pub.

'Lift up the rod tip, roll to your right, arch the tip down and cast in a D-shaped motion aiming the fly for the far bank.' Poor George must have said it a hundred times, patiently showing me again and again how to do it, as my brow beaded with anxious sweat. 'Keep that fly away!' implored George. 'You were looking good till you collapsed at the end, and that brings the fly closer into you.' He wasn't kidding. We spent a good few minutes extracting the salmon fly from deep within the neoprene that covered my rear end.

We were attempting to fish the very top of a milk-bottle-shaped stretch of water. The far bank was severely undercut by the flow of the Findhorn, red stone warped into attractive-looking coves and flat platforms, good fish-holding areas if only I could reach them. Eventually I learnt to keep the fly away from my underpants but I just couldn't get the distance no matter how hard I punched the rod out. 'You need to relax and feel for a rhythm,' said George. 'The best casters are the lady fishers,' he continued, reaching gently for my wrist. 'Relax your grip.' I did, and a couple of hours later my casting had improved markedly.

'Let me have a look at that fly,' George said after a time. I swung it in towards George's fingers. 'Blimey, it's as bare as a baby's behind!' he exclaimed. He was right – my fly was ruined from the constant whipping through the air and contact with objects other than the water. He flicked open a box of flies as colourful as a tub of Quality Street chocolates and selected a double-hooked and bright-blue number. 'Let's try that all again from the top of the beat.'

Almost immediately a shuddering take developed into a short but firm fight. I landed a fin-perfect brown trout just shy of the bottle's neck, and consecutive casts brought me two more fish: tiny salmon parr this time, my first Scottish salmon, of sorts. 'I think I'll celebrate with my disgusting habit,' George laughed, and sparked up a cigarette.

Clearly Spey casting wasn't supposed to be as brutal

as I had thought, and even with a stiff thirteen-foot rod, 15lb leader and enormous fly I had really felt the bites I'd had. Even those salmon parr, fish of no more than a couple of ounces each, had given a satisfying thump. Goodness knows what a fully fledged salmon must feel like then. 'Just make sure you get through the first line of the national anthem before lifting into it,' advised Nigel at lunchtime. 'The absolute worst thing you can do is strike,' added Dave, 'just tighten down on the fish gradually and you'll soon find it's on.'

The first day closed out with a single small salmon taking a swish at my fly. 'They are in there if we can just find a way to switch them on,' remarked Dave as we packed up the gear. 'I saw one of about five pounds up the top. She was bootiful,' purred Nigel, 'scarpered as soon as she saw me, mind.'

That evening Dad told me how Grandad had taken him to fish Ireland's Blackwater River. 'It was one of the best day's fishing Grandad had ever had.' I could tell by the way Dad began the story it was far from his best day. He took a sip of his beer and continued. 'We fished at the mouth of a waste pipe flowing from an abattoir. The anglers lined up and waited for the squeal from the pigs inside, then the pipe would churn out enough blood to turn a whole section of the river red. "Quick, son. Get the net and hook out all the blood clots," he'd say; stringy, worm-like, woollen lengths of clotted blood which he'd hook and trot downstream in the hope of big bream.'

It was a horrific tale and I could palpably feel Dad's sense of revulsion in the retelling. 'I remember catching a massive dace that day.' He indicated the fish's considerable size between his palms, but his tone was one of disgust. 'It was horrible. Its gills poured with pig's blood. I put it straight back in.'

The next morning we all stood outside in the mist as Dad diligently checked the moth traps he had set up overnight, his friends indulging him as he gleefully called out the names of each species: 'Red and green carpet! Hebrew character! Oh! Wonderful! A nut-tree tussock!'

It was hard to reconcile Dad's character with that of his father. Grandad was simply a product of a very different era. Dad was all peace and love, punk and revolution, tight trousers, big hair and open-minded, blue-sky thinking. Grandad, in spite of his rebellious, anti-authoritarian streak, was still operating within the confines of an ultra-conservative world that had just survived one of the most severe wartime periods ever. Back then animal welfare and ethical considerations were the indulgence of those who lived in lands of plenty and peacetime. Any small edge offered was exploited to its maximum advantage at a time when the screws were really being twisted. You simply never knew when, or if, any edge might be offered again.

Perhaps catching fish on pig's blood wasn't the end of the world. You could argue it wasn't exactly adding to the harm of the slaughterhouse, simply by using its waste product, but that day at the Blackwater the war had finished a very long time ago, and, clearly, Grandad's actions were upsetting his young son.

Grandad remained tough and uncompromising throughout his life. He never seemed to take a backward step over anything; I can't even recall him ever apologizing. I used to admire his doggedness, his ability to laugh off almost anything, and interpreted his stubbornness as strength. To no little extent, I modelled myself on him when I was a young man. Only now it seems a little excessive, inconsiderate even.

The moth collection was so much fun we lost track of ourselves and turned up quite late at the river. Grandad would never have done that, I thought, he would've fished a burning ghat on the Ganges with a human head for bait if he'd thought it would have put him onto a monster. For Dad, though, the Findhorn was more than just the sum of its fish.

'Dad . . .' We sat together on a rock promontory looking directly down into a pool. '. . . this is as close to perfect as I think it's possible for a salmon run to be.'

We had headed further up into the gorge than I had been before, scrambling over rocks and occasionally pulling ourselves along the smooth, rock-slab sides by rope to get right to the very top of the beat. It was steep and tight but there was still a prevailing quality to the air of a sort of breathy alpine atmosphere that is only really felt in the bands of forest at the extreme ends of the globe. It didn't feel claustrophobic in there in the slightest. Pungent pine and birch forests stood tall above a maze of warped and twisted boulders, the largest of which tapered high above me as if dropped from a giant Mr Whippy ice cream machine. In spite of the lack of water, the pools in the gorge still looked very deep and alluring.

'I'm sorry, Dad.' I picked myself off the stone and reached for my rod. 'I can't wait any longer, I've got to have a cast.'

The water cascaded down in great steps of a dozen or more. At points the entry to a pool was little more than a foot or two wide, the full force of the Findhorn's flow channelled through a natural gap you could quite easily hop across. It seemed highly improbable that any living creature could be able to swim against such power, but clearly the salmon here had found a way; of greater concern, then, was what might happen if I hooked a fish in one of these pools and it decided to exit via such an opening? Surely it would be impossible to stay in touch with a fish if that was its will? It was a prospect that was both inviting and intimidating in equal measure.

We took the pools on methodically, covering the water twice over before moving on down the staircase. I came nose to nose with a deer at one point and we both watched a goosander chase, then swallow whole, a trout. The salmon, though, continued to evade us.

We headed ever deeper into the gorge. Our nets and rods slung over our shoulders or held in our teeth as we were forced to rock-climb with greater regularity. 'It's guerrilla fishing, Dad!' I called out, as he swung on a rope. Finally, I was about as far from the commercial fishery as it was possible to be. The sense of relief was palpable and, to no small degree, I felt I had achieved one of the major ambitions I had set myself at the outset of this journey. Unquestionably, I had dipped a line in some wonderful places before coming here, but the Findhorn was in a different class of magnificence; a big fish now would be very nice indeed.

In the last pool of the beat Dad makes a long cast and lets his fly drift along the edge of some rocks and out across the deeper water. It sinks into the depths and he begins a jerking retrieve, lifting the fly, which I notice looks very much like a small carrot, up through the water column and towards the surface.

I'm sat high above the pool so I get a very clear view of what happens next. Just as the fly looks like it might break the surface, right at the edge of the deeper water, a salmon resembling a silver submarine emerges directly underneath the carrot, swims to within an inch of the hooks, and then drifts back into the shadows.

I am utterly stunned, but I know I can't exactly start shouting down to Dad and risk scaring the fish. I stare at his head. Trying to project the scene into his brain, or at least get some sort of telepathic communication going where he might think to look up at me. It's pointless though; he's locked within his own little world and definitely did not see the fish. He re-casts and nothing happens. Maybe I imagined it? He casts again and up it floats once again. It really is huge, comfortably the biggest salmon I've ever seen, clearly over 15lb, at a push possibly even 20lb.

'Dad!' I can't help myself. 'Dad!' I try again in my best shout-whisper. I can see he's considering changing his fly. Bollocks to it. 'Dad!' I really shout it this time. He looks straight up at me, smiling. 'There is a massive salmon in that pool! He's gone for that fly twice!' He wasn't smiling any more. The fly was cast and re-cast, right back into the hole.

How many times has that happened when I've been fishing, I wonder? How close have I been to my own leviathan and not even realized it was there? Surely that fish is going to go for it this time though. I watch on, holding my breath, and Dad gets that great fish to rise up again.

Many months later I read the following words by Michael Wigan: 'A salmon that has dwelt in one place for a month may have watched innumerable flies swinging over it and pays them no greater attention than the man on the park bench does who subconsciously watches buses looping their circuit.'

I wish I had known that then. The fish, like a jealous boyfriend removing his girlfriend from a club, nosed right up to Dad's fly and chaperoned it from the pool. We tried every fly in the box after that, but only Dave managed to get that great fish to move again. However, it was not going to make a mistake for any of us. That salmon wasn't interested in anything other than rain and spawn.

*

The story of Dad fishing with the blood clots hadn't actually been news to me. Grandad had told me about that treasured memory before – of course he had, he broke his bream record twice that day. It was the other fishing memories that spilled from Dad's head, mundane stories when records weren't on the menu, that were much more telling about their relationship.

'I would have to trudge behind him for miles carrying his gear,' recalled Dad, 'off to some distant swim where we would sit in the cold for hours and if I tangled my line that was it. I was on my own. It would reduce me to tears trying to unknot those bird's nest tangles as he just carried on fishing.'

Grandad was extraordinarily blinkered when it came to his determination to catch for himself, and even when Dad did manage to cast a line and hook into something it was hardly a cause for celebration. 'I remember him putting a huge lobworm on my hook and me then landing this really big perch. You'd think he'd be pleased, but he was absolutely green with envy!'

We both laughed. I could picture it perfectly.

It was all beginning to add up. It had never been about sharing his world with others, it was about catching well and winning. It felt obviously and immediately familiar. It was me.

I was strangely relieved. All this time I had been chasing Grandad's higher wisdom it had never actually occurred to me that he had been bound by exactly the same failings as me when he was on the banks as a younger man; but he must have changed at some point later in his life. Grandad may have resembled his younger self at times, but he was undoubtedly a lot more relaxed on the banks we had shared. I wondered when the transformation in him had occurred, and why?

When he taught me to fish he spent far more time paying me close attention than he did actually fishing himself. If I tangled my lines he would make me untangle them, but he would always help; he would never have fished on. Two stories stuck in my mind as Dad recounted his experiences: the first was an evening when Grandad and Grandma were babysitting us and Grandad spent the entire night carefully untangling one of my rods for me; the second was the absolute pleasure he took in seeing me catch a big fish. When I was eight years old he helped me land a thuggish and powerful tench, scooping it out of the river with handfuls of lily stems, embracing me and cheering with joy.

The late, great fishing godfather Bernard Venables famously noted the three stages of an angler's evolution, summarized by Luke Jennings in the excellent *Blood Knots*: 'To begin with, as a child, you just want to catch fish, any fish. Then you move to the stage where you want to catch big fish. And finally, with nothing left to prove, you reach a place where it's the manner of the catch that counts, the rigour and challenge of it, at which point the whole thing takes on an intellectual and perhaps even a philosophical cast.'

Fishermen reflect their life in their fishing. Grandad

just didn't have anything left to prove, to himself, to the world of man, fish or his son, by the time I turned up with my 'Argos Introduction to Fishing Kit'. Grandparents often become second parents, but they get second chances too.

'I make a very close link between our belonging here and the will to fish,' Bernard Venables said towards the latter stages of his own career. 'Most of the things which are least pleasant about life now are the things which are most antithetical to fishing.' Fishing, he believed, was sullied by competition, by men taking on other men, by obsessing over size and records, by inviting self-promotion and all the jealousy that came with it. It took my Grandad a long time, but as we headed towards our last casts together he cared for nothing more than company.

There was more to Grandad curbing his enthusiasm for competition than simply a mellowing with age, however; if he really had always been obsessed with just catching, then the commercial carp fishery would have represented the absolute zenith of his angling ambitions, and the modernization of the sport, the carbon elasticated poles, the baitrunners on reels, the bite alarms and synthetic baits, would all have been must-haves in the decades before his epiphany. Yet, even when he was at his most addicted to the sport, his methods barely changed from when he was a child.

Grandad despised the commercial carp fishery as it suppressed the wild and precarious element for which he fished. Fishing rivers was a distillation of his character: unpredictable and bold. He felt changes in fishing eviscerated the sport of its elemental sense of fairness and dulled the angler's wits and skill. On that, he had common ground with his son; plus, they were both fantastic observers of the natural world.

Fairness and a keen eye for nature. For all Grandad's faults, they were two great traits to pass on to his son. Dad had just applied their uses to different ends and standards, but he was still his father's son.

Stepping out of your dad's shadow can be hard. Grandad had been a legend in his own lifetime, and my dad, the local doctor, was known by everyone in my area. I occasionally found it hard too. A lot of people really looked up to my dad and I felt, as the doctor's son, that I was expected to behave in a certain way. People knew who I was, and even though it wasn't ever said, I felt whatever I did would be held up for extra scrutiny as a result of my dad.

I wonder whether that influenced me in my determination to plough my own furrow later in life. I knew my expeditions were something that Dad could and would never do. They were dangerous and risky, and they had no obvious outcomes, pay cheques or prospects. He made it very clear he didn't approve of me leaving steady jobs to pursue those dreams, and that served to spur me on even more to make a success of what I was trying to do.

It was hardly a wholesale rejection of him, though. I

massively coveted my dad's attention and approval, more than anything else in fact, and when he showed any interest in what I was doing I gratefully embraced him within my world.

It's the curious dichotomy of growing up, the desperate rejection of figureheads while secretly wanting to imitate them at almost every stage of our lives. For most of us a predictable pattern inevitably follows that sees us steadily morphing into a version of the very role models we spent so much of our energy and time denigrating. In that, I was no exception.

More and more I see my own father in me. Not just a zero-tolerance attitude for lateness at airports, but an appreciation of life's details and an interest in how the world ticks, for both good and bad. I don't feel like I am in such an enormous rush any more, that it's me versus the world, or that I'm constantly having to prove myself to other people, but I haven't quite abandoned Venables' second stage of the angler's evolution either. So I still occasionally seek big fish and big challenges, but at least I know enough now to try to live and fish for the things that make me, and the people closest to me, happiest. I have always loved my dad, and only hope I might be half the man he is one day.

I was alone in the gorge as my fly descended neatly into the mouth of a salmon. It rose up from behind a rock and sucked it right in. It was so close I could see the sun reflecting off the white on the roof of its mouth. Indeed,

I was so close I was also able to perfectly track the frame of the fly leaving the fish's mouth and disappearing around the bend.

The old suck and blow. It had done me in.

It was as close as I got to snaring my first salmon on the fly but I wasn't too disheartened. As Dad, Nigel and I made to leave, Dave stayed on with his new recruit, another superb salmon fisherman named Jon. 'We used to fish all the time with a friend who once went thirteen years without a salmon,' Jon began. 'He'd come with us and we would always let him take the first cast in the top pools or the water that was easier to fish but he just caught nothing. It must've been so disheartening, especially when we would catch on a pool he had just left. Then, one day on the Dee, he caught two grilse to start, then a springer salmon. It was like a curse was lifted, he didn't stop catching after that.' I just needed some more time.

Nothing was caught for the rest of the week but I emerged from my time on the Findhorn deeply satisfied in a way I hadn't been for years. If I had already been surprised to learn that it doesn't matter if you don't catch anything big, I was quite shocked to realize that it actually doesn't matter if sometimes you don't catch anything at all.

'Grandad, I've got someone I would like you to meet.'

I had seen Grandad almost every day when I lived with my sister and James back in the Fens, but since I'd moved back to Cardiff to work on the BBC series my visits to his home had become inevitably more infrequent. His dementia had been steadily worsening over the last year, but in the last few months it had become really quite severe. He was living in a residential care home away from Grandma and spent the greater part of his days asleep in a chair, not really aware of where or who he was most of the time, and barely speaking at all.

I squeezed his hand and repeated my words. I had warned Emma about his state, but I had wanted him to meet her anyway, even if it was only to be a token gesture.

She took his hand tenderly and, quite suddenly, some light penetrated the dark clouds that had previously been puddling his mind. He woke up, and in that moment seemed to return to the saddle of his motorbike. Screaming into the nurses' quarters with his shock of black hair and that 'devil may care' attitude.

'Grandad, this is Emma.'

He took her in through his big brown eyes and flashed her a handsome grin.

'Hello, Ken,' Emma blushed, 'is Will a good fisherman?'

'He thinks he is,' he replied.

The cheeky bugger.

I held his other hand. They were the last words we would share together.

Three years after I caught that first Taff salmon, Emma and I returned to the very spot where the fish was caught. It was cold and the River Taff was in a foul mood. I had a couple of casts but sometimes there is no serendipity to fishing. I knew I didn't need that fish any more. Perhaps the river knew it too.

That weekend we were married.

Coming Home

For all our time together in the Fens the thick-lipped and fat-chested chub was very much Grandad's fish. He talked about catching them from the running water around Bedfordshire with relish: 'Large lumps of bread crust or a plump slug, that's all you need for a whackin' great chub, my boy.' I caught my first one on a metal spinner and wisely elected not to tell him anything about it; my second came twenty years later and told me with certainty that he was finally on his way out.

Dad took him out fishing just one more time. It was to a local pond in the centre of a town park, and, despite a cancer beneath his right eye and floating blobs that cruelly obscured his vision, he still managed to winkle out a tiny perch or two: the tiny perch, the fisherman's escort in and out of the sport. On the front cover of the order of service at his funeral was a picture of him holding the monster perch caught from our favourite swim at Popham's Eau. I felt my chest heave and eyes fill with tears as I looked at it. He had been on his way for a long time, so there was no sense of robbery at his loss, but time did little to dull the impact of actually losing him for good.

The gathering of friends and family brought out many of the old stories. Some were familiar, such as the time his friend was so thoroughly depressed at being out-fished by him they swapped rods, only for Grandad to continue to catch more; other stories were new even to me, including one outrageous tale involving Grandad's knowledge of the Russian word for 'ice cream' and an interrogation at the hands of the KGB. I made a small speech about what he meant to us grandchildren, but I struggled to talk about his relationship with his son. It felt uncomfortable, as if all the awkwardness of his alpha-male posturing and the resultant shunning of real emotions had been transferred directly onto me for the day. Grandad was very different to Dad, but he was none the less extraordinarily proud of his son and loved him deeply. He just couldn't bring himself to publicly show it. If I had my time again I would say what he once told me on the riverbank. The banks always were his confessional box. 'Just aim to be like your dad, Will,' he said. 'Aim to be like your dad.'

I wanted to end this journey back where it began. I wanted to come home. I wanted to see the Creek again and fish Popham's Eau. I needed to see the Fens. I hadn't been back since his funeral over two years ago, and I hadn't fished Popham's Eau since I carried Grandad off the banks on our last fishing trip together. Almost every fish I've tried to catch from when this challenge began has been influenced by what he tried to teach me there. I need to go back now to really see what else I have learnt. Going full circle, right back to where in effect it all began, is the only way I will know if I've really changed at all.

It was the week before Christmas when I began the long drive cross-country from South Wales to fenland. I had returned from a honeymoon in Zambia and headed straight back out to New Guinea for more filming with BBC Two, so I really wasn't ready for the cold on my return, and nor was the van. Strong cross-winds and exposure made it a bit like steering a sail between the great concrete pillars that hold up the M4 bridge into Wales, fittingly rising up like giant rugby posts in this rugby mad nation. I love crossing the River Severn in bad weather, though, just so I can see the bleak savagery of the wind-whipped tidal currents, the coal-black exposed rock at low tide. The fish are probably impossible to catch in conditions like this. I gaze into the turbid waters and imagine the advancing squadrons of bass as the tide changes, the flatfish and the elver eels on their way up on the ride. I've rarely seen it worse than this down there but the fish are just fine; humans, though, would stand no chance. Stripped down and bare, without technology or clothing, the far bank would hang tantalizingly in view but your body would slide away on the savage current long before you froze to death. I sail over the bridge and on into England.

There is great value to keeping an eye out for wildlife, even on motorways as barren in feel as the M4. There are always red kites to be spotted, cutting through the sky and seeking roadkill, and a great many deer species hang on the fringes of the woodland set aside at the road's edge, staring forward with their twitching ears and glassy, doll-like eyes. Everything drops away as the sun fades. Three hours in and the earth is flattening around me, an indication I am entering the far east of the country.

By the time I finally reach the outskirts of the Fens it is already pitch black. Fen black. It should be its own colour. The density of the darkness on the long roads between communities here is something you can only fully experience on a clear winter's night like this. It feels like I've been ejected into deep space, ploughing my van on through some infinite void. Wispy, frozen mist envelops me as I head out onto the fields; but I am calm. I learnt to drive in these conditions and am far more fearful of driving in big cities than I ever will be driving out here.

A buzzard rests near the royal-purple sign that welcomes me back into fenland proper. I catch its feathers in the headlight beam of my car. Its wings are angled down and flattened by the moisture in the air. It looks like the large, leathery hood of an axe-wielding executioner from the Middle Ages when it hangs in the trees like that. The bird is waiting until first light to hunt. We both are.

This darkness, especially nightfall, had a big role to play during my childhood. It was the time all activity, fishing and war games must come to an end. No matter how far from home we were, we all knew the consequences of arriving back through the front door in the Fen black. My life was one without mobile phones, or even clocks, we ate when we were hungry and used the passage of the sun across the sky to dictate what we would do next. Everything else could be pushed to the limits, but there was no justification for a post-dusk homecoming; besides, we respected our parents and valued our liberty far too much to ever push our luck too far.

It was only when I left this area and met people from outside that I began to realize how different my childhood had been to most. As long as we were home before dark, and didn't speak to strangers, my friends and I pretty much did as we pleased. We looked after each other and stuck together. As long as we kept to the basic rules, we had the chance to be free. Really free.

Although the draining of the Fens began in 1630 it would take right through till the 1850s for the fertile farmland to be effectively free of water. The introduction of Victorian engineering and the first steam-powered pumps saw the land increase in value some four times over; the Fens would become the vegetable basket of

Britain, and people flocked to help with the massive harvests on the exposed blackened peat.

Soon the sense of familiarity is so intense I feel I can almost close my eyes and drive the rest of the way home: Ring's End, Guyhirn, Wisbech St Mary, Leverington, Wisbech and the spectral glow of the old factory site I used to work on; all so well-known yet so distant, as if they were locations cast off from another life I had once led.

The A47 leads me on down to the roundabout by the Elm Hall Hotel. This is the place where I turn towards my village, but I always knew it for the little roadside fishing pond stocked for the workers in the local canning factory. My friends fished it once and spoke of catching dozens of little common carp on sweetcorn. I was much older when I eventually made it there to fish, but it was already long barren of its anglers and carp. At one end the wind was corralling hundreds of super-strength cans of Polish beer on the water's surface. When change came here, it came quickly.

The modern-day mechanization of farming practices after the Second World War both dramatically reduced the number of labourers needed and boosted the land's productivity to stratospheric proportions. By the late 1980s the Fens were accounting for more than one third of the national output of vegetables, and the supermarkets' use of new computer technology meant orders could be placed the moment a product had been purchased. With the scan of a barcode and click of a mouse, the supply chain was essentially streamlined and retro-fitted around the exact buying habits of the consumer. Massive orders of fruit and vegetables were now capable of doubling or halving overnight, so farms and their factories took to calling in their workers to pick, pack and process at the shortest notice possible, but supermarket competition and customer expectation demanded the product price was still kept as low as possible. There was no real rise in wages for the legions of workers who had survived when the machines replaced people, but the uncertain shifts, unpredictable hours and now the crap wages on top meant many locals finally felt that enough was enough. There were still many jobs that needed the human hand, though; the farmers and factory owners were going to have to look elsewhere.

I was sheltered from these monumental changes as a child, particularly as I was still able to find local work fruit picking as a teenager well into the 1990s, but in the time it took me to leave school and finish my degree I went from being able to walk onto a factory line any-where to finding it virtually impossible to get a job at all.

Many of my friends in the fields and factories blamed the migrant workers for 'coming over here and taking all the work', but this was as far from the mark as those that pointed fingers at the 'lazy benefit-scrounging' local population who were 'all just racist'.

When the locals had started to refuse to meet the new demands, farms and factories simply turned to foreign gangmasters and agencies to pick up the shortfall.

Eastern European workers from the poorest parts of the former Soviet bloc, Poland at first, but latterly Latvians, Lithuanians and Russians, flooded to the area on the false promise of good wages and regular jobs, but when they arrived they discovered that the meagre wages they were to be paid were largely siphoned into the hands of criminal gangmasters under the guise of being 'back payments' on transportation costs, or taken as outlandish rental rates for the overcrowded houses they were placed in. Away from the houses, I began to notice tents cropping up, concealed deep within hedges and patches of trees. Out on the banks, fyke nets and long lines turned up for the first time in my lifetime. People were desperate. Desperate enough to spend winter in a tent, desperate enough to risk a criminal record for poaching fish; accruing debts with terrible people and sinking into a worse state of poverty than the one they had left behind.

The rate of new migrants coming into the area was higher than anywhere else in the UK – it had to be, no one else would tolerate that sort of treatment longer than they had to. Soon, some of the worst examples of poverty in the country were to be seen right on my doorstep, but that should hardly be surprising, should it? When we demand our food is available at bargain prices, around the clock and throughout the seasons, there was always going to be someone paying the cost somewhere.

There were times I felt like we were still all cast adrift

in flooded Fens. I grew up in a Bermuda Triangle of land where the county borders of Lincolnshire, Norfolk and Cambridgeshire all meet. We had one train line a half an hour's drive away, a scattering of main roads and definitely no motorways, and our nearest McDonald's took two bus journeys and a change at Wisbech. In the Norfolk Broads or on the north Norfolk coast it is all part of the charm, but visitors rarely came to my neighbourhood through choice, and yet I still love it here. There is a sense of the truly mystical to the big skies and open fields, and the greatest sunsets and starry nights I will ever see have always been here. A comic once said if you stand on a milk crate you can see the curvature of the earth. As a child I would sneak out the back of the house in the depths of winter and climb the last apple tree in the orchard. From my vantage point I could see across the earthen sugar beet fields, stripped bare of their crop and frozen solid like the sea. I used to imagine it was the point where the world was stitched together, an elongated patch atop the earth's surface sewn in the same way my school trousers were when I holed the kneecap.

Fenland people are mocked, of course. We are the uneducated, slack-jawed inbreds. 'NFN' – 'Normal for Norfolk' – the outsiders like to joke. Folk-of-the-flat interned in a land where people go mad because of the lack of hills. Later the madness was actually attributed to malaria from the swamps, but we never shed the rest of the character stains, and everywhere I go people like to poke fun about where I'm from. It doesn't bother me, though. I liked the people I grew up with here, and I actually felt sorry for people that took the piss out of us, as I knew they had missed out. Most of all, I liked the adult contentment of feeling small in a vast, unbroken landscape. I am grateful to this land: for the respect and interest in water it has given me, the lack of fear and sense of control I have in the wild. I now realize that it is something special, and not something simply innate in everyone.

Perhaps I am indulging my nostalgia now I no longer live here. I couldn't wait to leave this place when I did. I felt a sense of suffocation as I grew older, that the whole place was getting perversely smaller and more inward-looking with each year of my life that passed. New Year's Eve and when Glastonbury was on as a teenager were always the worst. Watching mass celebrations on the television I would feel frustrated and jealous of every-one else. Worse still I couldn't shake the feeling that we were the sorts of people that would never be invited to the party. However, a decade after all of my friends and I had been released from the Fens and headed to jobs in the big cities of Britain, I realized that it was now that we were actually trapped for real and that what we had as kids would never be ours again. I never really felt at home in cities, and thought that any day soon someone in a suit would tap me on the shoulder and remind me where I was from, that I was wearing the emperor's new clothes, that it was time to go home now and that my performance was over. It took another ten years before I realized everyone else working in the city feels exactly the same.

According to the Wilson *Encyclopedia*, the 'Roach is the most commonly caught British freshwater shoal fish.' It was the footsoldier of the Creek, the fish that made up the bulk of my keepnet as a child, but, as a result of their sheer volume and small size, I feel they never really received the respect they deserve. Coming home, it had to be the roach I went for.

The eyes are a virulent, violent red in colour, but there is something of the underdog spirit in the way the rest of its curved and downward-facing mouth appears. Its neat head fronts a classically fish-shaped body, and with white-silver sides and orange-red fins it is, unfortunately, the prime target for live-baiting for pike. A Finnish friend of mine even uses their eyeballs to catch perch: 'But they shimmer with an animation you just can't get from any bait,' he said, in response to my disgust at his practice. As I said, the roach deserves more respect.

Before the opening day of the coarse season on 16 June I would walk the Creek and look under the bridges at Popham's Eau. Thousands of roach in great shoals were to be seen basking in the sunshine together and the day couldn't come quick enough when we could try and catch them. The greatest catch I ever made came in that opening week. I was on the River Delph at Welney with Grandad, Dad and my friend Lee. We had happened upon a truly vast shoal of roach that would not stop biting. We baited with maggots and threw in breadcrumbs by the handful till we had precipitated a feeding frenzy so great that even when we ran out of free-feed they still just kept on coming. They continued to bite through pike attacks, they even continued to bite when I fell in. It was simply an incredible day's fishing, and when it came to tip our keepnets up and return the roach to the river I can still remember that feeling of amazement that such a great quantity of fish could be living in such a small patch of river.

Numbers, though, are one thing. There were other days when the roach came on strong for a time, but, out of the thousands and thousands that came to my hook, the biggest I ever landed was well under the 2lb mark. Jack Hargreaves writes: 'It took me thirty years to catch a two-pound roach, even fishing in the best southern roach-waters.' The current record roach, standing at 4lb 4oz, was caught from a lake in Northern Ireland, and the only river to feature any fish in the current top ten record roach list is the Stour in Dorset. Truly, the Fens were never likely to trouble the roach record books then, but some very fine roach have been landed here, many fish over 2lb, and I even once heard of a fish in excess of 3lb coming from the Great Ouse near Ely. In angling, there is always a chance, but, really, how much did I actually care by this stage?

I approached the outskirts of my village a little before dawn. My entire childhood world had just been compressed into a little under an hour in the car, but fifteen years after I had left it was heartening to discover my village had hardly changed.

I chose to drive the long way to Popham's Eau so I could pass both houses we had lived in. The first, a beautiful Georgian doctor's house in the middle of the village, had electronic Christmas candles in the window; the second, on the outskirts, had a new shed on one side, and that seemed to be the sum of the modifications. I drove beside the Creek, noting the nonsensical new sign that declared it the 'Nene–Ouse Navigation Link', then on past the butcher's, the hairdresser's, the corner shop and Navrady's, which still sells the best fish and chips in Britain. Out towards the end of the village I closed in on Grandad's place but flicked the indicator to signal right, just before I made it to his bungalow. Following the nail-straight road towards the Sixteen Foot Bank I headed instead towards his spiritual home, travelling just a few hundred metres before pulling into a small lay-by beside a field.

You wouldn't know the river was here in light or dark. The pancake-flat landscape creates an optical illusion that hides Popham's Eau perfectly in its dip, but I knew it was there. I opened the boot and lifted out a large bucket filled with groundbait and a couple of tubs of maggots and casters. It was cold but not as cold as it used to be at this time of year. When I was a child the winters here could be savage, days of sub-zero temperatures would freeze the fields solid and turn the flooded

Welney Washes into a giant ice rink that produced many a champion speed skater, but the walk along the edge of the field towards our spot was still just as long as I remember.

The fen drains intimidate some anglers. They appear as a blank canvas, miles of unrelenting uniformity in both directions with very few obvious fish-holding features to cast at. When Grandad came here he would walk from his bungalow, across the road and alongside a small orchard between the field and the river. He followed a fence line to a concrete post at its end. Here he would tie off a length of rope for safety and, effectively, abseil his way down the bank to the water's edge. That was where I needed to be and I did eventually find the post, still standing proud; but it would take till the sun was fully up for me to realize the fence and the entire orchard were all long gone. One solitary old apple tree remained, surrounded by long grass.

I grip the cold concrete post and feel an overwhelming sense of belonging. I used to sit right here when I was old enough to come to the Eau on my own. I would wait for him, his heavy steps along the bank, his 'all right, my beaut' greeting. It would never come again now, but I can still feel his presence here, far more than I could at his funeral service, or by holding his rods or reading his books. This is where we both once belonged. Wet mist soaks the banks. I had been nervous walking here, warning myself repeatedly to take my time and watch my step, that one slip in the darkness could see me plummet from height and into the drain, but the post makes me feel secure and the banks are nothing like as steep as I found them as a child. I move down easily and quickly towards the water's side.

I doubt many people have been here since I last fished this spot with Grandad all those years ago. The bed of common reeds on this bank stand some eight foot high, forming a caramel-yellow fence between me and the water, but there is still a gap just big enough for me to squeeze into my seat and cast my roach tackle. I begin rolling apple-sized balls of groundbait laced with maggots and casters. The sluice gates are open downstream at Denver so the water is pushing through at a real clip, plus there is twelve foot of deep water in front of me: if I want to guarantee the balls make it to the bottom of the river I will have to squeeze them really tight. This is where I want the roach shoals to find them, and then, once the shoals are here and feeding confidently, I'll flick out a hook. I must remember to keep the bait going in, though – it won't last long in this flow and I'll want to hold the fish here for as long as I possibly can. 'It's not little and often, it's a lot and often, Will', that's what Grandad would have said had he been next to me now; then he would have told his old story about the fishing match he once lost because he only brought ten kilos of groundbait with him. 'Don't be afraid to keep it going in, as once the roach are gone you'll never get them back.' I throw the bait in as accurately as I can and return to the car for the rods.

Two hours slide by and the sun gently rises without bringing much warmth. The river elects to retain its misty coat and small jenny wrens buzz around in the reeds like hummingbirds. On the far bank a pair of swans dance neck to neck out across the water, but mostly it is very quiet. I didn't realize how much I miss the silence. The real fenlands personify a rare brand of solitude. Many can't hack it. I can understand that and I've always felt for the occupants of the remote farm-houses out here, miles from people and each other. Clumps of rotting water lily leaves float past on the flow. The living plant that formed them is firmly on the retreat now, back towards the silty riverbed where it will safely wait until the weather warms once more. In the spring the lily beds are dense and sometimes many metres thick. I used to love fishing off these lilies. It produced some of our finest fish, but a monster lived in there too, a fish that contained unstoppable power. It was our Moby-Dick. I hooked it just once; Grandad managed it several times, of course, but neither of us ever saw that beast – it simply tore the line from our reels and straightened our hooks right out. Looking back, we never once scaled our gear up to actually attempt to land the creature; we simply tolerated its occasional intrusion, probably in much the same way as it tolerated us. Many years later a young lad from the neighbouring village of Three Holes landed a carp well in excess of 20lb from this very stretch of water; perhaps that was all the legend had ever amounted to, but we never liked to think so.

I have set up for the roach exactly as Grandad taught me, with one of his handsome handmade floats, thick and well weighted, set at twelve feet in depth with the bulk of my shot strung out close to a small hook. I want to get the bait right down in the river, but if I don't get a bite down on the river bed that doesn't mean the roach are definitely not present. I'll just have to adjust the float and bring my bait off the bottom a little, an inch or two every ten minutes or so, just to check that they aren't shoaling a little higher up and intercepting all my groundbait as it sinks through the water column. Even with the heavy float and weights, I still have to steady the tackle in the flow, mending the line almost as if I were float-fishing the River Taff. I keep the bait trickling in with one hand and fix my eye firmly on the bright-red tip of the float for any possible indication of arriving roach.

Roach can be extraordinarily cute when they take the bait and sometimes a gentle bite might only register as a tickle on the float tip. In his prime Grandad could seemingly catch roach without any indication whatsoever, though: he would give a sudden crack of his wrist and there the roach would be, writhing on his hook as if spirited there by some unseen force. When the poet Ted Hughes wrote of float-fishing in 1967 he commented that 'your whole being rests lightly on the float'. That's the state you must look to achieve to be a truly successful float-fisher like Grandad, a condition of such intense concentration that there is nothing more in life than you and your float; when a pulse, a flick, a tremble on that tip will register in your body as if an earthquake has struck under your tackle box. It sounds tense – it really isn't, and, even if you fall short of such a lofty goal, float-fishing still offers its junior practitioners a shot at pure escapism. Staring at a float erodes stress at a far greater rate than any trip to the gym, pub or psychiatrist's couch ever will. It alleviates anxiety and leaves the angler fixed within a world where there are no bills to pay, no pieces of work to deliver and no problems at home. Time both slows down and speeds up. You can spot micro-details like how a cloud of nymphs expands and contracts on a river's surface, or how a kingfisher dramatically throws its neck forward as it strikes the water, but while observing the translucence on the wing of some damsel, or watching a toad crawl in animated slow motion, you suddenly realize it is getting dark and that you didn't even touch your lunchtime sandwiches.

I always feel better after a day's float-fishing, even when I miss all my bites, and if I were allowed to fish only one method for the rest of my life then the float would be it.

I tried to settle into the rhythm of my float that morning but it was impossible to get over the piece of my personal history I was sat in. Why did Grandad fish here almost exclusively for the last twenty years of his life? I had always put it down to the Eau's close proximity to his bungalow, but he really could have lived just about anywhere in the village. I blew some hot air and life back into my fingers. Popham's Eau didn't have the obvious aesthetics of the Creek even; you had to look hard for both the beauty and the fish down here. Maybe that was part of it, the idea that it was a bigger challenge. The fish here were definitely bigger if you did find them but I knew there was more at play here too.

I flicked a lily pad off the float. I never want to return to fishing just one set of venues for just one fish, but the immense enjoyment to be had at seeing a river change its shape and character from just one vantage point seemed pretty clear. Only by returning to the same place over and over can you see that no one day is ever the same as the next. Watching a river change its character through the seasons somehow ballasts us as anglers and people. It reminds us of our own mortality in the face of natural forces that are out of our control. It should not be an intimidating or frightening prospect. There is great comfort to be found in the discovery of something larger than your life. I can very well imagine that bearing witness to the changes in your grandchildren has a similar effect. Eventually we all get left behind, of course, but at least we can take steps to make sure that when we do go the things we love continue to grow without us around. Grandad kept his grandchildren, and this place, close. I know he was proud of us all, and now, against all odds, I've found my way right back here to check all is well on his behalf. I bet he always knew I would as well, the silly old sod.

Jiang Taigong was a statesman and strategist who lived in ancient China in the second millennium before

Christ. According to legend, he had served the tyrannical Zhouwang, the last king of the Shang Dynasty. Zhouwang was a debauched slave owner who took enormous pleasure in torturing, then executing, anyone who objected to his rule. Jiang Taigong hated him with every inch of his being and was desperate to overthrow the despot. However, despite being an expert in military strategy, Jiang Taigong was old and had no army to call on.

Jiang Taigong left his position with the king, but knew that one day his special talents would be needed to defeat him. He took to fishing and lived in seclusion for many years. As time slipped by it became clear to those who lived around the riverbank where he fished that Jiang Taigong never actually seemed to catch anything; in fact, on closer inspection, they discovered he wasn't actually fishing with a hook at all. Jiang Taigong believed that the fish, when they were ready, would come to him of their own volition. And so it was that King Wen of the powerful Zhou state found Jiang Taigong, at the ripe old age of eighty, fishing without his hook and, through pure curiosity alone, engaged this peculiar man in conversation. The king soon realized that Jiang Taigong was a uniquely gifted person, as well as a military expert, and hired him as his mentor. Together they would go on to overthrow Zhouwang and eventually establish the legendary Zhou dynasty throughout China, the longest dynasty in Chinese history.

Jiang Taigong gave out the image of a man fishing, when in fact he was waiting for an army to overthrow

King Zhou. It was a cunning piece of sleight of hand: he had a hidden purpose that was heavily masked by an obvious one, but it took him time. The morals of the story: good things come to those who wait, and things aren't always as they seem.

My bite alarm has just gone off.

Gently, I place my roach rod down on its rests, leaving my seat behind as the bleeps start to sing out in a string. Forgive me, readers, for slightly pulling the wool over your eyes with the roach-fishing lark, and forgive me, Grandad, for the blatant use of technology in your treasured spot, but hidden at the end of the reed bed a heavy rod baited with a single smelt has been lying in wait this entire time.

I scoop that rod off its rests. Its feels like gripping the trunk of a tree in comparison to the roach rod but this is no time for clever comparisons: the line is pulling alarmingly taut, signalling that it is high time to strike, and strike hard I do.

At first I feel solid resistance and the line grinds horribly. It is locked up against something but I sense instinctively that now is not the time to ease off on the pressure. Suddenly the line pings free and I can tell from the opening, steaming, pile-driving run which follows that this is going to be the biggest fish of my journey by an absolute fucking mile.

Despite the mammoth run I feel strangely in control. Don't let the fish bully you. I pile on strain when I feel it is trying to rest and give it line and space to run when it decides to assert itself. After ten minutes I get my first glimpse of the fish and it is, as expected, a very big pike. It shakes its head angrily at me, like a bullock caught in an electric fence, and, to my absolute horror, I notice that there is only a single, barbless, hookpoint left in the fish's mouth, sat right between its bony teeth like an after-dinner toothpick. It is, as they say, brown-trouser time.

The pike steamrollers towards the dead lilies and reeds on my side of the bank so I apply as much side-strain as I dare; if it goes in there I know I'm done for. Mercifully, she turns her head at the last moment and drives back into open water. It's definitely a female pike: the solid belly, shoulders and head are unmistakable. The reel whines and my hands and knees begin to rattle with adrenaline. I know now that this is not just the big-gest fish of the journey, it is the biggest fish I have ever seen in Popham's Eau. It is the beast.

In front of me, in a flash of a second, I swear blind that a giant shoal of roach rolls on the surface of the river, momentarily rippling the place with a life I haven't seen in a hundred winter visits here. In the middle of them all is my great fish, wallowing like a hippo just out of reach of the net. I hold the rod up to its maximum extent and slowly win back the line, gently heaving the magnificent animal back towards me. The weight of the fish leaves my rod the moment it hits the base of my net; at the same time another, unseen, weight slides right off my shoulders. I stare up to the sky and feel my eyes heave with tears.

Thank you, Grandad. Thank you for teaching me how to fish and thank you for everything else. Thank you for just being there.

I didn't break any angling records during this journey and, in reality, I was always quite some considerable distance off the mark. That greater sand eel is still as close as I've been to a submission to the hallowed British Record Fish Committee and its list, but, still, I had a lot of fun and did break several personal bests. In my own way, I did at least avenge the memory of that greater sand eel.

The fact is, you just can't drop into any old swim and hope to catch a record on wild water. Yes, the chances are significantly narrowed when you know there is a record fish trapped within a lake, or even behind a lock gate, but you still need to learn that creature's habits and harmonize yourself to the natural rhythm of a place. That all takes more time than I had, and yet I still wouldn't have changed how I approached this challenge one bit.

I realized ultimately that I'd had infinitely more pleasure catching fish from ridiculously unlikely spots, meeting new people and discovering new places to try, than I ever did from actually chasing a record fish. The sand eel was beautiful not because it was a record on some other man's list but because it was a total surprise and the first I had ever caught. What is fishing without the element of surprise?

There have been many failures in this book and plenty of days when I caught absolutely nothing at all. In the past this would have been a major problem, rectified quickly with a trip to my nearest carp stew pond to confirm I hadn't lost the magic. In fact, this very act confirmed I *had* already lost the magic. Fishing is our way of tapping back into something we have lost in our comfortable and cosseted lives, a throwback to a time when we did need to catch to survive; it should not ever be reduced to purely a competition to catch the biggest fish. The baited line is our link to the secret underwater world and it reconnects us with nature in an immensely powerful way that few other pastimes ever could. We are a part of a much wider, wilder system, and not simply above it. Failure to catch demonstrates we do not have full dominion over nature all of the time and plugs us back into the notion that we, as humans, should only ever be participating in a mutual and fair exchange with the natural world, one where we can't always guarantee a win.

At the end of it all I have discovered that I am still at my most relaxed when I am by water, but I am also at my happiest when I'm fishing a river. My river fishing, like my family, has always been there for me, and I've been at my lowest when I've abandoned them both. I now realize that it is the fishing, and not actually the fish, that has provided the levelling presence throughout my life. Even when I've neglected it, river fishing has waited for me. I promise I'll never leave the rivers again.

My hero, John Wilson, made 160 television programmes in a career spanning over twenty-five years. In 2009 he justifiably received an MBE for services to angling and eventually retired to Thailand, where he runs a fishing lake with his brother, Dave. I spent a wonderful evening drinking beers in the bath while watching episodes of *Go Fishing* back to back for hours on end, drunkenly raising a glass to the man who inspired a legion of young fishermen just like me. Thanks, John.

My grandad was not a second father. I already had one of those and never needed another, so what was he to me? He was my older best friend. He would do anything for me (as long as it didn't cost too much money!) and I would do anything for him. There was nothing I wouldn't tell him, and no judgement he would ever pass. He was a superficially hard and competitive man to his death, but his core held an utter softness. He brimmed with absolute and unwavering love for his son, his family, his grandchildren, and for me.

Grandad and I kept the secrets we shared with each other on the banks, but there was one of his musings that I knew I would eventually have to tell Dad about when the time came. I was ten years old and we were fishing Popham's Eau side by side. He was sat there with his floppy white hat on, watching his float while absent-mindedly moulding breadcrumb groundbait all around the cork handle of his rod. It was a fairly typical summer afternoon. Then he leant towards me and said: 'When I go don't put me in the ground with the rest of the silly buggers. Put me in the river, back where I was a boy, my boy.'

Dad found the exact spot he spoke of in words Grandad had written in *Bedford, My Bedford*, and one crisp spring afternoon my dad, my brother and I carried him back home: up the River Great Ouse above Bedford, below a bridge, across a field, and into a break in the eight-foot-high common reeds.

Grandad finished his journey where his passion began. Gently we eased his ashes between our fingers and let him slip into his infinite water.

Acknowledgements

This book has focused far too much on men at times. I would like to thank three of the most important women in my life: my loving mum, for everything she did for me growing up, giving me my self-belief and providing an environment for all her children to flourish; my brilliant twin, Anna, for being there for me and having my back for, quite literally, my entire life; and, most of all, thank you to my wonderful wife, Emma, for always believing in me, for keeping me going, and for putting up with me heading off to catch fish in the same year we got married.

Grandparents are quite often the unsung heroes of any family. Thank you to both sets of mine for the unconditional love they always gave. I wish you were all still with us, and that you can forgive my occasional swearword in this book; I don't really mean it. I'm blessed with some really awesome friends and a fantastic wider family. I won't turn this into a mammoth love-in as I hope they already know how much they've helped shape me and my writing, but I would like to single out my brother Tom for special praise. Thanks, Tom, both for putting up with a brother who was as obsessed with fishing as I was as a child, and for giving me the metaphorical boot-up-the-arse I needed when I was spending too much time watching fishing on satellite TV and not enough time writing about it.

I am very grateful to the Society of Authors for their generous grant for yet more tackle and miles more in the petrol tank. Huge thanks to everyone who has helped along the way at Viking, Anna-Sophia Watts for her beautiful illustrations, John Hamilton for his superb cover art, Mark Handsley for his copy-editing patience, and to Emma Brown for handling the latter stages of the book edit. Emily Robertson has been the best editorial partner I could have ever hoped for. Without your guidance and encouragement this book would never have happened. Thanks for convincing me this would work, Emily, and for understanding what I was struggling to commit to words.

On the banks, my thanks go to the Canal and River Trust and especially John Ellis for switching me on to the wonders of our canals, Jake Finnegan at Wykeham Lakes for relating the story of his monstrous pike, John Horsey for his exceptional knowledge of Chew, and for letting me blow his chance at a big pike, Peter Rolfe and Pam for their incredible hospitality and introduction to all things crucian, Verulam Fishing Club for being so kind in letting me fish their pond, Dr Carl Sayer for his patience in explaining his research to a dullard like me, Glamorgan Anglers Club for the access to all the excellent fishing to be had in South Wales, the guys at Garry Evans Tackle Shop, especially Rich and Andrew, for all of their advice and help, and to Dad's salmon mates, Dave, Nigel and John, for letting me gatecrash their trip. Thanks also to my childhood friends Lee Wales and Paul Woods, who picked up where Grandad left off, and helped create some of my fondest fishing memories.

The final word of thanks must go to Dad, Grandad and John Wilson. Thanks for the inspiration, guys. May your lines be for ever tight.

He just wanted a decent book to read ...

Not too much to ask, is it? It was in 1935 when Allen Lane, Managing Director of Bodley Head Publishers, stood on a platform at Exeter railway station looking for something good to read on his journey back to London. His choice was limited to popular magazines and poor-quality paperbacks – the same choice faced every day by the vast majority of readers, few of whom could afford hardbacks. Lane's disappointment and subsequent anger at the range of books generally available led him to found a company – and change the world.

'We believed in the existence in this country of a vast reading public for intelligent books at a low price, and staked everything on it'
Sir Allen Lane, 1902–1970, founder of Penguin Books

The quality paperback had arrived – and not just in bookshops. Lane was adamant that his Penguins should appear in chain stores and tobacconists, and should cost no more than a packet of cigarettes.

Reading habits (and cigarette prices) have changed since 1935, but Penguin still believes in publishing the best books for everybody to enjoy. We still believe that good design costs no more than bad design, and we still believe that quality books published passionately and responsibly make the world a better place.

So wherever you see the little bird – whether it's on a piece of prize-winning literary fiction or a celebrity autobiography, political tour de force or historical masterpiece, a serial-killer thriller, reference book, world classic or a piece of pure escapism – you can bet that it represents the very best that the genre has to offer.

Whatever you like to read – trust Penguin.